"My Real Job is Being an Artist"

How to produce a body of signature art and build the foundation of an art business

I0473272

Aletta de Wal, M.Ed.
First Edition
Artist Career Training
www.ArtistCareerTraining.com

My Real Job Is Being An Artist: *How to produce a body of signature art and build the foundation of an art business*

Author: Aletta de Wal, M.Ed. Artist Advisor & Certified Visual Coach, Artist Career Training

Published by: Artist Career Training
Cover Design by Finesilver Design. Illustrated by Rachel Ann Lindsay
Author Photo by Trish Tunney Photography

Artist Career Training
Telephone: 250-549-2615 Pacific time
Web Site: www.ArtistCareerTraining.com

The information contained in this book represents the views of the author, her research and editorial team input, based on practices and regulations in the United States at time of publication. The author makes no warranty about the ongoing accuracy of the information. Although this publication is designed to provide direction in regard to the subject matter covered, it is sold with the understanding that neither the author nor the publisher are engaged in rendering legal or accounting services.

The author and publisher shall have neither liability nor responsibility to any person or entity with respect to any loss or damage caused, or alleged to be caused, directly or indirectly by any information contained in this guide. Be a responsible entrepreneur and always consult your paid professional advisors regarding financial or legal matters.

Library of Congress Control Number: 2014922116
ISBN-13: 978-0-9833531-1-9

Dedication

This book is a tribute to all the artists who make a living while making a life, and to all the people out there helping them do so.

I keep on keeping on because of the example of Johanna de Wal – my 95-year old mother who has more curiosity and energy than many teenagers, and who reminds me that things in life just are the way they are, so smile and get on with something.

I do what I love and live where I do and I am healthy and happy because of my forty+ year relationship with Andrzejko, acoustic guitar genius, amongst his many other talents.

And dedicated to the memory of Molly, the greatest English Labrador Retriever companion in the world.

Aletta

Thank You!

Thank you for buying this book. What you have in your hands is the result of four years of writing, rewriting, more rewriting, still more rewriting and editing, all with the support of a great team. I've worked long and hard to give you the best resource I could produce so that you can make good decisions about the real job of making a living as a visual artist.

The information I share in this book is an artist's career and business roadmap. You'll understand where you are in your journey, what you need to do next and when to take specific actions to further your career.

If you take action as you read, much of what you do will produce results right away. Other outcomes will happen over time, as you intentionally grow your art career with the knowledge found here and through your own experiences.

I appreciate it when you tell other artists about this book and let them know where to buy their own copy. I love it when you quote what I say and post comments on social media, along with a link to http://www.artistcareertraining.com/realjobartist.

Please respect my work and my copyright so I can continue to serve artists like you and run this business profitably. Please treat the intellectual property in this book, accompanying recordings and images as you would your own original art. If you purchased an e-book, you may download one copy, bonus content related PDF(s) and audio(s) to your computer and other personal listening devices (iPod, etc.) or burn to a disc for personal use. Your receipt indicates your agreement with these terms of use.

If you are serious about making a better living while making art, be sure to check the full range of programs and personal coaching services at http://www.artistcareertraining.com.

Aletta de Wal, M.Ed.
Artist Advisor & Certified Visual Coach
Artist Career Training
http://www.artistcareertraining.com
http://www.artistcareertraining.com/realjobartist
(250) 549-2615 Pacific Time
Aletta@ArtistCareerTraining.com
http://www.facebook.com/pages/Artist-Career-Training
https://plus.google.com/+ArtistcareertrainingAlettadeWal
http://www.linkedin.com/in/alettadewal
http://www.pinterest.com/artistcareer
http://www.twitter.com/artmktgmentor

Foreword

"My Real Job is Being an Artist" is an indispensable reference book about the art business and how to prepare for success as a fine artist. Author Aletta de Wal, who is both an artist and art business coach, provides a fresh look at exactly what an artist needs to do to become self-supporting. Aletta draws upon more than twenty years of relevant experience to explain how she and other successful artist clients have achieved their goals.

For artists who are not sure where or how they fit into the art world, this book provides detailed information on exactly what to do to break into the next stage of their career. Chapters on how to plan your time, visualize goals, and monitor progress are especially pertinent.

Readers will appreciate Aletta de Wal's practical advice on how to make the most of their limited time, energy and resources to land that perfect day job… as an artist!"

~Margaret Danielak
Owner of DanielakArt – Art Sales & Consulting Services
Author of "A Gallery without Walls: Selling Art in Alternative Venues"
www.danielakart.com

"Even if you only read the third section this book, 'The Basics of an Art Business,' you would be well on your way to a successful career in the arts. But wait, there are two other outstanding sections filled with everything you need to know to grow your business and build your career. This is a must read if you are serious about your success."

~Lee Silber
Award-winning author of the Business Books For Artists series
Founder of Creative-Lee Speaking, www.creativelee.com

Reviews by Artists

"Though I've been a professional artist now for almost two decades I found this book to be a compelling read and one I wished I had when I was starting out. Aletta de Wal details practical advice and organizes it in such a way that you would want to keep this book out on your desk for quick reference.

What I enjoyed most is that the advice is spot on, well researched and cuts through all the "what if" scenarios to "what works."

Even as an established artist, I found myself taking notes in order to look at some of my perspectives in a different way. I can say without a doubt there isn't an artist on any level in their career that wouldn't find this book an absolute necessity. 'My Real Job is Being an Artist' is a roadmap to a profitable and fulfilling art career."

~Eric Armusik, painter

"'My Real Job is Being an Artist' is a thorough guide to what it really takes to create a professional career as a visual artist. Aletta de Wal's understanding of the stages of an art career and what it takes to succeed at each stage is enlightening.

*I love her no-nonsense attitude about the nuts and bolts of business, all the while addressing the primary importance of doing your art. What I found most impressive and useful was Aletta's emphasis on really honoring and creating the art you love, **then** finding a market.*

I can see much of this book being useful to other kinds of artists, including writers. I found myself wanting to implement her suggestions right away, especially when it came to creating the vision of what I want next in my career.

Aletta really gets what it takes to create a successful artist career because she's been there, both as a working artist and through her work with hundreds of artists as an Artist Advisor. Follow her tips and see your professional art career accelerate and soar."

~Beth Barany, writer and book coach

"Aletta de Wal has been committed to the success of international artists for more than two decades. As a Coach, Mentor, Entrepreneur, Artist and Muse, Aletta continues to support the art and creative world with great humour and empathy. With this book, she continues to prove this commitment.

I know that my own commitment to my craft is not always consistent — Aletta encourages me to take up the challenge and to continue to "make art." As an entrepreneur, I now have the tools to not panic about the mechanics of the business."

~Susan Birkenshaw, photographer

"If you are or want to be a visual or performing artist, organization and linear thinking — business thinking — is usually elusive at best.

Aletta de Wal with her summaries, lists, questions and charts draws a road map for your individual growth and success from wherever you are in your quest — beginner, mid-career or even successful professional — to your dreams. It's like broccoli with chocolate sauce — easy to swallow and good for you, too."

~Connie Bransilver, wildlife photographer

"I've stated for many years that there isn't a manual on how to be an artist, as if it were a badge of courage inherited by choosing this career path. After reading the detailed information compiled by Aletta de Wal I'm happy to say that statement is no longer true. 'My Real Job is Being an Artist' is the solid, no-nonsense advice I always wished I had. Finally a manual that demystifies how to start, build and continue a career as an artist.

'My Real Job is Being an Artist' lays out, in easily understandable terms, how to approach your career as an artist. This book is not only relevant to the emerging artist, but to the mid-career artist, and the established artist as well. More importantly Aletta helps you identify what career stage you're currently in and the steps you should take to advance your career."

~Peter Bragino, painter

"'My Real Job is Being an Artist' is the book I wish I'd had years ago! In fact, it should be required reading for every B.F.A. program in the country! Chock full of art world savvy, artists' real experiences, step-by-step actions and incredibly well thought-through lists, I can only look back on how many false leads I could have sidestepped had Aletta de Wal's book been at hand along the way!

Having read many books to improve my art career, I can honestly say this is the book I wish I had found from the beginning. 'My Real Job is Being an Artist' is a definitive bible for artists at any level of their careers and creative paths.

In a practical and nurturing voice, Aletta guides you through a journey where you discover where you really are as an artist, where you need to be and the steps you must take to get there. It is not a book just to be read, but also a reference tool to keep going back to in your creative growth."

~Frank de Las Mercedes, mixed media artist

"Art business authority and marketing coach Aletta de Wal shows us how the right self-knowledge coupled with true art-world business savvy can equip any determined artist to step it up, moving from wherever you currently find yourself toward the deeper satisfactions of both creative and financial professional success.

Aletta takes the clueless and wandering among us and leads us through her remarkable thought processes, equipping us with a full backpack of perfect tools and the confidence to hike toward our own creative and financial mountaintops.

With deep empathy for the daily practical challenges every artist faces, Aletta guides us to the self-knowledge and practical business wisdom we must possess to fully reap the financial rewards we deserve to experience in this lifetime! Chapter by chapter, Aletta shows us the way with assurance and warmth."

~Huguette Despault May, MFA, drawings

"'My Real Job is Being an Artist' is relevant to all artists seeking to earn recognition and income through their unique forms of expression. Aletta de Wal has successfully 'peeled the onion' of life as a working artist in the 21st century.

This book is the perfect read for those new to the business of art, to learn, in bite-sized chunks, the steps to take. If you are already immersed in the art world, this book will take you deeper. The contents got me all jazzed up to recommit to the on-going personal development necessary for continued success as a professional artist."

~Patrice Federspiel, watercolor artist

"In 'My Real Job is Being an Artist' Aletta de Wal provides a comprehensive guidebook for life as a professional artist. Aletta provides the real stuff — not fluff — of what it takes in terms of work ethic and habits, signature style artwork, nuts and bolts of business and what to expect during different stages of your art career.

Aletta may not always tell you what you want to hear, but she gives you the straight story on what you **need** to hear to successfully develop and manage your career as a fine artist. As a full time artist for the past ten years and business executive for twenty years prior to that, I have read many art business books and this one by far is the most practical and realistic in terms of what it actually take to succeed."

~Pat Fiorello, painter

"Highly recommended! Aletta de Wal lays out the practical realities of making a living from making art with clarity, detail, and a dash of inspiration.

This book is a must-read for anyone contemplating or struggling with a career as a visual artist. Whether you're an art student, an experienced artist already selling, or someone who hopes to turn their talent into a business, it's all here.

From a frank assessment of where you are now, to tips on developing a signature style, to advice on starting and running a business, this book is filled with useful and practical information."

~Jennifer Mason, painter

The Purpose of This Book

Do you want to make your living from making art?

If you answered, "yes" to that question, then I wrote this book for you.

Whether you're a "Sunday painter" or already have an art business, this book will help you identify the mindset, skills and resources you already have, as well as those you'll need to develop in order to navigate a professional art career.

- You'll gain the tools you need to create and develop your own "signature style," which will make your art memorable and marketable to collectors and gallery owners alike.

- You'll have a framework you can use to build up your level of art production, so you can keep inventory levels high as your career grows.

- You'll understand exactly what to expect as you enter and move through each of the various career stages of being a professional artist.

- And while it's not the sexiest part of being an artist, you'll also learn how to set up and manage your art business — from record keeping and inventory systems, to tax and liability issues — so you can establish and maintain a professional art business, as well as experience the joy of deducting your own expenses!

Over all the rewarding years of coaching entrepreneurs and working with visual artists, I've gained many solid insights while helping them build professional art businesses that last. I'll share those experiences with you.

I've also been privy to the major stumbling blocks that many artists encounter while on the path to a professional career. I'll give you ways to go over, under or around what could otherwise trip you up.

I've discovered that, while there are many fine blogs, books and programs available that discuss art marketing, what's missing from the large body of artist career advice publically available is a more robust treatment of what comes *before* art marketing. My motivation in creating this guide for you was to fill in that very important blank.

Artists frequently ask me questions like:

"How exactly do I create a signature body of work, and how will I know when I have one?"
"How much art do I need to make before I can show it?"
"How do I keep up with both creating art and running a business?"
"If I am not yet selling any art do I really have to set up my business officially?"

These are all valid questions, and the artists who ask them are smart to do so. Consider the answers in this book the "prequel" to art marketing. (If you want more marketing help, you'll find plenty of that online at www.ArtistCareerTraining.com.)

If you have not yet started your art career, the contents here will help you decide when to quit your day job (or switch to part-time.)

If you have already made forays into the art world, you may want to find an extra source of support until your art income matches your needs.

Whether or not you have other income, you can still be the "real artist" you are. (Don't let anyone tell you that you're not!)

I consistently hear good news from my clients about their accomplishments, from completing their first body of work, to being interviewed for an international art magazine, to having their work selected for a national gallery. That's what I want for you — to build and celebrate a successful, satisfying and financially sustainable art career.

Now it's your turn to take this same timeless business information and make your art the jewel in the crown of your creative life. Bottom-line, there's no drivel here — just friendly, focused information.

P.S. Again, this book is not about art marketing and sales; rather, it's about making art that is marketable and saleable. Artist Career Training has e-books, classes, workshops and private consultations to help you learn to market and sell your work.

Epigraph

"Perseverance means that your essential identity is that of being an artist. Nothing changes that; no life circumstances, no economic lows, no outside criticism, nothing.

If you have to work a regular job five days a week, then you paint inside your head during those five days.

Life changes all the time, pendulums swing. Things are good, then they slow down, the situation becomes disappointing, and then one day something shifts and whole new worlds of opportunity open up.

If you are truly an artist you never give up. You don't listen to those outside voices that say to quit — ever. You only listen to your muse — your inner voice. You create and grow no matter what."

~Alexandria Levin, painter

Section Overview

Section 1: The Career Path of a Visual Artist

You'll learn what it will take to move from being a hobbyist to being an amateur, or move from amateur artist to professional artist. Next, you will understand how to transition through the three stages of a professional artist's visual art career: from emerging artist, to mid-career, and finally to established artist.

Section 2: The Work of a Visual Artist

Contrary to the myth that artists are only "right-brain" thinkers, it's not at all unnatural for artists to be business-oriented. You'll learn the methods I've learned, modified, or developed to help artists *plan* to succeed. Naturally, this includes how to accomplish your Number One priority as an artist — how to improve and increase your art production.

You'll apply time-proven ideas and exercises that will help you create a "signature" style and distinguish your own works of art in a crowded field of visual artists. You'll also learn what to do to continually assess and develop your unique signature throughout your career.

Section 3: The Basics of an Art Business

Many artists have a paralyzing fear that there are a zillion things to know, and a gazillion ways to get into trouble if they don't get everything about the business side of art exactly right. But the truth is simpler than that: you can rest easier once you learn how to take care of the "bare bones" of your business. You'll get all the basic bricks to give you a foundation on which to conduct your art business properly while avoiding many common legal or tax problems.

IMPORTANT NOTE: The information in this book is based on laws and business practices in the United States. It's unlikely that any book could cover everything that you need to know for every location. Besides local, regional, national and international differences, laws and practices often change. There are equivalent laws, regulations, requirements and practices for your country. It's up to you to find out how to do business where you live. Please use this book as a guide to research for your own locality, and to get legal counsel for the specifics of your own business.

Table of Contents

Section 1: The Career Path of a Visual Artist

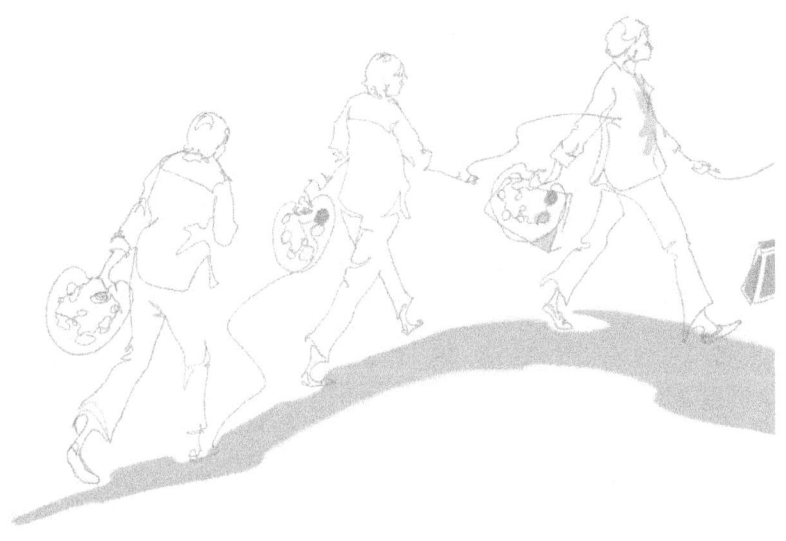

The Start of Your Journey

One comment I hear frequently, when I first work with new clients, is that their friends and family keep telling them to "get a *real* job," because, "come on, do you really think you're going to make it as a *real* artist?"

Despite the temptation to suggest that family members need to work on getting *real* hearts, I've been helping artists long enough to understand this — they don't mean you ill will, and they don't mean to be cruel. To the contrary: they want to *save* you from heartbreak and possibly bankruptcy.

My recommendation? Turn to them with love and thank them for their concerns about your well-being.

Then, if you are *driven* to create, regardless of where you are in your development as an artist — whether this is a full time profession or part-time passion — let them know that in your heart and soul you *are* a "real artist." Tell them that your determination is such that, after gathering the tools you'll need to move on to the next step, you will reap the rewards and feelings of validation you've always longed for. Ask them for their support no matter how things turn out.

Does that sound difficult to do?

Well, let's clarify one thing right now that you can help them understand — **whether or not you're a full-time artist has *nothing* to do with whether you're a "real" artist.**

A "real" artist is a state of being, not a state of employment. Being a real artist begins in your heart, develops in your head and emerges through your hands. I work with many artists who have part-time or full-time jobs and they're all *real* artists. In fact, because their art isn't tied to their finances, many of them face less pressure and are *more* creative during their studio time than some of their full-time artist counterparts who have the time to procrastinate.

Having a steady income and employee benefits like health care are key considerations for artists thinking about going full-time with their art, especially for artists with families. You are no less committed to your art because these factors play a role in your decision. I could even make the case that artists with other employment and/or family duties *must* be more focused and dedicated — after all, it's much harder for them to find studio time.

So I ask you to not doubt or judge yourself, or your potential future in the arts, by comparing yourself to other artists you know. Instead, stay open to all possibilities and then do the work to make your art career happen.

Every Artist Has a Path… What's Yours?

Artist James Thatcher's eloquence on what it means to be a real artist who balances art, life and marketing is the equivalent of a picture that is worth a thousand words:

> *"I once had an 8 year long break between artworks. I've also had stretches of sporadic art production, grinding out stuff as I've been able to cram it into spare time, doing maybe a dozen measly, incoherent pieces in a year; year after year.*
>
> *But that really is life…we're not art making machines, we're people; and we make art. Sometimes there are more important things than doing our artwork. We are multi-faceted beings, and our artwork is only one facet. Our other aspects must develop.*
>
> *And then we return to our work with a deeper experience to draw from; a greater awareness of love, responsibility, and commitment; and making amazing, deep, beautiful touching artworks.*
>
> *Have a little faith, gird up your loins, and believe. This is going in a dynamic and profound direction for you. You will do great and powerful things. It will work. You will not fail if you do not quit. Having responsibilities is not quitting; it is being admirably strong."*
> James Thatcher, http://www.jamesthatcheroriginals.com

Every artist has a unique path in life that contributes to the different ways in which they express their creativity. As I wrote this book, I kept in mind all of the artists who have contacted me over the years to learn about making a living making art, regardless of their other roles and responsibilities. If you are one of them, you are courageous and I applaud your dedication and tenacity.

Many of my clients are of the baby boomer generation, but I've also worked with artists as young as seventeen and as "experienced" as seventy-eight — a wide range of ages, and an even wider array of life experiences. Still, there is one thing they all have in common: the heart of a true artist beats incessantly inside their chests.

The following scenarios depicting the artist's journey may not fit you exactly, but there are probably bits and pieces that do. Feel free to select what fits to write your own story. You'll be telling your tale often as your art career develops. You may as well start now.

Scenario 1: Your art career got put on hold... and stayed there.

Perhaps you made pictures every chance you could when you were a little kid, and your art was proudly displayed on the refrigerator for all to see and admire. By the time you were in middle school it was tough to get you to stop drawing long enough to eat dinner, let alone do your homework! In high school, you lived for your art classes — they were so much better than any other subject. If you were lucky, your friends and the adults in your life understood your passion and encouraged you to keep making art. They supported your decision to go to art school (after all, couldn't you at least get work as a graphic designer?) where you earned your Bachelor's or Master's degree in Fine Art. Excited about your talent and an abundance of art styles, you couldn't wait until collectors came knocking at your door.

Then "reality" set in: you had rent to pay and a spouse or young family to support. The art world wasn't rushing to "knock at your door" like you thought it would. You made some tough decisions, then went out and got a regular job. You'd simply have to build your art career on evenings and weekends. But it wasn't long before life took over with parent-teacher conferences, soccer games and ballet recitals to attend, along with a lawn to mow. How could you continue to justify the time and money absorbed by your art hobby? So, you did the only sensible thing you could do and put your art on the back burner.

Still, deep in your heart-of-hearts, you think about what might have been... and wonder if you'll regret not "going for it," perhaps for the rest of your life.

Scenario 2: You've always dreamed of an art career... and still do.

Perhaps your parents weren't so supportive of your interest in art. They told you that it was fine, as a hobby, but art would never "pay the bills." So you drew and doodled in private, on the backs of your homework assignments, inside the covers of your school notebooks and on any other scrap of paper you came across.

You studied other drawings and graphic novels, copied other artists' styles and taught yourself. Your friends thought your drawings were increasingly "cool," and the art teacher at your high school encouraged you to go to art school after seeing some of your work, saying that you had natural talent!

Still, you followed the advice that the adults in your life gave you and went about getting a "real" education and a "regular" job. Deep in your heart, you had a dream: one day, someone would see your work… someone important in the art world. And just like your high school art teacher did, that person would instantly recognize your talent, insist that you quit your regular job and convince you to let them represent you because your art needed to be shared with the world.

Scenario 3: You're finally exploring being an artist.
Maybe you didn't start making art until later in life after your kids were grown or you had already retired. You'd always had an interest in art, but it just never seemed the right time to pursue your creative urges.

One day, when your neighbor told you about an art class at the local community center, you bought some supplies, cleared a space in the garage to serve as a studio, and, "Voila!" The surprising part has been the response from your friends and family — everyone's been so encouraging.

The art class teacher said you had the talent to do more with your art, so you entered a couple of local shows, actually won some awards and sold a piece or two.

Anyway, it's all been really exciting and flattering, but you're much too old to start thinking about an art career… right?

No matter which of these scenarios (or version of them) fits you, if you are a "real" artist in your own heart and mind, you *can* become a professional artist as long as you are willing to commit to building your career and take action consistent with that commitment.

Where Are You Now?

If you are a hobbyist or **amateur artist** you already know a thing or two about making art, but translating that into a money-making career takes a different type of knowledge and skill set. Just as you wouldn't normally hop into a car and begin driving randomly, without knowing how to drive or without knowing your destination or the best route to get there; so too you don't want to "jump" into an art career, without knowing where it will lead or the bumps and potholes to avoid along the way.

Let me be your guide to the destinations ahead; you'll see what you need for the journey, so you can decide if you're ready and whether or not you have what it takes to become a professional artist who makes a sustainable living from your art.

If you're an emerging artist, you may have struggled for years making sporadic progress. Or, you may have done very well and just don't know how to move on to the next stage. Even if you've had a few spectacular successes, it can be frustrating when your efforts feel "hit and miss."

This is your guidebook, too. You'll identify steps you've missed along the way, which may be impeding your progress, as well as the steps ahead that you still need to take to make your art business strong and primed for success.

If you're in mid-career, or returning to an art career after a lengthy break, you may feel as though you're pushing a huge rock up a steep hill alone, running out of energy, with no idea how to finally get to the top and stay there.

Whether you're an art school graduate or self-taught, you may have been unable to find — despite a glut of books, tutors, and teachers — just what you need to get over the hurdles. You're not in "last place," but you're not in "first" either.

This book is your chance to get off the blocks and start sprinting toward a fulfilling, functional, "first in class" art business.

What is Success to You?

Regardless of where you are now, **you** define your future success and decide how far, and how fast, you want to go.

Defining success is a little like trying to lasso happiness — it is always individual and subjective. Success is not a fixed commodity. Success is not the same for every – or any – artist. Success is not final or permanent. Success is strictly personal and is almost always a work-in-progress. For many artists, the journey is just as important, if not more important, than the outcomes or destination of the work.

> *"Success is not final, failure is not fatal: it is the courage to continue that counts. Every day you may make progress. Every step may be fruitful. Yet, there will stretch out before you an ever-lengthening, ever-ascending, ever-improving path. You know you will never get to the end of the journey…but this, so far from discouraging, only adds to the joy and glory of the climb."*
>
> *~Winston Churchill*

So before you read the rest of this book — ***stop***.

Close your eyes. Take a few deep breaths. Now let your mind find a memory of a time when you felt successful. Walk into that memory and experience it all over again. Use all of your senses: sight, smell, touch, taste and hearing to experience temperature, direction, pleasure and your awareness. Open your eyes and remember these sensations. **You** defined what success meant to you then and you will define success as an artist in much the same way.

Being a visual artist is a "real job" and wonderful profession. You contribute to the world in so many ways — through beauty, truth, thought and emotional connection, just to name a few. It's not always an easy path, but it *is* one that's worthy of your talents and efforts. When you run into obstacles, know that there are always opportunities just around the corner.

I believe in you. If you believe in yourself, at least enough to read the rest of this book, then you're ready to take the next steps to realize your dreams.

> *"I've had the usual obstacles artists face: lack of money, rejection and failure. Perseverance and a willingness to continually reinvent my approach along with the support of my wonderful husband and extended family members have been instrumental in my ability to overcome obstacles.*

I started out with very few resources and day by day made choices that wove together the life I have today. No matter what your life looks like today, be confident that what you do today will enrich your tomorrow.

Take the time to nurture yourself by creating a foundation around you that supports your interests and goals."

~Cristina Acosta, licensed artist

As long as there have been artists there have been "myths, mysteries, and innuendos" about the *business* of art. Can an artist actually make a living making art? And if so, can this be done without sacrificing every other aspect of life in the process?

Be assured: the answer is a resounding "Yes!" but it will take planning, relentless dedication, resilience, some hard work and constant learning. Making art and making a living from art are two entirely different pursuits, but if you have the drive and determination, this book can help you reach your goal.

Now let's get to work.

Are You a Hobbyist, Amateur or Professional Artist?

A common "path" for all artists except those who are child prodigies is to start making art as a hobby, become an amateur artist, and then decide to become a professional and develop a full-blown visual art career.

If you understand where you are on this path, you can avoid the heartache of spending time, effort and money that won't produce your desired results.

Instead you can make the most of even limited resources, as long as you have the commitment and are willing to do the work.

The Hobbyist Artist

Hobbyist artists may spend years, decades or even an entire lifetime making art strictly for personal pleasure. They may take art lessons but have no reason to professionally develop their skills. They simply want to create art and not turn art into work. (If this is you, please celebrate your joy in making art and don't ever lose that feeling!)

At some point a hobbyist might realize that art is an awfully expensive hobby and think that maybe it's time to put together some sort of business — at least to deduct the cost of art supplies on their taxes. They become amateur artists.

The Amateur Artist

Over the years, amateurs become more skillful at making art. Family and friends rave about how wonderful their work is and frequently say, "You should sell this!" At the same time, maybe a family member or spouse is concerned about the cost of this art hobby.

Whatever the case, the amateur artist sets up a business, sells a few pieces of art, and deducts their expenses. This is so exciting that they want to do more, and decide to become even more serious about their art.

Amateurs are willing to sacrifice personal time for the sake of their business, but are not always sure how to make it *really* pay.

As their confidence and skills grow, amateur artists may start to seriously consider art as a profession. They like the money they make with their art, and it's always great to deduct the costs at tax time.

With these thoughts may come a driving desire to make a *living* from their work. They start to pursue occasional art marketing opportunities and jump at every chance that comes their way, whether or not these actions make financial sense.

Amateur artists may spend most or all of their art income taking more classes and reading more blogs and yet never come up with a clear idea about what is required for them to make a living from making art. All they know is that it's time to find out how to succeed in the art world.

The Professional Artist

Most professional artists work hard for years before they succeed in the art world. Some years are better than others. While many people seem to like their art, for some reason, it doesn't all always sell. These artists often have many of the right pieces of an art business, but they haven't yet put the jigsaw puzzle together in a way that satisfies their need to make art *and* generates income from a large enough audience that appreciates it.

Unfortunately, in many such cases these talented artists eventually give up because they cannot detect a path to long-term success. Without a road map, artists in the early stages of their art career may give up too soon — or, even if they persist, these artists may spend a lifetime frustrated. (That doesn't have to happen to you!)
Artists who keep on going, and learn from others as well as from their own experiences, *can* make a life doing what they love. Remember, anything worth doing takes time, and often involves temporary setbacks before ultimate triumphs.

There are rites of passage in any career. Art is no exception. Artists "pay their dues" to move from being a hobbyist to a professional artist. Failed attempts by some artists to accomplish goals that do not fit their current abilities leads to confusion and doubt about the practicality of an art career. (You don't have to be one of them.)

I created a table to help you explore these three stages more fully, with notes about the capabilities, commitment level and attitudes of artists in each category.

The information below is a general overview — there are no hard lines between the phases, and you may be more advanced in some aspects than in others. This table is just a place to start your exploration.

Action creates progress! As you read, have a pen or highlighter in hand to check off each box ☐ where you are, so you can create a path to where you want to go.

Table 1: Hobbyist, Amateur or Professional Artist

Criteria	Hobbyist	Amateur	Professional
Artistic Motivation	☐ To explore ☐ For relaxation ☐ For pleasure	☐ To experience the joys of creation ☐ To get positive attention from friends and family	☐ To achieve success as a fine artist ☐ To explore and expand creative output ☐ To share a unique artistic perspective with the world
Art Skills and Knowledge	☐ Seeks personal enjoyment over gaining new skills and knowledge ☐ Takes classes "just for fun"	☐ Driven to learn new skills and knowledge (mostly for personal satisfaction)	☐ Understands that development of skills and knowledge are the foundation of a successful art career ☐ Makes a commitment to ongoing learning ☐ Teaches others as a way to "pay it forward"

Criteria	Hobbyist	Amateur	Professional
Subject Matter and Media	□ Changes media and subject matter as often as desired □ Focuses on experimentation rather than consistency	□ Chooses a preferred subject matter and media □ Develops methods of making art that satisfy and please self □ Does not consider audience when choosing subject matter and media	□ Masters methods of making art that satisfy self □ Works with subject matter and media that an audience wishes to buy □ Recognizes the importance of producing new bodies of work that the market desires
Business Orientation	□ No interest in establishing an art business	□ Shows some interest in developing an art business □ Undertakes business tasks every once in a while	□ 100% committed to running a successful art business □ Views art career as a business and lifestyle and makes choices accordingly
Work Hours	□ Creates art when the mood strikes □ Does not consider art a commitment or think about hours spent on it	□ Spends considerable time and effort even without financial reward □ Frequently pursues new ideas, techniques and art projects	□ Constantly makes new artwork to meet inventory needs, exhibit requirements and commission deadlines □ Commits all working hours (possibly more) to the needs of the art business
Audience	□ Self only	□ Self, first and foremost □ Family and friends second	□ Buyers, collectors and supporters □ Self (while still aiming to please audience and market)

Criteria	Hobbyist	Amateur	Professional
Reputation	□ No artistic reputation	□ Known by family members as "the creative one" □ Known to friends as someone who "does art" □ No artistic reputation outside of immediate circle	□ Understands the importance of making contacts in and out of the art world □ Knows how to build an art reputation □ Actively works to gain recognition as an artist
Credibility	□ Seeks personal credibility as an artist	□ Desires wider credibility as an artist but is unsure of how to achieve it	□ Seeks out strategies that establish credibility as an artist □ Consistently and deliberately takes action to build credibility
Visibility	□ Prefers working on art "under the radar" □ Does not seek attention for artwork □ May believe that artwork is not "good enough" to show	□ Puts some effort into increasing visibility as an artist □ Occasionally participates in art shows □ Confident in work being displayed in public	□ Understands how to stand out in the art world □ Recognizes the importance of visibility for a successful career in art □ Actively pursues visibility through many different channels

Criteria	Hobbyist	Amateur	Professional
Desirability	□ No desire to exhibit □ No desire to sell	□ May occasionally exhibit with other artists □ No desire to sell, but can be "talked into it" if someone wants the artwork	□ Actively seeks out opportunities to exhibit solo and with peers □ Regularly exhibits in order to build résumé □ Understands the necessity of continually showing artwork □ Sales and profit are a driving motivation for creating art □ Intention is to support self (and maybe others) with art sales
Attitude towards Art Shows and Exhibitions	□ Has a hard time letting artwork go □ Displays work mainly in home or office □ Gives some art away to friends and family	□ Keeps most work □ Exhibits in local arts organizations □ Occasionally donates artwork to a charity □ Gives some art away to family and sells to friends and acquaintances at various price levels	□ Keeps exemplar pieces in private collection □ Exhibits and sells most artwork □ Considers artwork to be inventory, having a financial value □ Donates the occasional work of art for a good cause or to build museum collections
Art Income	□ No income from art sales	□ Art sales are not a primary source of income □ Any earnings typically go towards future art supplies	□ Art sales are consistent enough to pay for living expenses

Criteria	Hobbyist	Amateur	Professional
Pricing	□ Rarely (if ever) needs to price artwork	□ Prices artwork on a case-by-case basis □ Aware of the need for consistent pricing	□ Skilled at pricing strategies □ Prices artwork consistently and in relation to the larger art market
Accounting and Taxes	□ Has no consistent income from artwork and no plans to deduct expenses on taxes	□ Declares income from most art sales □ Occasionally tracks art expenses for tax purposes □ Inconsistent or unsure about proper record keeping for taxes	□ Declares all art income on taxes □ Deducts all art expenses on income tax returns □ Meticulously tracks income, expenses and taxes throughout the year

Did you see yourself in any of these profiles, or perhaps in more than one? If you're like most artists I work with, you'll see different aspects of yourself in each profile.

If you decide to go ahead and move from being a hobbyist to an amateur, you don't have much to lose if it doesn't work out. You can always go back to being a hobbyist.

But if you want to move from being an amateur to a professional artist, you are making a big commitment, and you should know what is involved. Here's a short explanation of what's involved in both transitions.

Moving From Hobbyist to Amateur Artist

When you firmly decide to move from being a hobbyist to an amateur artist you also make a conscious choice to give up some of your other pursuits — or possibly the time that you used to spend simply doing nothing. This is not a light decision. You will need disposable time, energy and money to become a better artist. At this stage, you'll work on learning and practicing your art without any expectation of being reimbursed.

As an amateur, you may be just as talented as professional artists — or more so. You'll have the luxury of working at your art when it suits you, without the pressure of earning income from it. You can take workshops to guide your exploration of making art and have mentors to critique your work. When you make progress, you can simply enjoy it because your livelihood doesn't depend on constant artistic improvement.

Many artists choose to stay at this level. However, by doing so you'll be giving up many chances to show your work and get feedback from a wider audience. It is also unlikely that you will become well-known or get paid for what your artwork is truly worth.

> *"I have a degree in Recreation/Education. Early on I was an employed Recreation Director for an R.V. Campground. I created an art program for the visitors. I posted my work on the bulletin board to show examples of the classes that were being offered. Lo and behold people were stealing my work from the bulletin board. Well I decided if it was good enough to steal, then certainly it was good enough to sell."*
>
> *~Gayle Rappaport-Weiland, mixed media artist*

Moving From Amateur to Professional Artist

If you decide to move from being an amateur to a professional artist, you must love the life of an artist so much that you are willing to fully commit to art. In fact, you must be prepared to use most of your time, energy and money to make a living from your art. At this stage, you'll also need to develop a unique style and constantly build the number of pieces in your body of work.

As part of your strategy to become more visible and make more money, perhaps you'll teach others what you know. To remain competitive in the art world, you will also need to network with other artists and invest in professional development, whether that means mastering your medium, navigating the art world or doing business.

> "I began taking lessons as an adult. I was very lucky to find a teacher who encourages her students in all aspects of art and taught us from the beginning how to professionally present our work. Several of us bonded through class and started a critique group. We began meeting on a monthly basis and found we wanted to exhibit as a group. That was the beginning for me. "
>
> ~Vickie Martin, collage artist

Without a doubt, if you want to be financially successful you must be an entrepreneur with art at the core of your business. Any previous business experience you have will help you understand the administrative and marketing tasks that lie ahead.

I often tell people who are considering the move into a professional art career not to quit their day jobs just yet. It's a big decision and not one to be taken lightly. You don't want to have regrets or accumulate debt. You can continue working full time or part time while you build a solid foundation for your successful art business. That way, you'll be in a better position to succeed when it's time to leave your job.

> "Think about what you want out of your career. Remember that everything you do today is laying a solid foundation for tomorrow. Without that solid foundation, you won't be able to handle what comes. Be patient, be ready and be professional in everything you do."
>
> ~Bruce K. Haley, Jr., fine art nature photography

What Makes an Artist Professional?

There is still a lot of debate among artists about using the word "professional" to describe themselves. For artists who consider themselves "pure artists," that word often implies commercialism and "selling out." That's not how I see it.

When I interview professional artists and art world insiders, I ask them to define what makes an artist professional. You'll see that they each contribute a different perspective. Not one of them denies the right of artists to consider themselves professional and to define that term as it suits them.

"What makes an artist a professional is the unstoppable desire for success. You have to look at yourself as a professional and act the way a successful professional acts. I view my career as a thriving business, I am successful because I chose to be and I refuse to subscribe to failure. I've seen far too many people acting like they need to "pay their dues" or they aren't worthy to be successful - or worse, that there is no merit in success. This belief system impedes artists who have an inability to see beyond their own self-imposed limitations."

~Eric Armusik, painter

"Once you commit to being a professional, you don't just produce when you feel like it. What separates the professional from amateurs is a consistency of excellence, day in and day out, wet or dry, producing the images required on assignment or for self-assignment, telling stories in one frame. You also attend to relentless marketing combined with a thick skin. Ok, I have never learned to love rejection as advised, but at least it no longer bothers me much."

~Connie Bransilver, photographer

"Professional artists take themselves and their art seriously, and derive a significant portion (if not all) of their income from their art. Being a professional also refers to a level of business standards and in the documentation used, i.e. business cards, postcards, brochures, website. I wear an easy-to-read professionally made nametag when attending business networking functions and at art fairs. If I take myself seriously, it's more likely others will do so too."

~Patrice Federspiel, painter

*"In addition to producing work of consistent quality, I think a professional artist nurtures two essential attributes: The first involves **attitude**, the second, **action**. Artists must come to terms with the notion that the world isn't going to proffer us respect just because we say we're artists! Learn to respect yourself, your work: the value of your place in society. Without that confidence and conviction, it's tough to convince art world professionals to take us, or our work seriously."*

~Huguette Despault May, representational still life drawings

"Professionalism comes from creating commissioned artwork on time, in budget and as agreed. My professional approach to my career has brought me long-term clients who bring me many opportunities. We enjoy open communication and can count on each other. I also enjoy a certain amount of press coverage and that is a product of my professional approach to my career."

~B.J. Katz, glass artist

"Being a professional artist takes discipline. We have the luxury of being our own bosses, but in order to truly be a success, we must be responsible. A professional artist has specialized training in his/her artistic field and strives to uphold a high standard of artistic ability; works have impact and claim the attention of the viewer.

A true professional derives income from his/her art form, is recognized by his/her peers and is committed to devoting time to create."

~Lori McNee, painter

"A professional artist is one who creates high quality work with great commitment and focus, investing time and money to support both art making and everything else that goes into showing and selling art. This includes developing a plan, setting goals, registering the business, using business banking accounts and services, paying taxes, entering shows and exhibitions, and having an online presence and quality print materials. She knows when to seek advice and when to delegate."

~Karen Schmidt, sculptor

Every aspiring professional artist I know would love to achieve all of these things: unlimited financial success, national (or international) recognition and an unshakeable belief in the quality of their work so that they can proudly own the title of "professional artist."

Alas, there is no such thing as "one big break" that will bring you fortune, fame, followers and faith in your abilities all at once. Instead, you'll need to work your way through many different stages, in each of these areas, before realizing your dream.

Finding Your Driving Motivation

Which of these drives you to succeed: fame, fortune, followers or faith? These achievements are the ultimate reward for all the hard work, good habits and personal characteristics you need to go further with your art, whether you are an amateur or a professional.

A clear understanding of these motivating factors and a personal awareness of which ones are most important to you can help guide your choices as you start down the professional path. It will also help you enjoy the challenges and achievements along the way.

Here is a short explanation for each motivation:

Fame: Being recognized for your talent and the quality of your art.
For all career stages, fame offers recognition that validates your choice of signature style and your artist lifestyle.

- For the amateur, fame might mean being awarded a "Best of Show" ribbon at an exhibition.
- For an emerging artist, fame might be represented by a mention in a newspaper article, by gaining entry to an elite gallery or by an ever-expanding mailing list.
- For the mid-career or established artist, it might be having work shown in premier national or international galleries and exhibits, or even becoming a global household name.

Fortune: Being fairly compensated for the art you create.
The prices people pay for your art reflects its market value, both in the wider scope of the art market and in the enjoyment of the work purchased by collectors.

- For the amateur, the first measure of fortune is often selling a few pieces here and there so that the cost of materials and classes are no longer "out of pocket."
- The emerging artist might classify fortune as making enough consistent sales to be self-supporting with minimal additional income sources.
- For the mid-career artist, fortune could mean achieving a comfortable lifestyle, without financial burden and with some money in the bank for rainy days.
- For the established artist, fortune means having a choice of how much work to sell and how much to give to the world in other ways.

Followers: Having people who appreciate your art and support your career.

The number and kinds of followers that you have create a community of friendship and support, as well as sales.

- Amateur artists may count family and friends among their first fans.
- Emerging artists count viewers who come to exhibits or join their mailing list as followers.
- Mid-career artists add art professionals like gallery dealers, museum curators and arts writers to their growing "audience."
- Established artists attract attention far beyond their own doing and often beyond the art world.

Faith: having a solid, unwavering belief in yourself and your art form.

The source of this faith may be a higher power, an inner strength or a combination of both.

- For amateur artists, faith might be manifested by a level of inner trust and self-reliance in their ability to continually develop their talents, along with the courage to experiment with ways to express their vision.
- For emerging or mid-career artists, faith might mean persevering regardless of obstacles, or perhaps settling in to a personal style and no longer chasing after the techniques of other artists.
- For established artists, faith means believing that success will continue.

The Conduct of a "Professional" Artist

You will move from amateur to emerging artist and through mid-career before you are truly an established artist. Each of these stages requires many small breaks to bring success and movement into the next stage. You will need to work hard (and smart!) during every stage of the process. Make the journey as creative as possible to enjoy the challenge.

Many things may inspire you to keep moving forward in your art career, but one over-arching rule should guide your every move and action — to conduct yourself professionally if you desire to be considered a professional. So before delving into the more specific actions and efforts required to advance your place in the art world, let's lay a foundation of professional behavior by which to operate at all times.

Though it may seem like the world is filled with people trying to make it as professional artists, the truth is that the art community — like every other business niche — is really quite small. The people you meet, the connections you make and the impressions you leave will follow you everywhere in this tightly-knit market.

We're surrounded by stories of extraordinarily successful, high-achieving "professionals" in many fields and what made them that way. Identifying the attitudes, actions, personal characteristics and emotional maturity of professional artists is not as easy. Public knowledge (and media portrayal) of the sometimes crazed, sometimes tortured, antics of artists like Van Gogh, and Jackson Pollock have led us to expect irrationality, irritability and erratic (if not downright crazy) behavior from artists. Though often glamorized in film, few of us in reality would choose to live out our lives like this.

Read the following as though your entire career, respect and success as an artist depended on this advice — and rest assured that it does. Place a check mark next to the ones you already have in hand.

1. Decide to be known as a professional artist.
Make the decision now to be completely professional in *every* aspect of your art career. What does this mean? It means that despite the very personal, and often emotional, nature of your creative process, you will always conduct yourself with the same level of respect and regard for those around you as would any business professional or diplomat.

This advice may sound overly controlled. I've heard "My personality is part of who I am," or "I have to be free to express myself and my opinions if I want to remain true to my vision." You can do as much as you want in the privacy of your studio.

Bottom line: there is no excuse, in any profession, for being late, disrespectful, forgetful or otherwise not well-behaved in public. Ever. If you behave as a "flakey artist," you indeed will be seen that way.

> *"Artists who behave professionally are more likely to be treated as possible business partners. Gallery directors have complimented me on my professionalism. When I prepare for a show, I have things ready for the gallery before they even ask for it. Actions like this help me stand out from the crowd. Being professional in actions and attitudes has earned me respect from the people with whom I work."*
>
> *~ Lee McVey, pastel artist*

2. Present yourself professionally everywhere, all the time.

Make sure you are up to scrutiny, not just in behavior but also in appearance. Professional athletes might "go to work" every day in sweatpants, but they know better than to arrive at social functions looking that way.

Of course that doesn't mean that you have to look boring. Curate your own personal style. While a little colorfulness makes you memorable, use it in a way that is appropriate to the occasion. People will always look at how you present *yourself*, as well as your art.

> *"You can be making little money and be very successful at what you do. I never gave into the idea of looking like the starving artist. I always dress to feel good about myself when I am out of the studio. When you look like you are celebrating success (even if you're not selling art) and people ask what you do and you say 'I'm an artist,' their reaction is quite different than if you're dressed like a 'starving artist' for all to see. They become interested in you and your work. Leave the rags and the paint stained clothes in the studio. Look your best! People have bought art from me because they figured that if I look as if I am enjoying success, my art must be worth collecting."*
>
> *~Franck de Las Mercedes, abstract painter*

3. Respect everyone you meet.

Mind your manners and treat the people you choose to interact with in the way they want to be treated. You may not always know with whom you are dealing, or what they may tell others about you, so treat *everyone* with respect. This includes viewers, buyers, suppliers, venue managers, artist reps, art consultants, gallery dealers, museum curators, arts writers and anyone else you meet.

I have gone to gallery openings where the artist was more interested in drinking or talking with friends than connecting with guests. Art fairs and open studios may be casual, but having your feet on the desk or reading a paperback (yes — I've seen this) instead of greeting the people you invited is just plain rude and unprofessional.

A gallery dealer I know once told me that she had made a telephone appointment with an artist who had requested that she look at his work. When he answered the phone at the appointed time, he asked her to call back because he wanted to finish having his lunch. As you can guess, she crossed him off her list.

Respect is due for everyone inside or outside the art world. The next person you meet may help make your art career dreams come true. Respect and attention to others can be your most powerful public relations tools. Decide right now that you will behave in sharp contrast to the stereotype that artists are not dependable or reliable.

> "I've gotten to work with some incredibly brilliant people, who in the past I would have admired from afar, and whom I thought would not be not approachable. So now a lot of the people who would have been heroes, and are at the top of the food chain in whatever they do, are peers - they know what I do - and they have become friends. Having access to those kinds of people with those kinds of minds is probably one of the most rewarding things I do."
>
> ~John Unger, metal sculptor

4. Fulfill your promises.

To sell art, you need a network of trusted relationships. While it may seem obvious, *you* need to be reliable and trustworthy *first* to build that trust in others. When others are counting on you, make sure that you deliver so you never disappoint them or discredit yourself. Make only promises you know you can keep, and keep all the promises you make.

Last minute changes should be rare, and if they do happen, they should have reasons that would commonly be regarded as universally acceptable or unavoidable. "Traffic was heavy" or "Because I don't feel like it" are not valid reasons.

Communicate immediately at the first sign that there could be a problem keeping an agreement. The only thing worse than being unreliable is being unreliable and unreachable. Think about the hardships your change of plans may be causing the other party, not on the endless list of reasons you aren't able to perform. Offer whatever help you can to alleviate any inconvenience or difficulty your change of plans created.

When something goes wrong, don't "pass the buck" or try to make someone else look bad instead of you. Own up to your responsibilities and make all the reparations you can.

Any blame that belongs elsewhere will eventually find its way there without you pointing fingers. Speaking ill or gossiping about anyone, be they artists, dealers, artist representatives or collectors, will only make things worse and will kill your art career quickly. Remember, the art world is a small one — if people hear you blaming others, they may wonder what you're saying about them, and that thought alone could potentially "poison" future business opportunities.

In short, do what it takes to deliver as you said you would. When things do go wrong, if you have nothing good or useful to say, then say nothing. You'll be better respected for it.

> *"By the time I took the commission 'Stations of the Cross,' I was so worn down I would fall asleep randomly during the day and even at my easel. The commission would have normally been eighteen to twenty-four months worth of work. I had 3 months. Composing fifteen paintings in a classical style would be hard enough but painting them in that style seemed an impossible feat. In the end I succeeded. I learned more about myself during that time than all of my years painting."*
>
> *~Eric Armusik, painter*

5. React appropriately.

Being professional does not mean that you have to be stuffy, aloof or always in control. Things go wrong and you are entitled to feel your feelings. Just don't express your negative emotions publically and make a spectacle of yourself. If there is an issue you need to address, calm down, think it through and respond appropriately. Show restraint and you will win respect. Don't be a "high strung artist" and expect others to deal with your moods.

Most of the time you will discover that there was some simple misunderstanding or an unrealistic expectation. Refrain from reacting hastily and in anger. Instead, uncover the truth of the situation, then look for a reasonable explanation and find a respectful solution. By doing so you'll be respected both for your maturity and your considerate behavior.

Become known for your generosity of spirit, as well as for your professionalism, by understanding the needs and desires of those you work with. Support others in achieving their goals, and they will support you in achieving yours. Be kind, strategic and intelligent, and your actions will pay off for you, even if the offers you receive are one-sided. Again, you never know who else will learn about you second-hand, from the way you do business with others.

> "A man phoned after an Open Studios weekend. He wanted to meet and discuss representing my work at a big art fair. At first this seemed like a perfect opportunity to have my work seen by an audience who could afford my originals. I researched the art fair and it looked fine but found little about the dealer wanting to represent me. I ended up respectfully declining that opportunity. Though a fine gentleman, he was just not experienced enough, and had only an online brochure site representing art that did not relate at all to what I do."
>
> ~Huguette Despault May, still life drawings

If you can maintain these clear, simple standards of behavior, you'll be well-equipped to build a highly regarded, professional reputation along with your art career.

Making Money — Or Not

Perhaps you are fortunate enough that you *don't* need to make money from your art. If so, that's terrific — and also highly unusual. Most working artists want to at least cover their expenses. If you use art to support yourself, or yourself and your family, you must come to terms with the role of money in the lifestyle you want to create.

Which of the following is true for you?

1. You make art for play, not for pay.
There is great value in "playing with art" as a source of relaxation, creative expression or therapeutic catharsis. In this case, creating art is both the main event and the desired result. If you don't care about making money, or don't need to, then you're in a wonderful position to simply enjoy it. As I've said before, there is nothing wrong with making art for personal pleasure.

2. You want to cover your art expenses.
Some artists simply want to sell enough of their art to pay for the cost of materials and tools. By selling a piece now and then, they are able to make art "for free." The desire to cover your costs is a valid objective and also a good way to develop sound financial habits.

3. You have other employment to cover expenses.
There is much honor in having a "day job" to cover your living and art expenses. Your creative life may very well enrich your job life. Your job life may inspire your creativity and provide fans and followers. You might also use your art as a form of escape from the less enjoyable aspects of being employed. Having a reliable salary means that you can take your time building a body of work, gaining an audience and developing an art business foundation that will provide you with income.

4. Someone else covers your expenses.
If someone else supports you financially, make sure you have clear boundaries about what is expected in return. Your "backers" may feel that they are entitled to participate in all of your creative decisions, including how much you create or what you do with finished pieces.

One emerging artist I know, whose husband had been supporting her art career, received an ultimatum from her spouse to make $50,000 from her art in the next twelve months or get a "real job." This was unrealistic at her career stage. She had to decide whether to renegotiate the time frame with her husband, or get a part-time or full time job and keep working on her art in her personal time.

All of the professional artists I work with consider making money to be part of the deal. If you don't need to make money, you may be missing an important stimulant that drives many artists to go the extra mile.

The good news? You are doing what you love. As one of my clients once said, "Being an artist may be hard, but not being an artist would be much harder."

If all goes well and you are diligent at matching preparation with opportunity, the money will follow.

Your Attitude is as Important as Your Actions

> "My optimistic attitude, along with a sense of gratitude and wonder has been key to helping me go through the inevitable droughts of being a creative person."
>
> ~Anne Marchand, abstract painter

A positive attitude doesn't cost time, money or energy, and is entirely in your control — so turn it on and use it in your favor! Your attitude about your business is possibly the strongest influence on your level of success as an artist.

Read and commit to the following, and you will pave a smoother road for your success:

1. Be your own cheerleader.
You are the only one in charge of your motivation. Whatever motivates you, keep it at the forefront of your mind every day. Motivate yourself even when you are tired, uninspired or mired in life's "busywork" that has nothing to do with art.

2. Make space for better thoughts.
We all have days when things don't seem to be working as well as other days. Fussing tends to make everything feel worse though, so make space for better thoughts.

3. Say daily affirmations.
Come up with several positive statements of intent or accomplishment that you repeat often. Make sure that they are emotionally true and that you actually believe they are possible. Endless mindless repetitions of "I'm going to be discovered tomorrow," or "The world is ready for my brilliant vision" will just set you up for further feelings of failure. Consistent use of realistic, supportive "mantras" can help eliminate self-doubt when it creeps in. Establish the habit of having faith in what you can do, and it will be harder for doubt to take hold.

4. Meditate and/or pray.
Meditate to clear your mind of day-to-day distractions so you can build a clear space for your creativity to flourish. If you are religious, pray for guidance and the ability to overcome the obstacles ahead of you.

5. Turn obstacles into opportunities to improve.
Everyone's heard the saying "Necessity is the mother of invention," but have you ever truly contemplated the wisdom in it? Invention and problem solving have their basis in creativity… so any time you allow yourself to examine what's not working in your art, your solution cannot help but tap into new avenues of creativity, and just might turn that obstacle into a tremendous opportunity.

Looking at flaws is humbling — and good practice. The first time I was able to look at a piece and say, "Wow, that's really awful!" was a freeing moment for me, because I realized that I was developing a critical eye for my own work. I threw that particular artwork in the trash, but in later situations I was able to get past what was "wrong" and instead look for what was "right" with the piece — and then identify what I could do to save it.

Sometimes when there's "nothing to lose" you can gain the most. If you remain open to what *might* be, you can turn anything "less than successful" into something wonderful.

© 2015 Aletta de Wal, Artist Advisor, Artist Career Training
www.ArtistCareerTraining.com

The Three Stages of a Professional Art Career

There is no profession where you can leap from the bottom to the top — instead you must progress through a series of stages. First you have to "learn the ropes" in an entry-level job, pay your dues for a time and then move up the ranks. Though the creative path differs significantly from climbing the corporate ladder, artists progress through several distinct career stages too.

The terms "emerging," "mid-career" and "established" are all art industry shorthand to describe how far an artist has advanced. While the qualifiers for these terms are more evaluative than definitive, they generally include:

- The quality of art and the size of the body of work.
- The development of a signature style.
- The scope of the audience and market.
- The number and dollar value of sales.

Some artists dislike these terms and prefer not to be "pigeon-holed" by what they perceive as a linear description. I use these terms here not to box you in, but rather to allow you to step out — so please don't interpret them as limiting. Instead, choose to see these stages as a realistic context for evaluating your growth, as well as a tangible guideline for when to take certain actions throughout your career.

It's also important to realize that being an emerging, mid-career or established professional artist has nothing to do with age or talent. Many artists in their sixties have a lifetime of experience making art, but are still "emerging" because they haven't shown or sold their work. Other artists enjoy thriving careers early in life and are considered "established" while still in their twenties. Similarly, I've met many very talented artists who have never moved past the "mid-career" stage, and some very savvy artists with lesser "gifts" who moved well beyond mid-career because of their business acumen.

In other words, not all artists progress through all three stages — and not all artists want to. It's up to you to decide how far you want to go, and whether your skills and life circumstances will support that decision.

Sadly, it's very common for artists to overestimate the maturity of their work and under-estimate what it takes to build an art business. These artists end up disappointed and angry because they want unrealistic results in an unrealistic time-frame.

Other artists might be prepared for the workload of a full-time art career, but aren't aware of their true, current career stage. Consequently, they waste their resources, make unnecessary mistakes and find themselves in embarrassing, costly or thorny situations.

In this chapter you'll be able to identify which stage you're in, you'll get a handle on what to do next, and you'll learn how to plan future steps to further your career. With these necessary foundations in place you'll be able to side-step frustrations and move your career steadily forward, instead of sideways or backwards.

If you haven't yet made the decision to pursue your art professionally, understanding these stages will help you evaluate if, when, and how you want to proceed. By knowing what to expect at each stage you'll feel more comfortable along the journey and can stop being anxious about whether you're going far enough, fast enough or in the right direction.

Let's take a look at some typical markers of the three stages of a professional art career. While the stages do overlap, you should still get a good feeling for the main factors that define each level. This will help you determine where you are as an artist, where you want to go — or both.

The Emerging Artist

Artists in this stage develop their art talents, create their art business foundations and start to get local notice. They spend most of their time making art, staying focused on the thrill of creating and exploring. Their work ranges widely in style, subject matter and media as they seek to try every possible means of expression. Emerging artists are often enthralled with the romantic notion of being an artist and spend endless hours in the studio. As a result, their artwork improves, their speed increases with their ability and their production expands.

Though emerging artists commit major portions of their life to making art, they also begin to build an art business foundation. With typically very little art-related income at this stage, the emerging artist must be a "Jack-or-Jill of all trades" to get everything done and stay afloat. Luckily, the business aspects at this stage are fairly light: tracking income and expenses, building a basic web site, starting to exhibit and promoting to a small audience.

Emerging artists are often inexperienced or uncomfortable about pricing and may choose to give art away to family and friends to avoid the awkward question of "How much?" They are still in the process of discovering their audience and letting the public know about their art. Over time, they do start to gather a following from which they begin to build a mailing list and perhaps even make some sales.

At this stage artists often go through alternating periods of exhilaration and frustration. They produce work that pleases them one day, then looks unfinished the next. While this may feel like a roller coaster ride, the variations are actually a hallmark of progress —it shows a developing ability to objectively evaluate work produced. Removed from the jubilation of creation, the critical eye begins to identify potential improvements.

What should be done with these less-successful pieces? I often suggest to emerging artists that they should keep everything they make as long as they have the storage space. There is a wonderful sense of accomplishment when you can see the progress in your work across an expanse of time.

It's also highly rewarding to accumulate a body of work as a measure of your diligence and dedication to create each piece. These rewards help make the downside of the "roller coaster ride" a little less discouraging.
At some point the emerging artist will have to decide what is precious enough to keep in a personal collection, what is worth considering for exhibit and what is too far "off the mark" in subject, style or quality to be considered for either. These last, lesser pieces should then be discarded or recycled into new work. While relegating a piece to "the woodpile" may not be easy — after all, you invested a good deal of time and energy in its creation — it must be done occasionally for an artist to continue to emerge. Consider it a rite of passage.

The Mid-Career Artist

The passage to mid-career always has an indefinite time frame because artists emerge at varying rates of speed. Eventually, however, their growing production rate, increasingly cohesive style, and expanding body of quality work gains mid-career artists entry to multiple venues, including galleries and museums.

Mid-career artists are committed to making a living as an artist. Income from their art may not be as predictable as they'd like, but by actively working on the business side of the business, they begin to achieve a more consistent cash flow.

Mid-career artists have good business habits and have many record-keeping and marketing systems in place. They use their ever-expanding mailing list to promote their work while also managing a website, often with e-commerce features, so collectors can buy from them online. This allows them to supplement any gallery income with direct sales. They spend considerably more time marketing art than making it, though many are never fully comfortable with this loss of studio time.

The studio time they *do* have, however, is more focused than before. They are "settling in" to a particular blend of subject matter, medium and technique that will, with more honing, become their signature style. Because of this, mid-career artists have a well-defined audience and a growing following of committed collectors hungry for their increasingly recognizable work. Mid-career artists are knowledgeable about art pricing and take steps to ensure that their work is priced appropriately for their talent and market size.

As their audience grows and their market expands (from local to regional to national) mid-career artists may increase their capacity for sales by offering limited editions or prints, or grow their income by licensing their work.

The Established Artist

Again, time is not the deciding factor for when artists are considered to have "established" themselves in the art world. The most important qualifier is consistent sales of a strong, recognizable signature style, evolved over many bodies of marketable work.

An established artist's signature style is distinctive and notable to the degree that other artists want to emulate that look in their own art. Many times emerging artists will also wish to study with, or apprentice with, established artists.

Established artists often have people helping them with every aspect of their business as demand for media exposure and premier gallery appearances begins to encroach on office tasks and studio time. Some established artists might even take on studio assistants, if demand for their work increases beyond a level that can be maintained by the artist alone. While still personally directing the overall vision, an established artist may delegate less creative and more time-consuming tasks to others. If their career spans decades, established artists may end up building an "art empire," supporting numerous employees, assistants, and multiple studios.

Artists in this stage usually have multiple streams of income from their artwork and produce steady financial results. Their inventory is large enough to supply concurrent shows as well as private sales to their avid collector base. Established artists have well-developed pricing strategies, and of course, their work commands top dollar in the art market. With their national and possibly even international acclaim, collectors begin to acquire their work not only as beautiful pieces but also as investments that may increase in value.

Comparing Emerging, Mid-Career and Established Artists

I've created another table that will help compare each of the three career stages of a being professional artist.

If you're still contemplating a professional art career, or if you're in the early stages, read through the table one stage at a time beginning with the full profile of the emerging artist. After you've finished each column, take time to clearly visualize the activities and responsibilities needed to attain and maintain that stage before moving on to the next one.

Can you see yourself as a professional artist, after reading what's involved? Try to honestly evaluate if you can commit to all of the categories, and be satisfied with both the sacrifices and the rewards. Thoughtful reflection will help you decide if this life is for you.

If you are already an emerging or mid-career artist, you can use this table to identify areas you may have overlooked or neglected, as well as areas where you might be stretching ahead. Read across each row of criteria and check the item in the column that most accurately describes your current attitudes and achievements, whether it is within the emerging or mid-career column. Any checkmarks in the emerging column will be focus areas for future work, so you can advance your art business.

So get out your pen or marker, and take stock of where you are now.

You'll reference this chart in future chapters, as we work through techniques for advancement from level to level. Remember, the boundaries between the three stages are for the purpose of comparison only, and you may straddle more than one column.

Table 2: Career Comparison Chart: Emerging, Mid-Career and Established Artists.

Criteria	Emerging Artist	Mid-Career Artist	Established Artist
Motivation for Making Art	□ Still caught up in the early excitement of being an artist □ Artistic creation is its own reward □ Loves making art and wants to be a full-time artist	□ Joyful creativity persists, but is tempered somewhat by the need to produce saleable artwork □ Occasionally feels constrained by commission requests or gallery direction	□ Making art is both pleasurable and also a means to an end □ Work includes legacy projects that will outlast career
Style and Quality	□ Working to develop a signature style □ Still sees some fluctuation in quality of work exhibited	□ Constantly refines signature style, which is quickly becoming recognizable □ Exhibits only high-quality work	□ Attained national/international recognition with well-developed signature style □ Signature style is being imitated or copied □ Exhibits only best quality, impeccable work
Subject Matter and Media	□ Experiments with different media, subject matter and styles	□ Has discovered and developed a preferred media, subject matter and style	□ Expertly develops new techniques in preferred subject matter and media □ Explores new areas without losing enthusiasm or signature style

Criteria	Emerging Artist	Mid-Career Artist	Established Artist
Work Hours	☐ At least 75% of time is spent in studio making art ☐ 25% of time is spent researching and implementing business and marketing tasks	☐ About 60% of time is spent making and improving art ☐ 40% of time is spent on business tasks and marketing strategies	☐ 30% of time is spent making art ☐ 30% of time is spent managing team members ☐ 30% of time is spent making personal appearances and building relationships
Business Orientation	☐ Not fully committed to building an art business ☐ Works on business tasks "when there is time" ☐ Prioritizes business tasks by preference instead of need	☐ Completely committed to growing an art business ☐ Feels "stretched thin" by the amount of work required to run a business ☐ Prioritizes business tasks by urgency instead of personal preference	☐ Art business is both an ongoing commitment and a lifestyle ☐ Delegates many business tasks ☐ Prioritizes tasks by importance, timeliness and potential for gain
Audience	☐ Has a small local audience made up of family, friends and acquaintances ☐ Reception of new works is unpredictable ☐ Occasionally sells to people outside of local audience	☐ Commands a growing regional audience, far beyond personal circle of relationships ☐ Reception of new work is predictable and stable ☐ "Followed" by many collectors who regularly seek out new work for purchase	☐ Known by top collectors, galleries and museums ☐ Exhibits are "must-see" art events ☐ Maintains a waiting list of buyers for upcoming work

Criteria	Emerging Artist	Mid-Career Artist	Established Artist
Credibility	□ Has an art résumé of one page or less □ Receives few awards or merits beyond immediate circle of relationships □ Still encouraged by friends or family to get a "real" job □ Submits to galleries but is largely unsuccessful	□ Has a growing résumé of career accomplishments □ Has already received several awards and mentions that build credibility □ Full member of regional art clubs and organizations □ Seriously considered and often accepted for representation by galleries	□ Has a lengthy, impressive résumé of accomplishments □ Has won many prestigious awards □ Signature member of national arts organizations and prestigious art clubs □ Considered a top artist, in demand by blue-chip galleries nationally and internationally
Visibility	□ Occasionally appears in local newspaper mentions or articles □ Cannot afford to advertise in art publications □ Has a basic "brochure" website	□ Receives regular mentions in local or regional newspapers, art publications and local TV spots □ Places small ads in art publications □ Maintains a website with available work, accomplishments, gallery links and updated PR information	□ Consistently appears in regional and national newspapers, art publications and TV programs □ Takes out large ads and full page "spreads" in art, décor and lifestyle magazines □ Has a complex website with the latest e-commerce functions
Desirability	□ Has not yet attracted attention from local art reviewers or commercial galleries □ Unsure of how to get in front of influential collectors, reviewers and critics	□ Has successfully attracted attention from collectors, art reviewers, critics and nationally recognized gallery dealers □ Consistently creates opportunities to be seen, and then makes the most of them	□ Gets positive feedback from recognized collectors, art experts and big players in the art world □ Keeps up with or sets trends and influences collector preferences within the art market

Criteria	Emerging Artist	Mid-Career Artist	Established Artist
Inventory	□ 20-25 finished two-dimensional pieces of work (fewer for larger works or sculptures)	□ Enough inventory on-hand to keep up with demand, typically 60-100 pieces of finished work in a variety of sizes	□ Large, constantly-updated inventory used for collector purchases, gallery shows and museum exhibits, typically 150-200 pieces of finished work in a variety of sizes
Art Shows and Exhibits	□ Displays artwork in studio, art fairs, local artist organization events and co-operative gallery exhibits □ May exhibit in a few group gallery shows, locally or regionally □ Submits artwork to open competitions online and local exhibitions	□ No longer exhibits at art fairs except for a few prestigious or highly profitable exceptions □ Regularly exhibits in regional (and sometimes national) commercial galleries, with some solo shows □ Enters selective juried competitions	□ Selectively chooses events and representatives □ Consistently exhibits in solo shows at top galleries (and some museums) regionally, nationally and internationally □ Juries exhibits and competitions
Art Income	□ Not profit driven □ Sells enough art to cover costs	□ Makes a profit from art sales □ Beginning to explore multiple income streams (originals, prints, licensing, workshops, etc.)	□ Business is highly profitable □ Maintains multiple sources of income beyond original artwork

The Career Path of a Visual Artist

Criteria	Emerging Artist	Mid-Career Artist	Established Artist
Pricing	□ Lets emotion influence pricing □ Changes prices from show-to-show to align with other artists or to make a sale □ Price increases (or decreases) may be unfounded and drastic □ Offers sizable discounts on direct sales when no commission is owed to a third party	□ Uses a solid pricing strategy based on costs and market factors □ Keeps prices consistent across all venues and shows □ Increases prices incrementally when supported by sales and desirability □ Keeps prices consistent for buyers regardless of commission owed	□ Makes use of a well-established pricing strategy and competitive bid management □ Increases prices according to market demand □ Adjusts artwork prices when resale or auction results require it □ Maintains consistent pricing although preferential terms may be negotiated with important collectors and/or third-party representatives
Accounting and Taxes	□ Keeps basic records of income and expenses □ Resists or resents tracking business finances for tax purposes	□ Keeps exceptional financial records to track expenses and manage cash flow □ Meticulously declares income and deducts expenses	□ Strategically invests earnings to build savings and retirement income □ Employs professionals to handle taxes
Team	□ Does not employ paid team members □ A spouse or family member may help with some tasks	□ Retains a small outsourced team plus local interns or apprentices □ May contract with an office assistant, web designer or marketing professional	□ Employs a well-developed team (employee and contract) consisting of studio assistants for art production and presentation, administrative helpers, financial managers or accountants, web designers and developers, graphic designers and marketing professionals

Criteria	Emerging Artist	Mid-Career Artist	Established Artist
Marketing	□ Considers marketing to be overwhelming and something to "get around to later" □ Concerned that marketing may "cut into" studio time	□ Maintains a full suite of marketing materials □ Promotes exhibits and events as they occur	□ Consistently involved in marketing as an ongoing activity □ Creates and promotes media-worthy exhibits, events and experiences
Sales*	□ Not very sales-oriented □ Keeps multiple saleable pieces because they are too "personal" to sell □ Most sales are to friends and family (or by chance)	□ Competent salesperson with regular sales. □ All finished work is available for sale □ Sales are split between regular buyers and new collectors	□ Expert salesperson □ Keeps some works or series "off the market" temporarily to create scarcity □ Sales are "top dollar" and usually out of reach to everyone but top art brokers, collectors and museums

*I want to make a point about using terms like "Sales" and "Sell." I use these words for convenience, to represent the actions taken to facilitate an art purchase. However, I strongly believe that art is **purchased**, not sold. It's a fine distinction, but an important one.

Where Are You?

Now that you've seen the path of a professional artist's career and have check-marked boxes to indicate where you are on that path, take a moment to reflect:

- Are the stages what you expected?
- Are there aspects/elements of stages you find unappealing?
- Would those elements prevent you from pursuing that stage?
- How far do you want to go?

If you're already well on your way, answer these questions too:

- Are you part way or between stages?
- Have you "jumped ahead" in some categories, and skipped over others?

- Are there categories you don't feel apply to you?
- Are you able to commit the time, effort and energy required, in every category, to move to the next level?

Be honest with yourself — this is a private assessment of your goals, progress, and feelings. There are no wrong answers, with one exception:

Every category is necessary, for every person, at every stage.

While you may be moving forward into a new stage in some categories, you will not be able to move fully into that stage, nor will you begin making progress toward the next stage, until you've made significant advances in every category.

Let's use a comparison:

> A young ice skater takes to the sport quite quickly, and just by watching the more advanced skaters she is soon able to copy their movements and execute a few simple jumps and spins. In fact, the new skater performs the tricks so well that there's no discernable difference between her movements and those of the advanced students. Within the qualifying categories of those jumps and spins, the amateur skater is equal to the advanced skaters.

So should our novice enter a competition with them? Not necessarily.

Like our skater, you may be well ahead in certain categories of your art career — but if you try to move too quickly to the next level, without advancing in all of the categories, you're bound to end up "on the ice."

If you're just getting started, you can use the table to track your current capabilities while readily seeing where you need to develop further. If your career is already underway, you've just narrowed down your list of things to focus on next.

If you've experienced disappointments while pursuing your art business, this is likely the reason — you may not have had the proper foundation in some of those categories to support your position.

Don't worry though — now that you're able to identify those missed areas, a little "remedial" art business effort can take care of it.

In the coming chapters I'll address the categories of each stage in-depth. You'll understand fully what they are, why you need them, and most importantly, how to attain them. When you're finished, you'll have a strategy to master the skills you don't yet have, build the foundation you need and achieve the art career you desire.

> "When I was at the Museum School, I took a field trip with a class to New York City. The instructor's wife had work in major contemporary museum collections there and she gave us an informal studio talk on what it's like to be a professional artist.
>
> One thing I remembered well was that there are two ways that artists out of school become known. They either get recognized almost right away through their thesis shows and become an instant sensation (at least for a while), or, more often, it usually takes about ten years of hard work and exhibiting before anyone in power takes them seriously."
>
> ~Huguette Despault May, still life drawings

Read on to learn what awaits you in each phase of a professional art career.

The Emerging Artist

There's a sense of euphoria during the first stages of an art career, much like the first few days of a new romance. It can feel as though you've finally found your place, and you need do nothing more than let your creativity flourish in your studio until the art world comes knocking at your door.

As an emerging artist your art is your passion. You'd love to live happily ever after this way, even though most aspects of your art making, and your art business, are still in flux.

Most of your family and friends like your art and tell you regularly that "it's good enough to sell." In fact, you've already sold a few pieces (just not to your family — how could you? You happily *give* your art to them). The art sales you made were "fantastic," though they didn't quite cover your show admission fees. Still, they covered the cost of some new materials so you're satisfied. A few skeptics in your family do continue to ask you when you're going to "grow up and get a real job" but you don't let that dissuade you.

Most of your time is devoted to making art, and you're constantly experimenting with different media, subject matter and styles. You may have attended art school, community classes or developed your skills on your own. While your art education has improved your skills, it taught you little, if anything, about the business side of art.

You may have shown your work at local and regional art fairs or at co-op gallery exhibits. You've submitted your "best" piece to a few open and juried competitions, and you'd like to enter more (depending on the entry fee). You've not yet attracted the attention of serious collectors, art reviewers, or prominent gallery dealers.

Marketing is something you'll "get around to later." You're not completely sure what's involved with promoting your art, but you know you can't afford to just start buying magazine ads. Still, there are enough blogs on the subject that it must be important… although they sometimes contradict each other. You've got a one-page résumé and a basic web site that you're going to update with your newest work… soon. The local paper might have featured you, but you've gotten nowhere with your submissions to art magazines.

If you recognize aspects of this description in your own art career, then you are, at least in part, an emerging artist. Read on to gain a more in-depth perspective on this stage of your career and learn specifically how to pursue success both within this stage and beyond it.

Motivation for Making Art

This is the most romantic stage of an artist's career, when the love of art and its creation are almost reward enough. I say "almost" because, while we all crave the personal rewards we receive from our studio time, the reason most artists build an art career is to reap financial rewards as well.

To achieve those rewards, you'll need to make some shifts in your approach to your craft — and for some emerging artists, that shift can be one of the most challenging aspects of their art career.

If you find yourself struggling in this manner, remember what I said earlier:

Selling art is *not* selling out.

Success in *any* business requires paying close attention to production costs, inventory levels, returns-on-investment, bookkeeping, marketing and all the other tasks that form a solid business foundation. Doing these tasks does *not* mean you're no longer passionate about art — it means you're *also* passionate about making a living from art. Don't let the critical voice of a family member or friend, or the critical voice in your own head, tell you otherwise.

You have not sold out — quite the contrary! You have embarked on a path few have the courage to trek, by risking in pursuit of your dream.

In poker terms, you're "all in." Despite how it might seem in televised celebrity poker tournaments, it's rare for a card player to put all his chips on the table. When someone does, it usually means they believe their hand is a "sure thing." With your art business, you don't get to look at your hand before placing your bet, and all the talent in the world still doesn't translate to a "sure thing."

So hold your head high, because you're not *selling out* — you're *investing in*. You're laying everything on the line for your art and your future. It's a noble and courageous choice.

Art Skills and Knowledge

The biggest mistake made by novice artists is "trying" everything and landing on nothing. You may even pride yourself on the variety of artwork that you can produce, and believe that if you have something for everyone you will be more successful.

Unfortunately this is not the case. Variety may be the spice of life, but it can also be the kiss of death for an emerging artist. While sticking to one style or genre may seem dull, to be a successful artist you must develop a robust body of related, identifiable work.

When I work with emerging artists, I ask them the following questions:

- What work can you make in the time, space and budget you presently have?
- What has most energy for you and inspires your creativity to flower?
- What gets you in the flow and keeps you there?
- What medium, subject matter, and style could you do all day long?
- When you lose track of time, what kind of work are you making?
- What work does your audience like the best?
- If you have sold work, what sells the best, the easiest and the most?

Of course, it can be tremendously difficult to remain objective when evaluating your own work. Emotions and memories may prevent you from making truly unbiased assessments.

It's a common mistake for emerging artists to include works which don't quite measure up in their portfolios — the quality, the media or the subject matter doesn't fit well with their better pieces. They include those pieces in exhibits, shows and gallery submissions because the "reflection in the water looks so realistic," or because they sold one just like it, or because it's their spouse's favorite or any other subjective reason.

Be proud of those works, keep them in your archives and share them privately with those you're close to — but be disciplined enough to take them out of your public portfolio.

You can improve your ability to objectively evaluate your own body of work by studying that of other artists. Go to art exhibits or fairs where many artists have set up their own display booths. With just a quick glance at each booth, can you get a clear feeling for the identity of the artist? Is there a singular style, or does it seem like more than one artist's work is hanging on the walls? Do the works seem to belong together, or are they a jumble of different subjects, styles and media all thrown together? You'll soon be able to differentiate between the artists who have found their niche, and those who simply want to do (and show) it all.

Next, take a closer look at some of the jumbled displays that seem to have multiple styles. Are there any consistent traits you can identify? Which pieces appear best together? Which pieces, if removed, would allow the remaining art to appear more cohesive? By repeatedly asking these questions and practicing how to "edit" other artist's exhibits, you will greatly develop your ability to assess your own collection.

Subject Matter and Media

As an emerging artist, now is the time to master your medium, subject matter and tools to build your competence and your confidence in your art talents.

Competence and confidence reinforce each other. The better you are technically, the better you'll feel about your work. The better you feel about your work, the more confidence you'll have to take risks and make distinctive choices. This, in turn, makes it easier to refine and define your signature style, and to know when a new piece is not up to your standards. A piece like that needs to be reworked before being shown — if it gets shown at all. It may simply belong in your personal collection.

So study the work of other artists, find teachers and mentors to help you, ask questions, read blogs and books - and most importantly - get into the studio regularly. Master the fundamentals of your art so you can be proud of what you create.

Business Orientation

I admit that there's more thrill and pleasure in creating art than in handling the business side of things, but it's very important that you don't subscribe to the myth that you will simply be "discovered." Because that's what it is — a *myth*! If all it took to "make it" as an artist was to make great art, there would be millions of successful modern-day masters right now, making heaps of money without ever leaving their studios.

The truth lies closer to the reverse of that image. Our world is full of "would be" artists who devoted all of their energies inside their studios, bitter at never having gotten their "big break." Even the most successful and well-established artists don't always love the business side of art, but they recognize that it has to be done in order for their work to find an audience.

Emerging artists who make it to mid-career are more realistic than romantic regarding their art careers, and are definitely business-oriented. If you are driven enough to persevere and diligent enough to do the *business* work as well as your *art* work, you too can be successful.

Work Hours

The amount of time each artist spends to create a single piece varies greatly. You might be a part-time artist who can only devote a few hours a week to your work. Perhaps you're a sculptor who works in hard stone, and it takes you months or years to complete a single piece. Or maybe you're a madly prolific creator who can turn anything and everything into a marketable piece of finished art in a relatively short period of time. However long your creations take, for every four hours you spend in the studio work up to devoting one hour to your business.

In one hour, you can, for example, update your resume, process photos of your newest work, apply to a couple of juried shows, write follow-up notes to new contacts, file a month's worth of business receipts or write a press release… all of which are tasks that will build your art business. Approaching these less-than-appealing business tasks as a "time trade-off" can make them more tolerable. Tell yourself, "I'm going to spend one hour updating my mailing list (or some other daunting or dreaded chore). Then when I'm done, I'll spend four hours in my studio."

Whatever system works for you, stick with it! If you track your hours and consistently devote about 25% of your working time to business tasks, you'll be making the progress you need for your art career to grow.

Audience

Learn to recognize "your" audience — know the people who like your aesthetic and are drawn to the styles, colors and media you use. You will find that there is a lot of crossover in art, and many viewers and collectors have tastes that are wide-ranging.

Some of them are more educated, or more experienced, and appreciate many different styles. The majority, however, are actually quite selective and focused in their art tastes.

Observe who is legitimately drawn to your art (as opposed to politely appreciative) and develop your connections within *that* group. Are there people in your audience more conservative in their likes and dislikes, or do their preferences run to the avant-garde? Choose carefully which types of events you attend based upon your answer — that way, you can focus on cultivating relationships within your audience.

Please don't misconstrue my meaning at this point: I'm not saying it's a waste of time talking with people whose tastes differ from yours… the art world *is* relationship-driven, and there's much to learn and benefit from interacting with people across all realms and preferences. By all means, enjoy those connections. Just remember, at an art show or opening, you have a limited timeframe available to meet and speak with others. Guard against devoting all your time and attention "converting" someone to your work, at the expense of losing an opportunity with those who already hold an appreciation for it. Yes, everyone is a potential collector, but some are far more *likely* than others.

Ask everyone who expresses interest in your work if they would like to be on your mailing list. Be prepared to describe how, and how often, you use your mailing list, and what you will not do with it (like share their names) to make it easier for them to commit to giving out their personal information. In the same conversation, don't forget to remind them to add your name to their online address books so your emails won't end up in their spam folder.

Make notes about all your contacts: where you met them, their art and color preferences, special dates or anniversaries, home-construction or remodel plans, etc. Use this information to stay in touch (more frequently than right before your upcoming shows) so you can build familiarity and turn acquaintances into art friends. Sales often happen through relationships like this, and relationships take time to develop. Start now.

Reputation

To be an artist today is to be a public figure — so be sure you are always prepared for your public.

You have to build your reputation over time, just as you need to build your artistic style and talents. At this stage of your art career, the best thing you can do for your reputation is to guard against developing a negative one.

While it might seem dauntingly large, the art "world" is actually a small, closely-knit community of regional clusters, so be careful of the impressions you make. In art's small circles, a negative reputation can grow much faster than a positive one… especially guard against the tendency to assert "proof of your knowledge" by making critical comments.

In all of your interactions, do what you say you'll do, how and when you say. Be prepared to be where you say you'll be, and be prepared to be there. Be polite, be respectful, and be supportive. Have a positive outlook and always act from integrity.

Credibility

While you may not yet have enough experience or credibility to apply to your first galleries and shows, you can start doing your homework to *become* prepared. Nearly every gallery and show website has a section labeled "Artist Submissions." Read it closely and respect the published methods of contact and rules for submissions. Adhering to these guidelines is essential because it shows your willingness and ability to follow directions and do what is asked of you. To a gallery owner or show sponsor, that translates to fewer headaches down the road — always a welcome trait in any applicant.

Keep in mind, you'll be evaluated on the overall quality of your submission long before anyone views any of your artwork. Pay close attention to the quality and appearance of your materials: no slang, no typos or spelling errors, no unlabeled images, no cut corners, no left-out sections, etc. Professionalism and credibility are judged on appearances and actions, so make sure your submissions not only fulfill requirements, but also are appropriate and well-presented.

For most submissions, you'll need your "Artist Statement" (a one-page mini-story about your inspirations, influences and artistic methods) as well as your art résumé. Like any other personal business document, there are a wide range of approaches and styles to consider. Go online and study a few artists you admire whose work or media is similar to your own. While you don't want to directly copy their work, seeing how they've styled their documents to reflect their artistic persona may help you in writing yours.

As you gain experience with shows, sales and gallery representation, you'll continually need to update your résumé and eventually use it to write your "bio." (Bio is short for biography — which will be a narrative about your accomplishments based on your résumé). You can combine your artist statement and bio for an "About" page on your website.

Visibility

Once you have art to exhibit and a business foundation, you'll need to also start thinking about marketing. We won't go into detail here, but gather examples of marketing tools like business cards, postcards, brochures and announcements, both printed and digital, from artists whom you admire. If possible, find out where they were made, what quality you get for what price, etc., so you can build a list of suppliers and resources to use when you develop your own promotional materials.

Your first website can be a simple "brochure-style" site which includes your artist statement, images of your work, a list of events or shows and a way to contact you. At this stage you can forego online sales features or additional links that will prove costly to develop. As your career progresses, you can expand the site to incorporate these features and perhaps add a blog to tell the "backstory" of your art and accomplishments.

If you are comfortable with social media, start exploring or interacting on sites like Facebook, Twitter, LinkedIn, Google+, and Pinterest and ask your contacts there to visit your website and blog. Give people a chance to get to know you, personally, and they'll be more interested in getting to know your art.

Desirability

To build desirability you first must be able to talk about your work. You must understand your creative process, your subject matter and your media thoroughly enough that you can explain your work to others.

You need to help viewers understand not just how, but *why*, you create the art that you do. This will likely take some personal review and soul-searching. Don't cheat and allow yourself empty catch-phrase answers like, "I just paint what's in my heart," or "I try to live in the moment and let my work evolve in the same way." Expressions like this might sound good on the surface but they don't create a specific impression for others, no matter how sincerely stated, and sometimes they sound downright trite and overused.

If you cite your influences, such as names of other artists or art movements, make sure that the general public knows them so that the reference doesn't cause confusion. What you want is a short, meaningful caption of your work, put in plain words that someone without any art experience can understand and relate to. You can reach a lot more people this way than if you use "art speak" and sound like a textbook.

Write out a description of what you do and why you do it (you may wish to include when, where and how you do it as well). This description may come very easily for some of you, but others may need to "try on" a variety of answers over time before finding what rings true. That's fine — even artists who have been describing their work for years "return to the drawing board" when their art moves in a new direction.

Jot down all the possibilities that come to mind, then honestly assess each one. Does it "hold up" next to your body of art? Does it bypass "art-speak" and empty catch-phrases? Does it resonate with you emotionally? And finally, one of my favorite tests — could you say it, with a straight face, to everyone you know?

> "My artist's statement is at the center of my art. It is like a mission statement for a corporation or a volunteer group. It is central and integral to my focus when I practice my art. It is a definition of my relationship to my art. I am producing a body of work and the direction of that work and the natural progression of that work is seen through my many mission statements over the years. Each time I come up with a new mission statement, I can see how my art is growing, being honed, and simplified to a clear shine.
>
> My artist's statement helps me talk about my art to clients, helps me define my art in grant proposals, and when I cannot find ready words, I rely on the words I painstakingly produced in my artist's statement to convey my deepest thoughts about my art.
>
> For me, the artist's statement has always been an important tool I use to understand why I go out there each day, get filthy dirty, so sore I can't use my hands at night, and smile when I come back each morning to see how far I've come. I have to know why I'm doing something...what its purpose is...and if it's really worth the enormous effort I put out in a given day. When I read my artist's statement pinned to the wall of my studio...and I believe it...then I know I'm doing what I came here to do...and I cannot ask any more of myself."

~Carol Mackay Mertz, sculptor

I've seen hundreds of artist statements that are bland and boring and a few that are bright and shiny. Your artist statement is an important marketing tool, so as I said earlier, start by looking at what has been written by artists you admire. Then write your own draft, test it, test it again, and rewrite. Writing an artist statement will require clarity and your best writing skills. Don't let that daunt you. The work is worth it in the end.

Besides understanding your artwork well enough to write about it and explain it, you must also be visible — in person at reputable art and society events, and online in a responsible, respectable fashion.

Go to art events as often as you can and get to know the different types of people who attend them: those who look at art, those who buy it (or know people who do), those who sell it and those who make it.

Don't restrict yourself just to art events, either. Collectors go where their interests take them, and you need to be there too. Remember, you might be *more* visible at non-art events because you're the only artist there! So make the most of *all* opportunities to become known to new people. One of my clients is a member of his local business owners' association and also attends Rotary Club meetings. Those gatherings have become a great way to promote his art events, simply by building relationships with others who share his business interests.

Art Inventory

Since your work is not yet in great demand, you have the opportunity to build an inventory of at least twenty to twenty-five small to mid-sized pieces. These pieces should be fairly cohesive in style and quality. Each should have a strong "family resemblance" to the others, and be works that you are proud to show and don't feel the need to explain or apologize for.

As you amass this starting inventory, pay close attention to the amount of time it takes to produce this number of quality, cohesive pieces. This information will become critically important as you begin applying to more shows and galleries. You don't want to overextend your ability to replace that inventory in your eagerness to gain wider and wider exposure. Nothing will upset a gallery owner more (or put you on a "no" list faster) than taking too long to replace your sold inventory — especially when there are willing customers waiting for your work. Guard your ability to continually restock your inventory just as vigilantly as you guard your reputation.

Art Shows and Exhibits

Naturally, people need to *see* your art before they can buy it, so find or create opportunities to show your work as soon and as often as you can. You can start in your studio, at art fairs and at the local co-op gallery. You will learn the most about how to exhibit your work by actually going out there and doing it. Once you have a track record of exhibiting at these informal venues, you will be able to consider more formal locations like commercial galleries.

Art Income

Few people without a benefactor, a stash of personal wealth or a high-earning and understanding spouse can afford to "jump in" to art full-time, right away. Art materials are expensive, and art income is often inconsistent (if not downright random) for artists just starting out.

At this stage, if you are exhibiting, one buyer can "make" an art show — but it's not uncommon to have shows with no sales at all, leaving artists longing for the "good old days" when they worked at a job with a regular paycheck. For this reason, I recommend a gradual transition so any art sales are supplemental to your steady income earned elsewhere, at least while your art business grows.

Keeping accurate and detailed financial records is one of the best ways to know when it's time to quit your regular job. Seeing evidence of consistent sales, over a long-enough period of time, will help you know that your artwork can support you.

Pricing

Pricing is often difficult for the emerging artist, for many reasons. Some of these pricing challenges stem directly from your artwork. With your passionate curiosity and exuberant sense of discovery driving much of your art production, you are still seeing some "swings" in work quality. Do you price these works equally? You're also occasionally producing breakthrough works, of better quality, which are creatively significant to you. Should they be priced equally? Still other pieces began as experimental "play" and look nothing like your usual body of work, but are very striking. How should you price them? Should you even show them? Other pricing quandaries exist depending on where you are showing your work.

Suppose you've just finished setting up your booth at an art fair, but upon walking the show, you realize everyone else's work is priced significantly lower than yours. Should you drop your prices to align with theirs? What if their prices are higher? Should you raise yours accordingly? What about shows where you have to pay a commission on sales, in addition to your entry fee? Can you raise your prices to cover the loss? If you don't, you'll make less than usual... and what do you do when a neighbor or a friend wants to buy a piece, before you've even displayed it? Should you offer a discount? After all, it hasn't cost you anything in show fees or commissions!

There are as many answers to these questions as there are artists, and most artists' answers will change along with their prices over the course of their careers. For the professional artist, however, there is one overarching rule that must guide every pricing decision:

Never make pricing choices that could hurt a collector, a gallery owner or an art representative.

Your ability to build a successful art career is as dependent upon your reputation as it is on your artwork. If you become known by collectors as someone who raises and lowers prices at will, or become known by galleries as an artist who "sells around them" to avoid paying a commission, your art career will be very short-lived.

Everyone expects some small fluctuations in pricing — but think about it from a buyer's perspective. Have you ever paid full price for a purchase, only to find the same item marked half-price the next day? Have you ever discovered that the discount the car dealer offered you was significantly less than the one your neighbor got? Remember how you felt in those situations, and you'll recognize the potential danger in using preferential pricing practices.

For the same reason, recognize the danger of "selling around" your gallery or representatives. By giving a collector a better price to buy directly from you, as opposed to through your gallery, you're giving galleries no reason to show your work. Galleries incur enormous expense on your behalf maintaining "your" exhibition space, providing "your" sales staff, advertising "your" product and cultivating "your" customer — all with no guarantee of income. If you do not believe they deserve every penny of commission you pay them, then don't work with them at all.

Accounting and Taxes

No matter how small your sales are as an emerging artist, always do business professionally and legally, with a business name registration, a vendor's license, sales tax ID and separate bank accounts and credit.

If you pay for art expenses through your personal accounts and credit cards without keeping records, you'll lack any information about how much you're spending versus how much you're making. You'll only have a vague idea of what it costs to produce your art, and you'll have no idea how to approach your taxes.

Aside from the obvious, immediate advantages (like tracking your cash flow and being able to deduct expenses), getting your business finances in order means you'll also be prepared for when your art business begins to grow. After you've added a couple of galleries or additional exhibitions to your work cycle, even the most basic accounting tasks become more complicated.

So set up your art "office" now, while you have time — because believe it or not, your time will only get more precious as your art sales start to grow. Keep track of everything you do, with files for expenses, business forms, your inventory (including work that's in your studio and at each of your galleries) and your mailing list.

Team

While you may not be able to afford hiring for many of your art business tasks, the assistance of willing family members or friends can lighten the load. Don't be afraid to ask for help! Those enlisted are often more than happy to feel that they've helped make your dreams come true. Whether offering a hand with bookkeeping or entering contact names in a database, a little help goes a long way in taking care of business tasks and freeing you for studio time.

Occasionally you will also need assistance in the studio. Cultivate an "art buddy." You can provide each other with inspiration, an outside eye and an extra set of hands in the studio — a realm where it can be difficult-to-impossible to utilize help from a layperson. Commit to assist each other and decide how to do so. You might have a daily ten minute telephone pep talk before either of you starts work, a once-a-week visit to each other's studios to give feedback on works-in-progress or an agreement to simply "be there" for each other, for whatever purpose.

Marketing

While this is frequently the last realm to receive attention from the emerging artist, there's been more written about marketing art than about any other element of building an art career. Take advantage of this abundance of material and begin to study art marketing now, so that you will be prepared to take action as your career begins to grow.

Immerse yourself in the culture of your local community to better understand the events, interests and ideals of the people you will be marketing to. You'll not only have an edge when preparing marketing materials, but your ongoing involvement may open up new venues for your artwork at the same time.

Pay particular attention, initially, to local and regional art shows and fairs, because these are the markets where you will be starting out. What are the submission qualifications for your local news media and radio? Can you get calendar mentions or public service announcements for individually-sponsored events? For in-studio shows? Are there any non-art related functions advertised that might benefit from an art tie-in? Who is advertising currently? Are ads for entire exhibits, or for individual artists showing there? Do news articles support the ads? Calendar mentions? TV appearances?

Sales

One of the most important transitions into the professional realm requires a "thought shift" in which making your work available for purchase becomes as important as creating it.

In no way does this mean you should abandon your priorities and hand over your art to the lowest bidder. You do, however, have to move beyond the frameworks of personal growth and accomplishment. Your art for sale cannot be too personally precious to consider letting it go to others, or too questionable in quality to offer up for purchase to begin with. When you are tempted to "pull a piece back" from a potential purchase, remember this: you have a lifetime of creating beautiful art ahead of you (not to mention a library's worth of digital records of the creations already behind you). You'll never be "without" some of your best work.

Once you've learned to "let go" of your work, you need to learn how to "sell it." I don't mean you need to use high-pressure tactics and learn the "ten most effective closes" — not at all. Largely, those techniques and the people who use them are overly aggressive, and should stay on the stereotypical car lot. And as I mentioned earlier, I believe that art is *purchased*, not sold. So, what's your role, when it comes to "selling" art?

I often tell my clients to remember that art is an emotional purchase. As an artist, what you need to do in order to "sell" your work is learn to tell your story, and the story behind each of your creations. Simple, honest words, spoken from your heart, will translate the meaning of each piece for your viewers and enhance their emotional connection to the artwork-
I do have one caution, however — have you ever walked into a furniture showroom and had a salesperson follow you around the entire store, all the while eagerly telling you about every sofa you see? I have, and it's never pleasant. In the same way, don't try to share the story of *every* piece of art on display, and don't "hover" over people as they view your work.

Just say "hello," then give them room to view your work on their own. If they become interested in a piece, you'll know, because they will *physically* return to it! If you're following too closely or talking a mile a minute about each piece, they may feel compelled to linger at every work just to be polite even though they're really not interested. Step back, be quiet, smile, and save your "story" until interest is expressed. That way, people will feel free to take their time to view, and possibly purchase, your art.

The Mid-Career Artist

It's hard to say where the line is between emerging and mid-career artists. Mid-career is a loose category, defined by exposure and experience, with signature work that has evolved over time and improved in quality for a number of years. As a mid-career artist, you fully enjoy the pleasures of making art but are also attentive to your audience's response to your work, both in exhibitions and online.

What your family, friends and acquaintances think about your art career no longer matters quite as much to you, although it's always nice to have their support. What's more important is getting positive feedback from both your collectors and those who are knowledgeable in the art world. This type of public praise has grown stronger and stronger in recent years, as you've fine-tuned your signature style.

To stave off boredom, you've started experimenting with some new subject matter and media, but so far you've kept those works private. Once you're confident that your new pieces are worthy of showing in public, you'll transition a few of them into your active body of work in order to gradually introduce them to your audience.

You've learned by experience how to make a profitable and satisfying living making art, though you never imagined it would take so much time and effort. You spend more time than before on marketing and administration, but you know it's a necessary part of running a business. To ensure that you still have enough time in the studio, you've begun hiring help for some of the administrative tasks. This business investment is already paying off — your new webmaster just added a payment feature to your site (which you had meant to get to yourself, but never had time for), and you've already sold a few pieces online.

Your work is shown in several commercial galleries around the country, though the majority of your galleries are regionally located. You've stopped doing art fairs except for extremely profitable ones where you've built a solid following, and either reduced your involvement or resigned altogether from your co-op gallery. There's simply not enough time for all of these activities, and besides, they're not the right image for you now, anyway. You focus instead on your collectors, some of whom have started traveling to your exhibitions and show openings. For your most loyal collectors, you sometimes hold private "previews" because they want to be the first to see your new work.

You've been written-up in regional and national art publications, and although it was small, your regional museum show attracted the attention of some art reviewers and bloggers. You've won a few awards and recently completed a good-sized public commission. You happily posted these achievements on social media sites where you've gained a following. You may wonder where you'll find the time to keep this up, and wish you had a weekend (or more) that you could devote solely to your studio.

If you recognize aspects of this description in your art career then you've moved into the realm of the mid-career artist. Are you enjoying it? Once you get a handle on the more challenging aspects, it's actually quite common for some artists to choose to stay in this stage since it can provide a satisfying and sustainable art lifestyle business.

While it's fun to contemplate taking your career to the next level, the prospect of sacrificing even more time and effort to get there may not feel worthwhile. If you're comfortable where you are, that's enough.

Read on to gain a more in-depth perspective on this stage of your career. You will learn specific ways to make the most of your success within it, and, for some of you, how to move beyond it.

Motivation for Making Art

As a mid-career artist, your joy of creative expression persists. In many ways, it's even been enhanced as you've honed your skills and solidified your signature style. Your work has grown more powerful, eliciting a more passionate response from your audience and providing greater personal satisfaction. You're also receiving financial rewards for your work, which increases your confidence and your certainty of vision. All of this positive feedback has you "pumped up" and primed for time in the studio where your creative juices can flow. The biggest danger to you is that you'll be tempted to neglect the needs of your business in favor of the rewards of your studio, or ignore the feedback from your galleries in favor of "staying true" to your vision. My advice? *Don't*. It's vitally important as your career begins to grow that you stay grounded in the disciplines that brought you success in the first place.

It's all too tempting to put aside essential business tasks and justify those choices by saying, "I need more studio time if I'm going to double my representation this year," or "My galleries should handle all the business now — isn't that what I pay them for?" or "I can't do office tasks before going into the studio… it ruins my creative flow." Stay away from those thoughts. You've learned that to build an art career, you needed to build an art business; well, to maintain that art career, you must also continue to *maintain* that art business.

Of course, you need to maintain the artistic vision that got you there, too. Many mid-career artists find success with their newly-honed signature style and cannot wait to show the world all of the other creative visions swirling inside their heads. They experience great rushes of energy and inspiration putting everything they've got into fresh new work in a whole new vein… and then become greatly disappointed and disgruntled when their galleries don't appreciate that new direction.

Resist this cycle and listen to the feedback from your galleries. Yes, they've chosen to represent your artwork because they respect your creative vision and talent, but they also represent it because they know they have a market for it. *You* are not the product. Collectors won't buy the work just because it's yours — that realm is reserved for the most elite, established artists. *Your* success depends on the artwork you produce. If you suddenly change your style entirely, it may no longer be saleable.

Let's look at this issue with another example:

A small women's clothing boutique exclusively features "special occasion" wear such as evening gowns, bridal, and formal party attire. The owners have spent years building their reputation for having the widest selection, the best quality and the newest trends in stock. They carry their customers' favorite brands, but also regularly introduce new designers to expand their selection. They're particularly excited about one new designer — though they've only carried him for one season, his gowns flew off the racks and they had to reorder mid-season.

The storeowners arrive at market during fashion week and rush to the new designer's showroom. He greets them warmly and gushes about how inspired he's been this season — he believes his designs to be the best work he's ever done! The storeowners are ecstatic to see his new creations. Yet, despite their heightened anticipation and their record of success with the designer's gowns, they leave without placing an order. Why? Because the designer's newly-inspired line features only casual wear.

While this story might seem a little extreme, it nevertheless perfectly illustrates the dilemma faced by gallery owners when their artists are inspired in completely new directions. Did the designer exhibit any less talent in producing his new line? No — it equally expressed his vision and showcased his skills, but in a product for which he hadn't yet built a market.

Remember, you've spent a lot of time paying your dues to get to this point, and your galleries have done the same. Don't undercut those efforts by allowing your inspiration to swing too widely. While you may occasionally feel constraints to your creativity because of gallery direction, remember that they are the retailers who have "made" your art career and they deserve your attention.

Art Skills and Knowledge

Early on in your love affair with art, you very likely studied other artists' work, copied their techniques and replicated their style. Now that you're a mid-career artist, your goal is the opposite — you want to refine your style so it looks *less* like the work of other artists and more distinctly like your own. The more you make art and learn to look at it with a critical eye, the more you'll be able to identify even the subtlest differences that separate you from "the crowd." Identifying those differences is very important.

Other artists are great sources of feedback in this regard. They know the language of art, they are familiar with a wide-range of artist's styles and typically they will have a more objective eye than you, the creator of the work. They also understand the challenges you face and will often be supportive and empathetic as they share their opinions. You may want to join, or form, a critique group for regular feedback, particularly with more experienced or advanced artists who are skilled at articulating their feedback to express *what* they feel and *why*, along with their suggested improvements.

You can also solicit feedback from your galleries who are on the "front lines" of art sales. They've spent years viewing and studying art, they regularly hear feedback from the public and they may be aware of private opinions that people are too polite to share directly with the artist. If they suggest that you change some aspect of your work, don't equate doing so with "taking orders." It's possible these small adjustments are meant to enhance the overall quality of your work, and are not intended to merely bend it to the market's whims.

Your galleries have chosen to represent you because they believe in your talent and your artistic vision. They're on your side, and they are just as interested in selling your work as you are. Their profitability and reputation depends on mutual interests. Listen to their assessments of market demand with as much objectivity as you can. If you incorporate their suggestions into your style it may mean an enormous difference in your success.

When I work with skilled mid-career artists, I ask them the following questions:

- What work can you make in the time, space and budget you presently have?
- What work holds the most energy for you, and inspires you to "step up your game?"
- What work holds the least energy for you?
- When you get excited and want to start new work, what sets off that desire?
- What work do people comment on the most?
- Of the art you have sold, what sells the best, the easiest and for the highest prices?

You've invested years to get to this stage of your career, and you take pride in your readily identifiable, distinctive art. The final element needed to continue elevating your body of work is to "raise the bar" on quality. Every artist has favorites within their body of work, and most also have pieces that they don't feel are as successful. The difficulty lies in determining whether it's personal preference affecting your opinion of a piece, or a difference in quality from the rest of your body of work.

Some artists develop systems to help them evaluate their work, assigning point values to various qualifiers (such as composition or color) with a minimum score required for the art to go into inventory. Others assign grades to their new pieces and, for example, nothing below a "B+" gets released to the public. One artist I know simply asks himself if there's anything about the new piece for which he wants to apologize; if he answers "yes" then the work fails the test. It's a difficult question to answer, and made more so by the fact that these "troubled" pieces usually eat up more than their fair share of time and energy — so you really didn't want to scrap them.

If you find yourself asking, "Does this piece need more work, or is it good enough?" the answer is simple:

"Good enough" is never good enough.

Do your reputation and career a favor and err on the stricter side when evaluating your work for public release. If you find yourself using any qualifying terms, such as "it'll do," "it's fine" or "somebody will buy it," move the piece in question to your re-work pile. Then, re-evaluate it at a future time when fatigue and frustration are not impeding your decision — or when you've got a completely honest and trusted second party to assist you with your decision.

Subject Matter and Media

As an emerging artist you explored a range of subject matter and media, but now that you've been building a career around those disciplines for a few years you may want to spread your wings once more. Maybe you're bored with producing the same thing over and over and want to try a new media or subject matter. Go ahead! All artists need to feel free to flex their creative muscles — just know that you'll need to continue producing artwork in your original subject matter and media as well (at least for a little while).

Building a career on a specific "look" doesn't mean you're restricted from venturing into other realms, it just means you need to do so gradually for the sake of your collectors and galleries. I encourage artists to think in terms of *transitioning*, as opposed to *changing*.

Let's say you're known for soft-hued landscapes, but your new fascination is intensely-colored high-contrast florals in close up, tightly-cropped compositions. The difference between the two looks is extreme, so building a show based entirely in the new style could easily cost you your audience (and possibly your galleries). Perhaps, you think, I can show a little of both? While at first that may seem like a good compromise, as transitions go, it too will likely be unsuccessful. Putting two such disparate styles side-by-side often subtracts from the power and appeal of both, and will certainly cost you the cohesive quality that a mid-career artist's body of work should exhibit.

The solution is to apply a bit of discipline, both in your studio *and* while curating your shows, to gently guide viewers in your new direction. Your heart and your passion may beg you to focus solely on the new style, but from a business perspective it will help more if you also commit to producing works in-between the two.

You might create some close up florals in the soft hues of your landscapes, or begin teasing some of the brighter hues into your landscape compositions, or add some mid-distance landscapes to your mix or create a few tightly cropped "detail" pieces pulled from one of your landscapes. There are infinite possibilities you can use to bridge the gap from old to new.

You'll also need to be prepared to speak about shifts in your subject matter or media. Just as you learned to tell the story of your old work, you'll need to be well-versed with descriptive language to romance the new pieces — their call to you, the new techniques you're using and your history with the new materials or subjects. The history can be particularly important — collectors who are not wholly enthusiastic about the new work may have a change of heart once they understand the reason for the changes to your style. Knowing that you painted the first of the florals at your mother's special request, or as a tribute after your grandmother's passing because she was a florist, can help existing collectors make an emotional connection to radically different new work.

Work Hours

As an emerging artist you likely spent about 75% of your time on art and 25% on your business set-up. Now is when those business systems will really come into play! Initially your paper trail was supporting just one or two galleries or shows, but now you've got to track inventory, shipments, commissions, promotional materials, expenses, photo documentation and the like, for many more places and events.

For the sake of comparison, let's say that as a mid-career artist your business and marketing tasks will take about 40% of your time, leaving you with 60% of your time available for studio tasks. The importance of establishing good business systems and employing assistance whenever possible becomes ever more meaningful at this stage.

Business Orientation

As a mid-career artist, you're now completely committed to your art business — you have to be! You're a small business owner who manufactures your own inventory, and you've (hopefully) become as efficient as possible in the office *and* in the studio. If you haven't yet, now is the time. Even if you're using streamlined systems with high efficiency you're still going to be stretched fairly thin. In order to make further growth possible in your career, you're going to need help.

This presents a difficult crossroads for many artists, both emotionally and financially. After working so hard to build your business you may find it challenging to trust someone else. Strapped for time as you are, it may seem more daunting to find and train someone reliable than it would to continue to do the work yourself. Let's face it — you do a million different tasks requiring a wide range of skills every single day. How could you possibly break that down into steps that you could teach someone else? And even if you could, how could you afford to pay them?

Like any seemingly insurmountable task, the answer is to do it bit-by-bit. Consider beginning with an accountant or bookkeeper to handle your financial tasks. After a few lengthier sessions early on to set things up, accountants can often handle your books for just a few hours a month. Similarly, you could hire someone to handle photo documentation and cataloguing of new inventory — a time consuming task, but one that is relatively simple in scope and easily teachable to someone already familiar with the necessary software. Imagine how wonderful it would be to gain back the hours spent adjusting images in Photoshop, assigning inventory numbers and saving works to the appropriate files. When you begin with singular tasks like these, it is much easier to find, train and afford a bit of help.

If you still struggle with the notion that paid help is an unaffordable luxury, I encourage you to consider the costs of *not* hiring assistance.

You might be capable of maintaining your own website, but if that task is taking time away from booking a commission, landing a new gallery or finishing a grant proposal, you might not be saving any money at all by slaving over that computer code. In other words, at this stage of your career you need to start considering the "cost of doing business" as an investment in your future, rather than as unwelcome expenses.

Getting help needn't be too expensive, either. Ask your local university or community college about creating an internship for students in finance or marketing, or team up with fellow artists to hire one assistant that you can "time-share." A little creative thinking goes a long way when it comes to finding office help — in the end, they'll likely be able to do the tasks better, faster and more effectively than you ever did, so you can just get back to making art.

Audience

Now that you're in your mid-career stage, your work is likely being featured in several group and solo shows at various galleries, giving you a tremendous opportunity to visit with your audience. Of course, you've had the chance to meet some admirers and collectors before, perhaps at art fairs or outdoor exhibits, but those venues are peppered with so many distractions that it can be hard to really focus in, one-on-one, with fans of your work.

Gallery events and shows are different. They're designed to create intimate pockets of art-focused time, allowing artists and patrons to mix. They're the perfect place to kindle new collectors and nurture key relationships. Be prepared to discuss your work — your unique techniques, inspirations, influences, studio rituals... whatever will help you share your "art and soul" to these potential collectors.

One caution, however: when attending events where your art is being showcased, avoid the tendency for all of your focus to be self-directed. I know — you can't wait to tell people all about *you*. Naturally, the people attending your events *are* interested in you and your work — they wouldn't be there otherwise — but they have lives and interests and pursuits *outside* of your realm, too. Don't make the mistake of being so eager to welcome them into your world that you forget to inquire into *theirs*. It's a delicate balance, but I'll tell you what I tell all my clients: when you are in the studio, you are in charge; when you are out offering your work, your audience is in charge — so focus on them.

Unfortunately, many artists are not as adept at sharing the limelight as they'd like to believe. We all know what it's like to be cornered at a party by someone who drones on and on about themselves, but we're equally convinced we've never been guilty of that behavior.

At the other end of the spectrum are artists who don't like attention. They'd rather fade into the background at public events and prefer the isolation of the studio to talking with strangers. This "wallflower" behavior can be just as damaging, and may mistakenly come across as aloof and antisocial.

Your goal is to strive for the middle ground, a feat most easily accomplished by remembering that while gallery openings are social events for the attendees, they are *working* events for artists. You are essentially at a job interview, and every patron is your new potential boss. So share your inspirations and methods with your would-be "employers" but don't forget to learn about their "company" as well.

Managing that give and take during group shows is a little trickier because you need to share the limelight with your fellow artists while still sharing it with the public. Again, with the goal of building lasting friendships, be courteous and allow other artists to "take the spotlight" occasionally.

Be careful not to dominate conversations or intrude on other artists' interactions, even if it's with a mutual client. If you recognize one of your collectors in a conversation with another artist across the room, don't rush over to greet them and interrupt the exchange. Be gracious and wait until they've broken away or moved on before making your own connection.

Not only does this give your collectors a bit of breathing room, but it also allows them to explore their other art interests. Yours is probably not the only work they admire. At the same time, it should prevent any disgruntled feelings or "turf wars" from developing between you and the other artists.

Finally, use these events to expand your network of contacts by inviting those you meet to visit your website or join your mailing list — gallery permitting, that is. Some galleries frown on those actions, for fear that the artist is going to sell around them. Make sure you have a clear understanding of your gallery's position on personal promotion and contact acquisition.

Reputation

You've demonstrated to gallery owners and the art professionals with whom you work that you are a competent and reliable business partner, as well as a fine artist. Now it's time to nurture those relationships further. Show your support by attending their events whenever possible, or by phoning with your best wishes a few days beforehand.

Keep them informed of notable events and accomplishments as they occur in your career and connect with them periodically to see if there's anything they need from you — like new promotional materials, image files for their website, new pieces to rotate inventory, etc. Always let them know about new work as soon as it's available. While they might not be in need of more inventory right away, knowing that you have new work available could be crucial when fielding a customer request.

The more you can do to help their business the more you'll help your own. Keep in mind, too, that gallery business is a difficult business. The occasional friendly call to lend an ear or offer encouragement will be much appreciated, and could deepen your business friendship into a life-long relationship.

Credibility

You build your experience and credibility in your mid-career by continuing to promote your work as an artist and by expanding your profile as an art *expert*. As an artist, you've been winning acclaim and merit at juried shows and competitions. Now that you're transitioning into mid-career, it's time to work toward jurying those shows as well.

You may need to start quite small, by approaching local and regional entities with artists who haven't yet reached your professional status. Check with community schools, colleges and civic organizations in addition to near-by fairs and expos. Almost all of them will have some level of art or design competition. Contact the organizers to outline your background and training and offer your services as a judge. Even if you haven't juried a show before, your knowledge and experience as a mid-career artist will make you an attractive candidate. Then, when demand for your expertise in these smaller venues grows, you can take that experience with you as you begin to jury larger, more prestigious events.

While you may not have considered a residency before (perhaps believing that it would require you to travel and live away from home for an extended period of time) in reality there are numerous art residency opportunities available within most local communities. With the budget cuts of recent years, many high schools, junior highs and grade schools are desperate to procure art instruction for their students. Parents and teachers often fundraise for the cost of materials and artist compensation, particularly if it means they can provide their children with a qualified art professional. Even if no pay is available, developing a short residency program for your local schools or community centers is worth considering since it will bring you additional credentials for your resume, a huge new fan base and the appreciation of your community.

If you have good writing skills, consider building your credibility by writing articles for publication. Local community tabloids would likely welcome your "insider's view" of area fairs and exhibits or your "artist's eye" interpretation of a touring museum show. Trade magazines and specialty publications serving the art industry might similarly be interested in articles targeted to their fields. Explore both traditional printing and online publishing opportunities, starting with submissions to smaller specialty markets and building your way up to bigger publications. While it will take some effort, imagine the credibility you'll gain once your articles are accepted by the national art magazines.

This is also a good time to start building your experience in the public realm. Use the Internet to find calls-for-artists at museums, public-venue shows or public commissions/installations for which you are eligible. Fully research these listings and carefully do your homework. Do they want work "on loan" for a set period of time, or are they purchasing commissioned work for permanent installation? These limited-time-frame, "on loan" exhibitions are a good place to begin.

Typically they will be looking for existing work in a particular theme, style or medium, so these submissions are relatively simple to put together, but do check the show parameters carefully. For example, the length of time an exhibition needs to hold your art may be considerably longer than the show length. You don't want the inventory you need for an upcoming show being held-up in return shipping.

You'll also need to consider the financial obligations. Not only is there frequently a submission fee for these shows, but often the artist is also responsible for paying shipping fees, in *both* directions, as well as paying for insurance.

Filling a permanent installation is a bit different. They might be looking for traditional, pre-existing works to adorn the walls or lobbies of government buildings or hospitals, or they might want something more customized. If the description calls for an "innovative solution," or a "conceptual design," don't simply send images from your latest exhibit. Again, study the parameters and be clear about your concept, compensation schedule and production time-frame before submitting the entry. And, as always, ensure that your entry materials are top-notch and professional.

Visibility

Until now, your visibility efforts have largely been interpersonal. While you should maintain these one-on-one efforts, if you want to expand your visibility at the mid-career stage you need to start accessing more than a handful of individuals at a time.

It's time to focus your efforts on mass-media outlets, such as TV, radio and the Internet. Of course, before you begin, you need to ensure that you're projecting a consistent, easily identifiable and appropriate image. In other words, you need an "identity."

© 2015 Aletta de Wal, Artist Advisor, Artist Career Training
www.ArtistCareerTraining.com

Creating a public identity for yourself and your art is a process you may have already started. First, you need a visual identity for your art business — a reproducible logo and word mark. It should be finished in black-and-white, as well as two-color and four-color camera-ready art, and should be vector-based so it won't pixilate when being reduced or enlarged. Your logo's style should reflect that of your artwork and include your name and perhaps a simple tagline or descriptive slogan. For example, Hawaiian watercolor artist Patrice Federspiel has a colorful image of tropical flowers with the tagline, "I paint the essence of living aloha." New Mexico pastel artist Lee McVey uses an image of a photorealist-style desert landscape, with the phrase, "I paint pastel paintings people feel they can walk right into."

Take your time creating your visual identity. Research other artists, consult with or hire a graphic designer to assist you, or "try out" a few design ideas on friends and family members to get their feedback. Then, pin your final candidates on the wall of your studio for a few weeks before making your final selection. You'll use this logo and word mark everywhere, and all of your other marketing materials will be based on this design, color and font — so make sure you're truly happy with it. Remember, people will begin forming an impression of you based on your visual identity long before meeting you or viewing your work, so be sure that your final choice conveys a true representation of you and your art.

Once you've designed your art business identity, use it everywhere that you promote your art — your website, your emails, social media pages, press releases, postcards, business cards, other print media, personal correspondence even your price tags… all must bear your logo and display your colors. Think of your favorite sportswear or beverage and an image immediately comes to mind. In the same way, your visual identity should instantly increase the memorability of your art by supplying a visual association with your name.

Desirability

By this point, you're quite skilled at describing your work — your techniques, your influences and your art's special meaning or message — to help people connect emotionally to your pieces. Your contact database contains notes on each of the collector relationships you've cultivated, listing their personal preferences, their purchases and where you first connected with them.

You've also built an impressive mailing list. By combining these two powerful tools — your emotionally-charged descriptions and your detailed contact list — you can increase your exposure and generate desirability in your artwork, just by communicating captivating details to your contacts that will spark their emotional connections with your work.

As you finish new pieces, write a few sentences about each one, focusing on intimate details or emotional aspects of its creation that aren't readily apparent to the outside viewer. Were you listening to a particular piece of music while creating it that you think is reflected in the final work? Is there one particular aspect of the piece that you most admire? Is there a feeling or memory it evokes in you? These are the details that draw people in and make you more accessible and your art more enticing. Put these short captions together with a couple of images of each piece and send it to your mailing list or post it on your social media pages. These customized, personal messages will provide a window to your world and allow your audience to immediately connect with your art, and with you.

You can also turn your contacts into your sales force by encouraging them to share the images with friends and associates. While they might not do so without prompting, most collectors and fans are happy to promote you by word-of-mouth or by keystroke when you ask them to.

Art Inventory

By now you should be fairly adept at managing your inventory. With each new gallery or show you've added through the years, you've "upped" your production accordingly. You wouldn't have made it to mid-career otherwise.

If you find yourself reaching your production limits, consider these options:

1. Expand into reproductions.
Consider offering limited edition prints and/or hand-embellished giclées. While some galleries carry only original artwork, many welcome the versatility of size and price point that comes with a line of high-quality reproductions.

Expanding your "product line" in this way can do more than ease the burden of production… it can make your artwork available to a whole new audience who might love your work but not have the budget for your originals. These same buyers may eventually graduate to purchasing originals, as their personal wealth grows.

© 2015 Aletta de Wal, Artist Advisor, Artist Career Training
www.ArtistCareerTraining.com

2. Bring in studio help.

Many artists readily hire administrative help but shy away from employing someone to assist them in the studio. Don't fall prey to the misconception that *every* aspect of your art production must be done by your own hand. Whatever your media, there are always many tasks that can be handed off to a skilled assistant or apprentice with a little instruction or supervision.

Imagine… how could your production increase if you no longer had to prime your own canvas? Or build your own wire apertures? Or cut or score every piece of glass? Take an analytical look at your process. Chances are there are at least a few time-chewing steps that someone else could handle, without sacrificing the integrity of your signature.

3. Raise your prices.

There may come a time when you've done everything you can to improve your output, but still find yourself with your "back against the wall." If there's no other way to keep up with demand, it may be time to raise your prices.

I've listed this option last for good reason. This should be your final recourse, because it's not actually a solution to an inventory production problem. Rather, it's the *result* of demand. If your galleries are selling through your work faster than you can resupply them, it *may* mean your market can bear a higher price. I emphasize the word "may" because this is not a decision to make lightly, nor is it one you'll make alone. Your galleries are at the forefront of the art market and are likely to know best what price your work can command. If you suspect a price raise is in order, quietly approach one or two of your gallery owners or managers. Ask for their observations and then respect their answers. If they confirm an increase may be in order, come up with an estimated amount to raise your prices, which you can then run past your other art representatives.

Art Shows and Exhibits

If they're not already doing so, approach your galleries about featuring you in a solo exhibition or limited group show of two to four artists. Mounting a show can pose significant effort, risk and expense, and it is no small undertaking for a gallery, so don't be impatient or "pushy" with your inquiry. Merely express your interest or idea. Depending on your sales history and what they perceive public interest to be, your gallery will determine whether your market will "support" a show in their location.

Do make sure to inform your gallery of positive results from other recent shows, and offer your assistance with promotion, using your own personal connections and mailing list. When mounting shows for "unproven" artists, a gallery may ask you to share the expense of mailings and/or opening night parties. As long as the request comes from one of your regular galleries and your marketing budget can bear it, go ahead — just protect yourself by qualifying your maximum financial contribution first.

Don't, however, get lured into paying for a show or exhibition at an "outside" location (usually a hotel meeting room, banquet hall or other rental space) by someone claiming to be an artist's rep or dealer. These are what the industry calls "vanity shows." Like their counterpart, "vanity galleries," these exhibitions are mounted based solely on the artist's willingness to pay, and the agents "hosting" them make their living by charging artists to display their work. Vanity shows and galleries can be a legitimate way of doing business, but don't confuse these third party fee-based venues with reputable commercial galleries that already have a defined collector base and pay commissions or purchase outright.

Some of these venues will work hard to sell your work; others may not be so ethical. I have worked with a few artists who didn't check carefully what was really involved, and one who'd lost $15,000 "paying" to have a show in a trendy gallery district. In hindsight, there were many red flags, but the artist wanted a show so badly he ignored them and did not verify what he was told before signing up. Remember, this is how they make their living, and they're very good at it. The "pitch" usually goes something like this:

> There is always effusive praise of the artist's work, along with certainty about its appeal "to the right audience." Names and dollar figures get dropped into the conversation with stories of the incredible success other artists have had. There are exuberant promises of great attendance for the event, usually with a celebrity or two expected to come ("because they never miss one of these events.") Of course, celebrities mean great media coverage, too. You'll have great sales, and you'll easily recoup, if not double, your investment.

If the promoters were really that well connected and their events truly that profitable, they wouldn't be asking artists to "front" all the expenses. While they may actually put your work on display in the promised location for the promised number of hours, what will often *not* materialize are the promised sales results. When the event is over and not a single work has been sold, they'll shake their head in wonder and say they just don't understand... then walk away with your money in their pocket. Don't let this happen to you.

Art Business Income

As a mid-career artist you're earning a relatively stable living from your art. Your healthy profit margin has allowed you to invest in future success by hiring assistants to help you with a multitude of tasks. Now it's time to invest in your future security by building up a savings account for those "slower periods." While it may be difficult to find the discipline to set aside some of your hard-earned income (after all, there are so many other things you could do with the money!) building a crisis fund is perhaps the most important and most overlooked safety valve for the artist-entrepreneur. The statistics speak for themselves: insufficient capital is the number one cause of business closures.

While an extended slow-period of sales won't necessarily have you putting up a "Closing" sign on the door (and unless you also own your own gallery, you likely don't *have* a door) it could mean being forced to give up a leased studio space, being unable to maintain inventory or having to return to other employment to supplement your income.

So plan ahead. Set aside part of your income to build a savings account that will serve as a self-created loan in the event of a lengthy soft market. This account should always be separate from your general savings or retirement fund — in other words, don't "dip from this well" when the car breaks down or when your child needs braces; those expenses should already be built into your household budget.

This money, whether in actual cash or reserved available credit, serves only as a safeguard in the unfortunate event that your art income suddenly "nose-dives." Whether caused by a sluggish economy, a natural disaster or health issues, there are many unforeseeable factors that could impact the sale of your work. If these issues were to befall you, or befall two or more of your galleries thereby limiting sales for multiple months in a row, would you be able to weather the downturn? Begin building an emergency fund now, so you can answer "yes," should the need arise.

Pricing

Now that you've reached mid-career you should have a clearly defined pricing strategy that is consistent between your galleries, shows, website and personal sales. Still, circumstances may occasionally arise that cause you to question your prices and tempt you to make adjustments. Should you? That's a difficult question to answer, for while there are many factors that go into pricing, there are no hard and fast rules that all artists use, nor are there any absolute benchmarks. "Price" is simply what people pay for your art, and it may be far less or far more than the value you place on it. As Warren Buffett said, "Price is what you pay. Value is what you get."

So how should a mid-career artist arrive at a decision about a change in pricing? The best answer is to use the following guideline:

Never change or adjust your prices unless it's for the right reasons.

What are the right reasons? Generally, they're all related to a healthy "sell-through." Sell-through refers to the rate of speed at which your inventory sells. When your sell-through rate is strong it means your merchandise is moving "off the walls" almost as fast as you can replace it. This indicates you either have extremely high market demand or are priced under market value — or both — and a modest price increase is justified. If your prices need to come up significantly, do it in multiple small steps, no more than ten percent at a time. This gives you a chance to evaluate what the market will support in stages, and also prevents "sticker shock" for your collectors.

What are the wrong reasons for raising your prices? Many artists are tempted to raise their prices because they want to make more money. They "believe" their demand is strong enough or their collectors loyal enough to bear the increase. There's no reason to "believe" this is so unless your sell-through numbers say so. If your sales rate is the same as it's always been (or "flat," in market lingo) then the increase isn't justified, and you could wind up hurting your income if you raise your prices.

Another wrong reason that I frequently hear is the notion that artists can somehow increase their perceived value, and thus their sales, merely by being more expensive. Higher prices alone do not imply greater value. If that was true there would be no discount stores, and department stores would *raise* prices for their sales events instead of lowering them. So be very cautious about raising your prices without the sell-through history to support it. You might just price yourself out of the market.

It can be similarly tempting, if you aren't selling as much as you'd like or are in need of cash flow, to temporarily *lower* your prices. Be careful with that strategy, however, for it may be close to impossible to raise them again.

Again, think in terms of the department stores at your local mall. There was a time when they didn't have a "sale" every weekend. Sales events were held twice a year to clear out old inventory and make room for new. The new merchandise itself was never put on sale — at least, until one year when the new merchandise didn't seem to be selling very well. Concerned they wouldn't "make their numbers," they decided to stimulate purchasing by putting the *new* merchandise on promotion... and the "sale treadmill" was born.

You see, if you tell your customers they can buy your goods for less once it goes on sale, you've essentially *handed them control of your pricing*. Whether shopping at Macy's, or at a gallery or art show, once the buyer knows you sometimes have "sales," why would they ever pay full price again?

What about the question of discounts? First, let's establish the difference between a discount and a "sale." A discount is an unadvertised, variable price reduction given to a single individual, whereas a sale is an advertised discount of a set amount offered universally to all buyers. Some artists offer a small price break to their frequent collectors that I like to call a "preferred customer price," or to people buying multiple items. Other artists stand firm and never offer a discount. There are pros and cons to both approaches and the choice is yours to make, but whatever you do — be consistent. If you're comfortable, go ahead and offer a small "incentive" at times, just make sure to empower your galleries to do the same.

My preference is to stay true to posted prices, because the "treadmill" effect applies to discounts too. Instead, I suggest that you offer those looking for a discount some extra value to their purchase — a signed copy of one of your art books, a complimentary frame or installation services. People simply want to feel they've spent their money wisely.

One further word on discounts: offering a set percentage off should never be used in place of proper sales technique. In other words, don't try to "sell" solely by dangling a discounted price in front of the viewer. Remember, the decision to buy art is an emotional one. Help the buyer build a true emotional connection to the piece and you may not need price adjustments at all.

Accounting and Taxes

Recordkeeping for accounting and taxes is one of the most important systems of your art business. How well is yours functioning? Do you find yourself uncertain, at times, of the commission due from any of your galleries? Have you ever deposited commission checks but forgotten to process the payment through your bookkeeping program? Have you ever been late preparing one of your quarterly tax payments?

"Yes" answers to these or similar questions signal that your accounting system needs to be fine-tuned before your business grows further. The addition of each new gallery and show complicates your recordkeeping exponentially. While you may be well-prepared to handle the increased inventory and marketing demands of additional venues, your accounting system must be up to the task as well. If it isn't, there will definitely be trouble ahead. Take the time to stop, assess the problems and fix your financial system now, before your reputation or your credit rating gets damaged.

Team

At this stage it's essential that you free up your time for the creative aspects of making and marketing art. You've been developing systems for every routine business task; now assemble and train a team of people to implement those systems. This includes sourcing, purchasing materials and tools, inventory documentation, framing and shipping, insurance, banking, taxes and website management. Delegate *all* standard business routines, as well as any art-related tasks that seem feasible, to others who are qualified. That way you can do what you do best, and do what only *you* can do: make art and build relationships.

Marketing

When I ask mid-career artists what would most improve their art lives, I usually hear, "Someone to handle marketing, so I can get back into the studio." When I ask them what their business goals are, over and over I hear nearly the same thing: "To increase sales, so I can afford to hire someone for marketing."

Any way you look at it, marketing demands a huge commitment of time and energy, but at this stage of the game you can't afford to scrimp or cut corners. If you're not willing to do the work to market your art, it won't matter how talented you are — you won't be able to sustain the momentum that brought you to mid-career.

The emphasis here is not to scare you but to motivate you. Too many artists reach the stage where they begin to see returns on all their hard marketing efforts, and think, "Now that the ball is rolling, I can relax a bit."

Unfortunately that's just not true. While there is a point where your "name and fame" are enough to generate interest on their own, it's usually in the realm of the top-tier established artists. At mid-career, your marketing engine just won't run without regularly fueling the fires.

Provided you can afford it, you may want to hire a freelance administration assistant or intern, just part-time, to handle aspects of your marketing. Writing and distributing press releases and announcements, providing a communication "bridge" between multiple media sources covering the same event, or even facilitating social media postings are all smaller tasks someone else can handle in just a limited number of hours per month. This won't take the burden off your shoulders completely, however.

The "ideas" for marketing are still yours — just *implemented* by someone else. But it can still be a big relief to have someone help you create a marketing calendar for events, expand communications with both the media and your audience and build your Internet presence under your direction.

Sales

In the retail world there are three ways to increase sales: get more people to enter the store, sell to more of the people that enter the store and sell more to the people who already buy from you.

As artists we may prefer to think of the transactions with our collectors as somewhat different from "regular" retail, but you can still benefit from these principles.

1. Get more people to enter the store.
Just because most of your work may now be sold via galleries doesn't mean that "getting more people to enter the store" is solely *their* responsibility. As long as you stand to benefit, it's to your advantage to shoulder a share of the load. Remember: you and your gallery dealers are business partners, but the gallery is seeking potential buyers for *all* the artists they represent. You are the only one focused solely on *your* audience.

What can you do to support more foot traffic into the gallery or show? Notify your mailing and social media contacts of *all* noteworthy events and interactions within each gallery. Did you just ship a new work to one of your galleries? Snap a picture and post the gallery location on social media. Did a gallery recently sell a significant piece? Share the excitement with a quick "tweet" to your followers. Was one of your galleries featured recently in a trade publication? Copy the article and include it in your next email newsletter. These are all relatively effortless ways you can promote your galleries at the same time that you're promoting yourself.

Don't overlook the possibility of driving traffic to your local galleries by doing a "live" event there. Many galleries are happy to free up some space near a front window for an artist to work "on site" for an afternoon. Not only does it draw in onlookers from off the street, but it also provides you with an opportunity to meet and discuss your work with a whole new cadre of prospects.

2. Sell to more of the people that enter the store.

Do you track sales statistics from each of your galleries? Not just dollar figures per month or year, but sizes, price points, subject matter and coloration? Artists and gallery owners often rely on their memories to determine which type of work sells best for them, but recollections are not always accurate and may not show the whole picture.

Make a habit of reviewing your sales history, separately, for each of your galleries. What trends do you notice? If there is a downturn in sales, compare the works they've sold in the past to the new inventory they've received. Are there noticeable differences? (Note: it may be easier to make these comparisons by looking at images as well as sales figures.) The point of this exercise is to determine if unintended shifts in inventory composition could be affecting sales. Does one of your galleries always quickly sell through your miniatures? Does another one only do well with your warm-toned work? Unless these trends are consistent for every artist displayed in the gallery, no one may have made the connection. The reason sales of your work have slowed could be because previously sold pieces were replaced with your newer inventory that is "off trend" for that location. By doing a little detective work and discussing your findings with your galleries, you can ensure they always have the merchandise that most appeals to their buyers.

3. Sell more to the people who buy.

Experienced gallery dealers will tell you that, "The first piece of your work a collector purchases represents the hardest buying decision." The concept is this: once a buyer has deemed your work's intention, appeal, quality and value are meaningful, future purchases not only bring additional pleasure but also reinforce the original decision to buy. In other words, your first-time buyers *want* to buy more of your work in the future because it means their first purchase was a good choice!

While this bit of insight to the human ego may seem crass, it's included here not as a sales tool but as a point of perspective. It really *is* in our nature to want "more of the same," and to want others to want it too. Ever notice how the crowd, at some art openings, seems to be rather laid-back about the work until the first red dot goes up? Then, suddenly, everyone is clamoring to claim a piece before someone else does. Every purchase made, whether another collector's or our own, reaffirms our decision to buy.

With this in mind, it should be obvious that by building relationships, treating people well, thanking them when they select your work and following up with them about future work makes additional sales within your collector base become a natural, and welcomed, occurrence.

The Established Artist

As an established artist, you are going "full throttle" making your living and building your legacy. Producing art that bears your unique stamp is as natural as breathing, and your work is not just recognizable but readily copied.

Some established artists choose to keep to one consistent style; others who have proven themselves can now afford to be more adventurous and introduce an increased variety of work to the public. While there's always the risk of alienating some of your audience that way, your name recognition means that there's an ever-increasing supply of new collectors ready to take the place of any disaffected fans. In a similar fashion, as your prices rise, wealthier collectors replace purchasers for whom price tags have grown too precious.

Still, as an established artist you make sure to keep abreast of changes in collector preferences and fluctuations to the art market. You know that it takes a constant vigilance, and working "smart" as well as working hard, to keep making a profitable and satisfying living through your art.

Collectors and curators now seek out your work. Public commissions receive preferential treatment over private requests, unless the private request comes from a prominent collector whose name would be a source of validation and referrals. You frequently employ managers for large projects in addition to your full-time team, which now includes apprentices in your studio for basic art preparation, custom suppliers for your tools and presentation materials, marketing and public relations advisors for your promotional needs and of course the experts who handle business administration and your Internet presence.

Your work is featured regularly in the best "blue-chip" galleries with regional, national and international locations. You also enjoy museum exposure in permanent collections and traveling exhibits.

National and international publications approach you for interviews or VIP studio tours and regularly review your exhibits. You're also in demand as a juror for highly prestigious art shows and competitions, some of which you won earlier in your career. Your résumé is crowded with these and other accomplishments.

Collectors have come to consider your pieces as more than art — they are *investments*. Your track history on the secondary market where collectors purchase work from other collectors serves to reinforce confidence within this elite demographic. Your art sales now provide you with resources and possibilities almost beyond your imagination. Fortunately, you're an artist, comfortable with dreaming about the impossible — and now, quite familiar with attaining it.

If you recognize aspects of this description in your art career, congratulations! You are a member of a very small and very rewarding club. Less than 10% of artists ever reach this stage (a percentage no different than what you'd find in the top tier of any other profession).

As a mid-career artist, you nurtured seedlings and tilled the soil of your art business in hopes that it would blossom. Now, as an established artist, you can harvest what you've grown and fully enjoy the fruits of your labors. Of course, that doesn't mean there isn't more work ahead — you'll need to maintain your "garden" for it to continue to mature.

Read on to learn about the activities you will pursue in order to maintain your status as an established artist:

Motivation for Making Art

For the established artist, making art is still pleasurable, but is also a means to an end. You want even more success, more recognition and more wealth from your hard work. Until this point, you've simply focused on building a career that provided you a living.

Now that you're established, you have the opportunity to build beyond an art *career* and toward an art *legacy*. Your art has already touched the lives of many individuals — now it's time for you to "stake your claim" on future generations. This quest has reinvigorated you to work on increasingly large installations, public commissions and legacy projects which will outlast your career.

No project is too big and no vision too wide — you have an unmatched level of funding and the workforce of your dreams. It seems, suddenly, that your only limitation is your own lifespan.

Art Skills and Knowledge

You couldn't have gotten to this stage without having a well-defined signature style. Now your goal isn't to refine, but to *intensify* the features that make your art so distinctive! You let go of every restraint and push your creativity to its utmost expression so that it is *always* recognized — *never* confused with the work of other artists. This will prove increasingly important as up-and-comers begin to emulate your look. Imitation may be the sincerest form of flattery, but in the art world you want to make sure that these "copies" never get too close to your originals. So take what makes you "you," and make it even more so. Solidify your name and separate yourself from any would-be protégés forever.

Of course, consistency and quality are two other great distinguishing factors. You can further establish your claim on your style by ensuring that your work and your exhibits are always "top tier." Make your name synonymous with impeccable production values in art quality, presentation and exhibition, and you'll always be in a league apart.

Subject Matter and Media

Now that you are known, you can afford to demonstrate the range of your talent. In fact, a certain level of exploration and variety is almost expected from your audience. Don't think in terms of abandoning your signature work, but rather think of it as expanding your scope while innovating. You can do this by developing new bodies of work featuring different subject matters within your *usual* media, or by "crossing over" into *new* media while maintaining your original subject matter. In both instances your signature style should still "shine forth," even if its glow is pointed in a new direction.

When expanding into new subject matter, many artists choose to define similar works by grouping them into different "series." These series are typically titled separately and/or presented under a new category. Distinctions like this are important because it helps to clarify and define your expanding repertoire for the public. Creating within specific series can also add value. Once a popular series is closed (i.e., you're no longer producing work in that vein) the value of each piece within that series may jump, particularly in the secondary market.

Work that crosses over into new media should be similarly separated by title and category. Your artist's website might feature multiple categories of works — one category each for all of your drawings, paintings, sculptures, installations and work which utilizes more than one media.

As with subject-based series, these media-centric expansions can open your work to new collectors as well as create new demand within your existing audience. For example, a collector who had no real interest in your metal sculptures might find your forms irresistible when translated into wood, and the collector whose walls are already "full" with your two-dimensional works may once again start buying your work when you offer free-standing sculptures.

Subject matter and media expansions will also open new exhibition and marketing options as your existing galleries clamor for the new line and "specialty" galleries, previously out of your reach, can now carry your new work that *is* within their focus. You'll also find new avenues of opportunity in the public sector by being able to offer commissions and installations for a wider variety of spaces and clientele.

Of course, as you did in your mid-career, you'll need to support these expansions with marketing and media campaigns to educate the public about your new direction — but this can be a great boon to your career, even if it does entail a large amount of work. Think of the media frenzy caused when a late-career actor chooses an out-of-type role in a film. Seemingly overnight, she or he goes from being "untouchable" to being the hottest star in Hollywood. With the proper marketing, your art career can enjoy similar peaks each time you stretch your wings.

(Please note, if you are reading ahead of your career stage, these opportunities for experimentation and expansion are intended for established artists only, and are not recommended for those in the emerging or mid-career stage. If you are not yet a well-known entity, such variations would likely weaken your brand identity and confuse your audience).

Work Hours

As a mid-career artist, you were spending about 60% of your time on art and 40% on your business set-up and marketing. Again, for the sake of comparison with other stages, let's estimate that now you'll probably be spending 30-35% of your time making art, another 30-35% of your time managing your team and the remaining 30-35% of your time making personal appearances.

Business Orientation

Like any small business owner, you need to keep up-to-date with economic changes and technological advances so you can be poised to make adjustments and improvements to your systems. Consider becoming a student of business management as well. There's no shortage of good information available on team leadership, interpersonal communication, creative problem-solving or any other business-related topic you can imagine. Take advantage of these resources, because by now you fully understand that it takes much more than great art to build a great art business.

Audience

Describing your followers as your "audience" has never been more appropriate. Your success has placed you on a premier stage — your name and your work are recognizable to art enthusiasts everywhere. The biggest change from mid-career is that the majority of your audience is no longer comprised primarily of collectors. Your fame has far surpassed that of your inventory, and your premier prices mean there are now fewer individuals with the resources to own your originals.

In spite of that, it's still in your best interest to cultivate your following within *all* economic levels. Like a stage actor performing in front of a sold-out house, you need to play to the patrons in the third balcony as well as to those in the box seats. Why? Because it's the clamor of the general public who *can't* afford you that provides the prestige for the privileged few who *can*. Playing to all parties is best accomplished by keeping yourself *accessible* to your fans in any way possible.

You may think it's unnecessary to "work" your mailing list, as you've done in years past, but in fact the opposite is true. The greater your fame and acclaim, the *more* valuable your personal contacts become. Why? Because even as your *need* for those personal contacts shrinks, the perceived prestige of being *on* your contact list increases. People want to be a "member of your club," and they want to show off their membership card.

So by all means, deepen your relationship with the top 300 people on your mailing list, but nurture the remaining names as well. Join art and business organizations where you can develop your relationships with wealthy art patrons, but contribute to under-funded community organizations and efforts too. Those contacts may not be equally lucrative for you, but they will be extraordinarily loyal — and your continued interaction with them will likely be more personally rewarding as well.

Reputation

The art world, and its caretakers, can be fickle. Galleries are under so much pressure to sell (and curators under so much pressure to earn good reviews for their shows) that it's not uncommon for them to consider trading their established artists for new names in the hopes of stimulating their market during a down cycle. And even at this esteemed level, there's still strong competition among artists to occupy the same few spaces of acclaim.

As an established artist, one of the best ways to avoid being pushed to the side in this manner is to build a stellar reputation for delivery and service. If you make it *easy* for gallery owners and curators to work with you you'll stand a much better chance of "making the cut." Be dependable, be on time and be pleasant to work with, and your reputation as "one of the good ones" will stand you in good stead.

In a similar manner, nurturing a positive reputation with collectors will add to their desire to own your work. As your exposure grows, the public's *perception* of your character may begin to affect its reception of your art. Make sure you are who you say you are, in public and in private.

Bad behavior may be responsible for adding to the limelight of a few "celebrity" artists, but they are the minority and they are notorious out of infamy, not talent. The art world grows ever smaller as you play at higher levels, so don't succumb to a swelling ego or choose notoriety over respectability. No matter how much people like your art, if you don't also have *personal* likability your career will be short-lived. Choose to build a reputation that inspires admiration, and it will help hold your audience and win their hearts.

Credibility

By now, your resume is filled with impressive awards and accomplishments from prestigious arts organizations and galleries who have acknowledged your work. Sales through your galleries are no longer a concern — they're a given. There is no question that you are experienced and credible as an artist. What you need now is staying power and a foothold on the secondary market, to prove that your work's artistic merit and investment value are credible too.

The best independent proof of artistic merit is inclusion in museums, whether in periodic shows or in permanent collections. Typically, there's little you can do to enable such inclusions— they're decided solely by the museum's curatorial staff, with just a few exceptions. For example, a museum may mount a show of selected works from a private collection (and your work is part of it), or a smaller regional museum might accept the donation of a work, whether by you or a collector.

As for investment credibility, that can only be established by auction results. As an artist, this is both the best and worst thing that can happen to you. Certainly, having your work sold at auction represents a level of accomplishment and fame to which most artists would aspire — but it also means that you and your galleries must relinquish control over much of your pricing. While a strong auction result signifies investment value, a poor auction showing may do the opposite, undermining your investment credibility and consequently deflating your prices and sales.

While there is little you can do to defend against poor auction results, by maintaining the highest standards of quality, staying true to your vision and being even-minded about the cyclical nature of popularity, you can weather their effects until things take an up-turn.

Visibility

At this level it seems hard to imagine that your visibility and persona could ever need additional work, and yet you've gained enough experience to know better. It may only be a short while before, once again, you need to update your approach to marketing. Make the process of staying relevant easier on yourself by being uncompromising about managing your image, even as you take advantage of different avenues of visibility.

See everything, and be seen everywhere. Attend important art events and exhibits (whether or not your art is being featured) in order to expand your national visibility and international recognition. Similarly, develop a presence at non-art venues by attending notable events held in honor of your collectors. Not only will these efforts enhance your visibility but they'll also deepen your relationships as you demonstrate interest in those who show interest in you.

The possibilities in this vein are endless: establish a foundation, contribute to fundraisers or spearhead a community service campaign. The only requirement is that you be genuine; even a whiff of a self-serving motive will quickly spoil any and all efforts at good will. Follow your heart and be true to your passions (but at the same time, always provide a press release!) and you'll keep your PR engine purring.

Desirability

Few artists who reach this stage make mistakes. If they do err, it's by assuming they've "made it," and that success will always continue to be theirs for the asking. Unfortunately, that's just not the case. The public can be capricious, and attention spans can be short. So capitalize on your desirability while your work is in demand, but look to the future as well. You'll have to *keep* proving yourself as the art market goes looking for the "next best thing."

Use your connections with art experts and "big players" in the art world to keep up with changing preferences and trends. Pay heed to whatever is grabbing the attention of your most recognized collectors, because it's guaranteed they're looking beyond your scope. While you won't want to drop what you're doing to run in each new direction, staying *aware* of the winds of change will keep you open to opportunities.

For example, there's a current trend in the music industry for collaborative work: pop artists' singles are featuring rappers, rappers are sampling classic rock on their cuts and old-style crooners are recording duets with as many pop stars and rappers as they can. These collaborations work great for increasing desirability because they open up the artist's appeal to a whole new audience.

This phenomenon is not limited to the music industry. Artists like David Hockney and Julian Schnabel influenced their desirability in the same way with cross-media collaborations in theatre and film, and Andy Warhol enjoyed tremendous success through collaborative projects with Jean-Michel Basquiat.

Are you a textural painter? Consider combining your talents with a well-regarded metal sculptor to create works that bridge both of your mediums. Or, approach your favorite dance artist to develop art inspired by or exhibited with a specific performance work. The possibilities to build your presence and desirability in this manner are infinite, and they'll doubtless jolt your creativity as well.

Art Inventory

As an established artist, much of your art inventory requirements will remain the same as earlier in your career, just amplified to reflect your increasing number of galleries, shows and exhibits. For example, occasionally your work may be included in lengthier touring shows or exhibits. Works featured in this manner will have to be "suspended" from your inventory for the duration of the show, but you should have no trouble incorporating them back into "active" status once the show is over. In fact, once they are back on the market, these pieces may enjoy an increase in demand thanks to this prestigious addition to their provenance. If you're doing extremely well, you may also have works accepted for donation into a museum collection, requiring that they be permanently removed from your available inventory. Of course, this is an honor for which most artists would be more than happy to relinquish *any* amount of inventory.

Though you shouldn't encounter any considerable shifts in inventory demands as an established artist (beyond growth, of course), there are two related issues that bear mention:

1. The secondary market.

In the secondary market, work that has been previously owned is returned to the market for resale, generally through an art broker or auction house. Typically, the artist has no control over the price, quality, distribution or subject matter of secondary sales — a reality that can be hard to accept after the careful consideration that's been given to these factors by the artist and galleries for so long.

Aftermarket sales typically have the most significant impact on pricing, but a ripple-effect can create small disturbances to your inventory as well. For example, the auction of an "older" item might stimulate requests for more work in the same subject matter or series — even one that you're no longer showing. If the interest is significant, you'll be lucky if you have stored inventory of similar pieces to satisfy the demand, otherwise that new momentum will be lost.

Conversely, when any of your advertised auction work bears close resemblance to your current inventory, the result can be a "suspension" of sales for all of your work in the same vein. In this case, the public forestalls purchasing until after the auction's conclusion, in anticipation of a potential value change.

As an artist, these circumstances are beyond your control, but by being aware and staying flexible you can be prepared to respond to them.

2. The concept of scarcity.

"Scarcity" refers to the practice of intentionally lowering inventory levels to increase product demand. The theory is that by restricting supply you can create a perception of scarcity, and thus artificially spur a "feeding frenzy" on work that *is* available. This technique is widely believed to be the brainchild of the diamond market and has been employed with great success in industries as divergent as children's toys and luxury autos. Artists, however, should approach it with extreme caution — if at all.

Why? Consider this: the auto industry is able to spend millions in advertising dollars to make the public aware of its luxury products. As for the toy industry, in addition to its huge advertising budget it has an incredibly dense distribution system. In other words, toy makers can *create* market scarcity because they *control* market saturation. But when your product is only available in a handful of stores to begin with, public awareness is likely too limited to make a scarcity campaign effective.

(Please note, the discussion above refers to attempts to artificially create market demand by intentionally manipulating inventory levels. It should not be confused with artists who release limited editions or have "wait-lists" for their work. The difference is simple — wait-lists are the result of market demand, while "scarcity" is the attempt to create it.)

Art Shows and Exhibits

As an established artist, you are already enjoying solo shows at your various venues. The goal now is to further elevate your status by courting even more elite representation and by making your exhibits "must-see" art events. Accomplishing these goals will require innovative investment of your time, talent and money.

Unless you're fortunate enough to have wealthy connections and top name galleries, breaking into the high-end art market will likely take an indeterminate yet lengthy amount of time.

Begin by researching the better regional art fairs that feature work in your style or media. Think of venues like Art Los Angeles Contemporary or San Francisco Tribal and Textile if you're on the West coast. Look at Art Basel Miami or ArtExpo New York if you're on the East coast. Why start there? Because these fairs can be costly, even for attendees, and by beginning your investigations nearby you can minimize your investment of both money and travel time.

You may be fortunate enough to already have connections into some of these shows, so don't hesitate to ask your galleries and art associates for possible referrals. If you know anyone who *is* exhibiting, arrange a site-visit, offer to "booth sit" or otherwise make yourself useful in exchange for the chance to attend with an "insider."

Once inside, take careful and copious notes. Is it the type of fair that allows juried artists to display independently? If so, try to get a feeling for the success of these "solo" artists. Is their subject matter, quality and pricing similar to yours? Is their goal to make sales, or find representation (or both)? Are they reaching their goals? And perhaps most importantly, would they sell at the fair again? This information will help you evaluate your own potential for success there, and whether or not you'd like to participate yourself.

Some shows are restricted to specific galleries by invite only, and don't allow solo exhibitors — making you ineligible, unless you are able to garner representation from one of those galleries. If this is the case, assemble a list of each gallery present for which your work might be an appropriate fit. Then, once the fair is over, you can submit for representation. As always, be professional in your interactions and respectful of that gallery's focus at the show. They are there to do a job, and in many cases have invested tens-of-thousands of dollars for the opportunity to do so. *Don't* monopolize their time with your questions or chit-chat unless invited, and *do* identify yourself as an artist right at the outset.

Getting involved in high-end art fairs and shows will help you attain better gallery representation, simply because that wider exposure in the "blue chip" market will help bring your work to the attention of gallery managers and representatives. The process is one of evolution; as your market demand and prices increase, you'll begin to outgrow your earlier audience. Remember, high-end galleries are just as interested in finding artists with strong performance records as their middle market counterparts. If you're on the cusp of their demographic, they'll take notice.

In contrast, the means by which you can turn your exhibits into "must see" art events is not as clear. Certainly, ensuring that all of your exhibits are first-rate events — in the quality of your art, the elegance of its presentation and the appropriateness of promotional materials — is a given. But what makes such events truly memorable? What generates a level of excitement so powerful that people are reluctant to leave or determined to come back? There's a trend towards making art events more experiential and entertaining, but in the ever-frenzied efforts of artists and galleries to engage an audience, it's become increasingly difficult to separate the merely *new* from the *noteworthy*.

Ultimately, the barometer for "theatrics" in fine art promotion is a personal one, and it will be up to you and your galleries to determine what works. Be creative when planning your exhibits and events, think beyond the art world when appropriate and strive for an experience your patrons won't soon forget — just remember, they've chosen to attend an art function, not the circus. Use good taste and you'll remain in good company.

Art Income

You've spent years developing and fine-tuning what is now a well-established, consistent pricing strategy, and you are incrementally increasing your asking price as the market will bear it. You've grown adept at negotiating favorable deals and terms with important collectors and art brokers (allowing you to "pocket" more from each transaction) and your income from sales of originals is considerable.

You've also developed multiple sources of income beyond selling your originals, through both limited-edition reproductions and licensing venues. While the profit margins on these sales are lower, their sheer volume makes them equally lucrative (not to mention that they require no new labor from you). In other words, business is highly profitable.

Of course, you've needed this increase in income because it takes more money to support the team of assistants and experts you've assembled to help drive your business, production and creativity. While it may seem that paying for this team of employees consumes the lion's share of your wealth, remember this:

Your assistants are the keepers of your lifestyle — pay, and treat them, accordingly.

I'm not saying your success isn't self-earned. It was *your* years of dedication and endless hours of labor that built the career you now have — but your team is an essential part of getting to enjoy what you've built. Think of it this way: you're not just paying your assistants, accountants, marketers and reps for the jobs *they* do, you're paying them for the jobs that *you* don't have to do. Not only do they keep your income engine rolling, but they keep you from those never-ending hours of work that ruled your life during your early days as an emerging artist.

Pricing

As you move from mid-career into the elite realm of the established artist, the ever increasing figures your artwork commands will lure some collectors to consider "liquidating their assets." They, too, want to capitalize on your success, and so a piece of art they purchased for a modest price years ago gets released for sale on the secondary market, usually through a specialty art broker or public auction house. While people are most familiar with the premiere auction entities like Christie's and Sotheby's, the majority of after-market sales occur through smaller, regional auction events.

As I mentioned earlier, having work in auctions is both a blessing and a curse. The fact that there *is* a secondary market for your work means you've reached a certain level of acclaim and validates your position in the upper-echelons of working artists. However, because these after-market sales occur outside your realm of control, you'll likely have to contend with price fluctuations and sales competition *from your own work* without enjoying any earnings. The exception occurs when auction houses request work directly from an artist with whom they have a good sales performance history. In these instances, the artist takes the position of the "lister" and receives the profits from the sale after the auction house takes its commission.

Work that does well on the auction block can bolster an artist's pricing, and you will likely enjoy price increases based on auction results. Occasionally, though, you may have works that "hammer out" *under* the current market value. While these sales may still earn a profit for the seller (because the work was older, and/or purchased for an extremely good price), they can spell disaster for the artist by undermining current market sales. Collectors at this level will hesitate to purchase art when recent auction results suggest it may have questionable investment value.

While you can't entirely control situations like these, you may be able to take action to lessen the downward pricing trends that can accompany low auction results. If a "poor performer" is from a very early period in your art career, don't be afraid to say so — especially to your galleries and art reps, since they're usually the ones tasked with overcoming a buyer's concerns. It's reasonable, after all, that these early works would bring a lower price. Similarly, any pieces created outside your signature style, or from one of your less-popular collections, might sell for less at auction but shouldn't pose a legitimate threat to the established pricing for your current work — particularly when that discrepancy is properly explained.

Accounting and Taxes

At this point, all of your accounting and tax planning needs are being handled by trusted professionals and should require little to none of your time. Do be certain, however, that their services include strategic investments and adequate savings plans, to cover future business needs and preparations for retirement income.

Team

By now your business will be running efficiently, with a paid team of studio assistants for art preparation, production and presentation; an administrative staff for record-keeping and documentation; business and financial managers for all accounting concerns; web and graphic designers for all Internet, website and printing needs; and PR and marketing professionals to handle all media relations and advertising. You may also have consultants with whom you work on a project-by-project basis, including interior or theatrical designers and tradesmen, lighting designers and electricians, stylists, shipping agents, etc.

Whether you confer with your staffers during brief, regularly-scheduled meetings or assemble less frequently for lengthier brainstorming and production sessions, they should be adept at managing their daily tasks with little time or supervision from you — and with little, if any, need for crisis management.

If this is not the case then you either need to hire more workers, or delegate more efficiently. If you don't, you won't have the freedom that you need for your creativity to flourish. Make sure you've got top people working for you, pay them well for their loyalty and expertise and then trust them to keep your business functioning smoothly.

Marketing

Ideally, your marketing will be as creative as your work itself, keeping you media-worthy and at the forefront of everyone's minds. As an established artist you now have more resources with which to work, so consider investing in new and unusual marketing methods (that befit your particular audience, of course). You'll need to be memorable if you want to have staying power, so extend your marketing creativity to include your public persona. Your art, your advertising, your accomplishments and even your events should all be characterized by your distinct identity and style.

Don't overlook social media — while different sites may come and go, communicating en masse and in "real time" is a trend that's here to stay, so keep your social networks buzzing with activity.

Sales

Sales are the ultimate form of feedback from any marketplace. Ironically, now that you've reached the zenith of your art career, you're more "removed" from it than ever before.

With blue-chip galleries representing your work to the world's top art collectors, museum curators clamoring for pieces representing different periods of your evolution, licensing continuing to provide a rich and steady flow of income and brokers and auction houses doing a lively secondary business… it's all too tempting to pay little or no attention to how the sales are made.

While you certainly don't need to monitor each piece, or each price, it's imperative that you stay connected with general trends in your sales figures. Why? Because they're the most reliable and objective feedback you'll ever receive. By using sales trends to stay informed you can implement corrections nearly immediately as the market changes.

Tracking sales figures and trends is one of the first rules of retail, and even the most successful stores that earn huge profits follow this practice. No matter how much it seems that your momentum will never slow, it's *not* self-generating. Public tastes change and markets fluctuate — if you're not tracking your sales trends you likely won't see those changes coming until it's too late.

Naturally, I'm not suggesting that you change your signature style or your subject matter to follow the fashion of the day, but you might discover trends *within* those elements that can be adjusted. Are you selling more unframed pieces than before? Has a specific series "gone hot" in one gallery? Have bronzes in a particular patina "slumped?" These are all trends that can be discovered and adjusted for, without compromising your artistic integrity, simply by tracking sales figures. Protect your future success by learning to read those signs, and you'll be able to sustain, and enjoy, your fine art career for decades to come.

Section 2: The Work of a Visual Artist

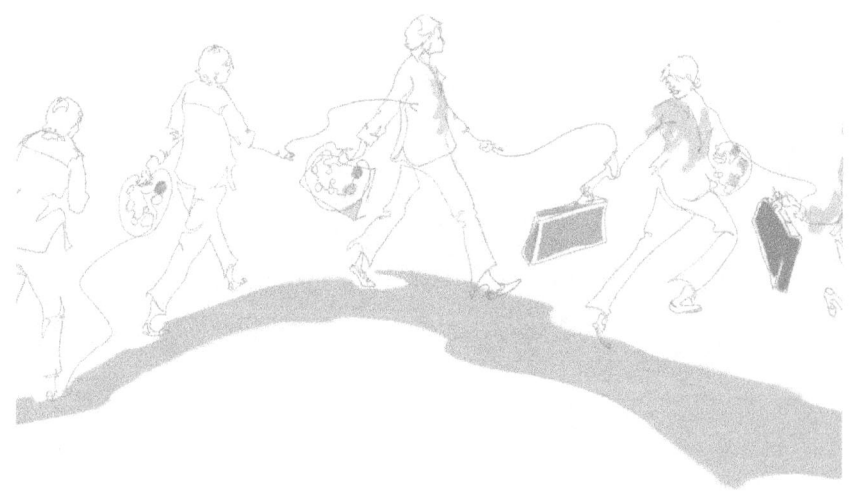

What Could Your Future Hold?

Please take a moment and finish this sentence as if you were already there:
"If I could have anything I wanted as my artist's lifestyle, it would be…"

Now, draw a picture or write down more details about what you want. Think of this brief exercise as a preliminary sketch for your art life masterpiece.

Don't try to make your vision more "reasonable" or achievable right now. Go for your deepest longings. When you can picture what you *really, really, really* want, you will be more inclined to find the unflinching dedication you need to get there.

We'll get the "how" later — for now think just about the "what."

Envisioning your future life is not simply playing make-believe. It's your own creative guidance device. When you shine "high beams" on your future, instead of groping your way forward in the dark without a flashlight, three important things begin to happen:

1. You increase your opportunities
When you continually imagine your ideal future, opportunities seem to "just happen" out of the blue. Your mind latches onto the image of what you want as if it were already real, and filters ideas of how you might get there.

2. You decrease your distractions
If you are clear on *where* you want to go, you can much more easily eliminate or reduce anything that doesn't move you closer to your desired goals. Your vision is the roadmap that helps you to decide the relevance and effectiveness of anything that pops up.

3. You grow your confidence and competence
As you develop your attitude, abilities and skills to become your future self, you *will* get better at what you do — and nothing reinforces your motivation better than getting results. It's a virtuous circle that will make you feel better and bolder with every success.

5 Ways to Visualize Your Future

When I work with artists to help them create a future vision, I use a combination of methods. We start with an audio to visualize the life the artist wants, who then makes a vision board of that life from images cut from magazines or found on the Internet, and we finish with a series of writing exercises.

The creative process of mentally seeing, sensing and feeling the artist lifestyle that you want is not very different from how you create art. In fact, your career may be one of your most creative works — so it may help to think of your future life as if you were about to create a work of art about it.

In the section below, you'll have an opportunity to put your imagination to good use and "design" an ideal art career and lifestyle that will satisfy and sustain you. Dream big at this stage. Don't let the limitations of others' advice, attitudes, past experiences or self-defeating thinking get in the way of what you want to achieve. Reality will impose enough obstacles; you don't need to add more.

Review the following five methods of capturing your vision and decide which of these techniques works best for you. If you feel wildly creative, do all of them. Make sure that you can set aside time when friends, family, telephones and visitors won't interrupt you.

1. Create a mental movie of your future

Athletes use this type of visioning exercise to imagine winning, while actors do it to put them in the correct mindset for performing. For this to work, however, you need to be *inside* the movie, not watching yourself from the outside. It also works best with an extraordinary level of detail. Engage all of your senses to imagine that you can see, touch, taste, smell and hear each moment occurring in your dream future.

While in a relaxed state of mind, visualize stepping into your future successful self and experiencing your ideal life through all of your senses. You can close your eyes if you like, to reduce distractions. Once your vision is clearly in focus, defined in both depth and detail, record your observations in written form.

The following questions may help you get started:

- What kind of art do you create?
- What type of lifestyle do you maintain?
- What is your studio or art creation space like?
- How much money do you make from your artwork?
- What does "success" as an artist mean to you?
- Do you have more than one source of income from your artwork?
- Who is in your art life?
- What kinds of supportive groups do you join?
- In what types of settings do you exhibit your art?
- What do people say about you and your work?
- Does anyone represent your art?
- Do you sell originals, multiples or both?
- How do you balance making art with an art business and all the other things you do with the people in your life?

If you've already done this kind of overall vision work for your career, use this opportunity to get even more specific about the details of your dream. For example, if you've already imagined finding success in multiple galleries, take your vision a step further by "attending," in your mind, the opening reception for one of your shows. Experience this "mental movie" from beginning to end — from hanging your work to greeting and socializing with guests, even to your satisfaction at the end of the night as you gaze about at the abundance of red dots on your title cards.

Remember to use all of your senses as you work through this exercise: *see* your art in the venue where you want to exhibit, *hear* the audience discussing your work, *smell* the fresh flowers, *taste* the refreshments being served, move through the crowd talking with people and *touch* the shoulders of those who come over to congratulate you. Employing all of your senses will help clarify your vision, and ensure a level of detail that will make it feel more real.

Repeat this for all the other ideas you've had about your future. Make your scenarios "juicy" and compelling enough to motivate you. If they're not making you tingle with anticipation, revise them until they do. You should feel excited and enthusiastic, and eager to do whatever it takes to create the reality you've just envisioned.

2. Free-write about your future

Some artists prefer to write about their vision by hand. For this exercise, you will only need to free-write — in other words, release yourself from worrying about spelling or grammar and just record words, thoughts, fragments and phrases as they come to mind.

You might find it even more liberating to free-write on a large, unlined notepad or sheet of butcher paper, using a variety of colored pens and markers (whatever you have at hand). Not only does this bring a more fun, colorful and creative aspect to the process, but it also has another added benefit. Without the limiting structure of lined paper, your finished product will likely show your biggest priorities for what they are — they'll be the largest, most colorful entries, with circles, arrows, hearts and stars drawn all about them. You can organize the bits and pieces of these free-associations into paragraphs or lists later.

As you write, record your answers to the following questions, along with any others you feel will help you define your vision:

- What do you want said of you and your career after you die?
- What is your epitaph?
- Who do you want to be as an artist, citizen, friend and family member?
- What do you want to do with your time, money and energy?
- What do you want to have by way of possessions and experiences?
- Where will you live and what is your lifestyle?
- What do you want to give to others and to whom?
- When will you have this life?
- Why is having this life important to you?

3. Envision your future life roles

Your life encompasses a number of roles *besides* your work as an artist. You can do this integration exercise through written narrative, free-writing, sensory visioning, or sketches.

Below are several "life role" categories to get you started. Make substitutions to tailor them to fit your ideal future.

Provider: Consider the contributions you make to your livelihood. Who is dependent on you for their financial survival? How will you pursue your art career while you provide for yourself and others?

Caretaker: Do you have children or other family members for whom you are a primary caregiver? How will you make sure that they are well taken care of? How will you take care of your own health and well-being?

Learner: What will you need to learn to develop fully into your many roles, even as the world continues to evolve at an increasing rate of speed and complexity? Which methods will you use to gain this knowledge?

Spouse or significant other: What will your relationship with your life partner be like? Will the amount and quality of time spent with them change? How will this individual, and your relationship, support your ideal life?

Spiritual or ethical self: How will you maintain your inner compass for your outer activities? Who will guide you? And to whom will you give guidance?

Neighbor, community member or volunteer: What activities will you engage in to contribute to your community and the wider society?

4. Take your "artist's life" inventory

Some of my clients prefer to begin with what they've *already* achieved before considering what they want to do next. One way to accomplish this is to create an artist's "bucket list" — but with a slight twist. Write down a list of all the things you want to do as an artist before you die, but also include the things you've already accomplished in your career. That way you can "cross them off" your list at the start and feel good about where you are now.

Some starting points:

- List 100 things you have already accomplished in your art career.
- Brainstorm 100 things you still want to achieve in your art career.
- Write 250 words about art you want to create.
- Write 250 words about where you want to be in your art career one year from today (or any other time period that feels right to you.)

Many of the artists I work with do this every year. Most are amazed at how much they've actually done, and it spurs them on to do more.

5. "Report" on your future

Imagine you're a reporter for a major newspaper or TV channel, tasked with writing a feature on your "future" artist self.

Use the journalist's approach and the six key questions: *what, who, where, when, how* and *why*. Don't forget to write a catchy headline that sums it all up, too.

WHAT do you ultimately want to accomplish in the future? Here are a few sample ideas:

- Create a signature style of art, or design a logo that matches your unique reputation.
- Clean your studio, organize your business files or increase your inventory.
- Coordinate a group show (or traveling exhibit) or join a community project.
- Start an art workshop or launch a fundraiser.
- Develop a marketing plan, design a postcard or brainstorm themes for exhibits.
- Plan an open studio, do some gallery research or send out postcard mailings.
- Build a studio, double your mailing list or grow your team by one.

WHO can help you with what you want in the future?

You may be able to achieve what you want all by yourself, but most art projects involve someone else at some point, so why not imagine your dream team? Consider who would fit your needs best. Do you need a teacher? An administrative assistant or a marketing advisor? How about a public relations person? Use this list as a jumping-off point.

WHERE are you going to have this future?

This is very important. You may need to address "where" before you can describe the rest of your vision. Is it at home, or in another building? Depending on your vision, "where" could be quite close, or very far away.

WHEN are you going to have this future?

It helps to have a date when you want this future. Some common time frames are by the end of the year, in 10 years, or "by the time I'm 60." Setting a time frame will help you treat your vision as real.

HOW will you do what you want to do, focus your energy and reward yourself for your hard work? What supplies must you have at hand? What do you need to learn and where can you learn it?

WHY is this important? The importance of asking "why" at this point is to make sure you really want to pursue this future outcome. Some possible answers are:

- So that I will have a body of work to exhibit, a brand for my marketing materials and/or recognition in my local community.
- So that I can reach out to more people with my art.
- So that I can be seen as a leader and pass on my skills.
- So that I will be able to get the word out about my art on a regular basis.
- So that I will be able to manage my time, money and energy.
- So that I can support myself/my family/causes I believe in.

(If you need a little more inspiration, check out Steve Jobs commencement address at Stanford in 2005: http://budurl.com/JobsStandford2005.)

Now that you have your dream career firmly in focus, and can envision what success looks like in your future, you're ready for the next step: converting that vision into reasonable, accomplishable goals and actions. In the chapters ahead, you'll learn just how it's done.

Setting Your Sights on Achievable Goals

When I ask artists to tell me what they want in life, their answers often express states of being — happiness, inner peace, self-esteem, a change of career direction, etc. These are wonderful wishes, many of them universal, but they're very hard to attain, at least in the way we tend to think about them. States of being are intangible, ethereal things with differing definitions for every individual. You can't take actions toward them directly, only toward things that you believe contribute to those states of being for you.

In other words, you don't work on "happiness," you work on the *things* that make you happy. The semantics can be a bit confusing, but the difference is crucial — goals translate your visions into actionable, *attainable*, deeds so you can achieve your desired outcome.

Now that you understand *why* you need to turn your visions into goals, there's still the question of *how*. How do you take your dream-like images and turn them into tangible, achievable goals? It's not as difficult as it might seem; when translating your vision into goals (and later, your goals into actions) the easiest method is to work backwards, from the top down. Imagine your vision as the uppermost point on a pyramid. Just below it are the individual goals that represent the components of your pinnacle vision.

Still further down, beneath the goals, are the singular actions you'll take to achieve those goals.

Let's look at an example: if your vision includes having your art exhibited in ten national galleries, then a good starting *goal* might be to get into a local gallery first. (In the next chapter we'll look at breaking these goals into singular actions, turning them into daily stepping-stones on your path to success. In this particular example, those stepping-stone requirements might include researching compatible galleries in your area, along with their submission requirements.)

Some artists like to work with goals that define *outcomes*, while others prefer goals that relate to their *process*. The difference between the two can be summarized by the oft-debated question, "Is it the destination, or the journey, that matters most?" There is no right answer, only what is right for you. "Outcomes" give a more definitive picture of what you are trying to achieve, but in some cases parts of the outcome are beyond your control. "Processes" are the actions you take, which you *can* control, so they may seem more real — yet without having concrete end results, they may not be quite as compelling to undertake. It's your choice whether outcomes or process, or even a combination will work best for you.

Move Your Goals Out of Your Head

You've done some visioning and maybe a vision board or a mind map. Now it's time to get your vision out of your head and down on paper, in words and numbers. Goals are worthless in the long run unless they're written down. This is an irrevocable truth — writing your goals down not only transforms them from the intangible stuff of your imagination to the tangible form of a task you can work toward, but it also *holds you accountable* for their accomplishment. Scary as that may sound, it's a baseline measurement of motivation. If there's no "evidence" of your intention, there's always an open "escape route" for not attaining it.

Think back to your high school or college days. If term papers had been assigned for the benefit of learning alone, but had no impact on a student's grade, how many would you have completed? Unless you're an extremely self-motivated individual, your answer is probably "one," or "none." This doesn't indicate moral failure, it's simply a fact of human nature. We're less likely to achieve or complete a goal unless we're held accountable for it — particularly *publically*.

An artist was experiencing a period of reasonably strong growth, but was eager to see her sales move to another level. She had a large and lengthy show coming up and had established a goal for the exhibition sales.

"Where is it posted?"

"Posted?".

"Yes,- Is it on the wall of your studio? On the front door of your home? In your exhibition plans?

The answer: it was in a computer document.

I asked why she didn't post it somewhere that was easier to see every day.

"Because this way, if I don't reach my goal, only I will know."

Not only was she unlikely to reach his goal, but by thinking this way, she was setting herself up to have little confidence in the exhibition outcomes.

Accountability plays a key factor in success. It's why people who join a structured weight-loss program tend to be more successful than those who "diet" on their own. It's why someone who tells all their friends that they are running a marathon is more likely to keep to a training schedule than someone who just considers it privately. As long as we leave ourselves a way out, there's a chance we won't accomplish as much.

When you get your goals "out of your head" and onto paper, you send your brain the message that your goals are important. Then, by posting these goals where you and others can view them, every day, you add accountability.

Remember the adage: "Out of sight, out of mind?" Don't allow your goals to drift out of focus. Instead, put a copy where you make your art, where you brush your teeth and where you make your meals. If they are in plain sight it will be harder to forget that you declared these goals to be "what you wanted." It will also make it easier to squeeze in even the smallest actions that will contribute to making them happen. There are many ways to create and record goals. You don't even have to rigidly follow the examples I give: you can draw, mind map, create an audio tape... even write them on the back of a napkin. Just make sure you *write* them!

By the way, I recommend that you experiment with writing them by hand, using a pen or pencil (remember those?) before typing them into your computer. That way you'll tap into a different way of thinking. So break out your visioning results, NOW, and start working backwards to find the short and long-term goals that will get you there.

Create Short and Long-term Goals

Combining short and long-term goals in a flexible plan gives you a "roadmap" to your dream without locking you into something that doesn't work for you. Your short and long-term goals will help you know what you need to do, both day-by-day *and* over the long run, to accomplish what you want to achieve.

Long-term goals are the "big-picture map" to the life you want (your vision). When you looked ahead in the visioning exercises, what did you see? Now, being as specific as possible, identify what you'll need to achieve in the next, two-, three-, five-, and ten-year time spans, in order to realize your vision. These are your long-term goals.

Artists often have trouble being specific about their goals. For example, just saying, "In the future I want to be making money from my art," leaves a lot of questions unanswered. How much money? How near in the future? To make the outcome of your goals clearer (and thus easier to take action on) try saying instead: "In three years, I will be making $15,000 a year from my art. In five years, it'll be $45,000 per year, and in ten years, I will be earning $85,000 per year from my art." Or, in process terms, "Each year, I will increase my income and/or decrease my expenses so that I am able to put aside money for emergencies until I build up enough for a year's worth of living."

Here's another example: instead of saying, "I'll fill my studio with finished paintings," say, "In the next ten years I'll create one hundred 4' x 5' paintings, 50 2' x 3' paintings and 300 miniatures." Or, "I'll work in my studio five days a week and work on increasing my speed while maintaining my quality, so that I can produce enough paintings to support my art business and living expenses."

Does this level of detail scare you? Don't let it! The more detailed and exacting you are with your goals the better you'll be able to see yourself accomplishing them. (In addition, being more specific during this step will help you move forward with the next one: figuring out the *actions* required to *attain* these goals.) So for now, put aside any worries about whether or not you can reach these goals... just focus on what moves you toward your vision.

As for your short-term goals, they're really no different than (and frequently work in tandem with) their longer-term counterparts — they're merely more *immediate* in nature, usually looking ahead to the next four to six months, or up to a year.

It may be easiest to think in terms of working "backwards" from your one- or two-year long-term goals in order to find your short-term targets. To continue with the earlier example, where the goal is to reach $15,000 per year in art sales within the next three years, you could say, "This year I am working on achieving a $500 per-month profit from my art sales. In four months my sales will cover my expenses with a little left over. By eight months I'll be showing a $200 profit, and by the end of the year I'll be pocketing $500 per month in profit."

Again, try not to get too hung-up on getting these goals "exactly right." Depending on your familiarity with the art market, the nature of gallery selections or even typical growth-rates in retail sales, you may need to do a little research before writing your goals.

Alternatively, you could present your pre-written goals to a trusted artist friend or teacher and then adjust your goals according to their feedback.

Keep in mind that your long-term goals may change over time — and as they do, your short-term goals will automatically need to change, too. Occasionally, though, the reverse can be true. While on your way to achieving your short-term goals, you may find they point the way to new long-term results.

Whichever direction, don't hesitate to adjust your goals to take advantage of unanticipated opportunities — just be sure you're doing it for the right reasons. In other words, don't abandon a goal because you were in danger of not reaching it, but only if you stand to gain *more* from creating a new one. Let your "vision" be your guide: as long as the goal adjustment stays true to your vision and keeps advancing you toward your stated "dream life," a small shift may be acceptable or even needed.

Are Your Goals Appropriate?

Many artists are afraid of writing goals that are beyond their reach, but it's equally possible to make the mistake of drafting goals that are *beneath* your reach.

Neither of these extremes is helpful, not for setting your goals and certainly not for maintaining the levels of confidence and enthusiasm necessary for achieving those goals. Like Goldilocks, you want your goals to be "just right."

Toward that end, let's take a look some pitfalls of goals that are too soft or too hard.

Safe goals

It's tempting to fall into the habit of "playing it safe" — after all, it keeps you in your *comfort zone* where everything is friendly and familiar, with a big buffer between you and anything dangerous or new.

The concept of "playing safe" is instilled in us as children to protect us from harm: don't go beyond the fence, don't walk home alone and don't run with scissors. Though we're no longer children, this safety message is often so internalized that we still fall under its influence… but at what price?
If you're not able to embrace the unknown, it's unlikely you'll make strides beyond your current "comfort zone" to achieve the success you desire. You will, in essence, settle for "hiding" from your dream future.

Here are some of the ways that artists play it safe:

- You show your art only to your family, your friends and the people you know — not risking exposure to a new audience.
- You "hide out" at public events and galleries, avoiding contact with new people and organizations.
- You delay seeking-out the career advances you're ready for, preferring the safety of your current status.

When you find yourself feeling timid about the next step in your art career — whether it's trying new techniques alone in your studio, submitting your work to a prestigious show or even placing that first price sticker alongside your work — realize this: even as a child, you likely did, at least once, go beyond the fence, walk home alone or run with scissors… and lived to tell about it!

It's time to reach beyond the safety of your comfort zone. Every well-known artist (and architect, and actor, and dancer) once stood where you are now, and similarly asked, "How could I possibly...?"

The answer, as you very well may know, is "one step at a time." With each step you take the unknown will become a little more familiar, and the frightful become a little less so.

Over-reaching goals

The opposite end of the spectrum from playing it safe is "over-reaching." This is where your stated goals call for a rate of progress or advancement that's simply not feasible.

You imagine your success; you can "see" your positive outcome clearly and it seems nothing will stand in your way. You then assess your capacities as "greater" than they actually are, and as a result, you set goals that are far beyond your abilities or resources.

"Resources" is a critical concept here — it's going to take more than your talent and determination to reach your goals: it's also going to take time, money and energy. If you establish your goals without regard for your available resources, you are "over-reaching," and may *retard* your progress and undermine your confidence in the process.

For example, imagine you've just had an extraordinary performance at an outdoor art fair: you sold ten paintings and "netted" $6,000 in just one weekend. Excited by your success, you set a goal to sell the same number of paintings every month between different weekend shows.

Sounds like a good goal, right? Well, there are a few problems — and of course, the first is whether it's reasonable to anticipate repeating this level of sales success every month. (It's not... that's why I described this result as "extraordinary.") No, the larger problem is your own resources. If your production rate is only eight finished paintings per-month, you won't be able to support a sell-through of ten, no matter how high the demand.

Here's another scenario. You've been enjoying strong sell-through at the art fairs and exhibits you attend, but so far you're not represented by any galleries. However, since you've been an artist for so many years and are selling "a lot" you decide to by-pass the co-op and emerging galleries in your area and apply instead to the "blue-chip" galleries in the neighboring city.

Is this a justifiable goal? Well, while long-shots do occasionally occur, generally speaking this would be considered an "over-reach." Going directly from having no gallery representation to hanging in the most prestigious is simply not a reasonable goal; there's no logical support to sustain it.

Here are some examples of over-reaching:

- You approach the "blue chip" commercial gallery in town after making a few thousand dollars in sale at local fairs, with only ten pieces of available art in your inventory.
- You apply for signature status in the national organization for your media without having won any awards or participated in their regional events.
- You approach an art representative to handle your work without a track record of sales or a contact database of collectors.

Stretch goals

Now, let's turn our attention to *stretch* goals, or "just right," Goldilocks option.

Stretch goals take you beyond your comfort zone, but keep you in the realm of what's possible. Not enough "stretch," and you'll fall flat: you'll continue to do what you've already done. You may get better at it, but you won't be moving forward toward your vision. Too much "stretch," on the other hand, and your goals could be too demanding, leaving you feeling as though you're making no progress. As a result, you become disillusioned and disgruntled. So what amount, you ask, when it comes to goal setting, is "just right?"

Perhaps the following exercise can help you feel the answer:

> Take an elastic (rubber) band and put both of your index fingers inside of it. Move your fingers apart until the band is taught but not stretched. To experience playing it safe, bring your fingers together until the band sags, without the surface tension or strength of its original form.
>
> Bring your fingers apart again. The elastic band once again becomes taut, as it reaches its original position. But now, pass through that starting point, stretching the band as far as you can. There's a certain point where it begins to feel unsafe — you know if you continue, the band will snap. Ouch!

Between these two extreme positions of the rubber band lies a "sweet spot" where there's enough tension on the band to provide strength, but not so much that you fear it will break. Target your goals for this same spot. When you do, you'll stretch beyond your comfort zone but not so far as to put your continued progress and confidence at risk.

Here are some examples of reaching that sweet spot:

- When setting networking goals, decide to attend business networking events where you may be the only artist.
- As you develop your Internet presence, set a goal to go *beyond* your own website to partner with non-art sites for wider exposure and to adopt the latest technologies.
- At public art events, make a plan to start five conversations with people you have not met before and with whom you want to connect.

Take honest stock of the goals you've set for yourself.

Does your goal move you forward, or merely repeat the same accomplishments over and over again? If you're not excited or ever-so-slightly frightened by what lies ahead, you're probably playing it too safe.

If, on the other hand, your goal looks like a "big leap" from your current position or requires resources beyond what's available to you, you may be overreaching.

When your goal is a logical extension of what you've done so far and is supported by your resources at hand, it's probably a stretch goal and is "just right."

Read on to learn about the widely acknowledged technique of writing "S.M.A.R.T." goals to help you aim for achievements that are always on track.

How to Use the "S.M.A.R.T." System of Goal Creation

The acronym "S.M.A.R.T." is a simple, memorable system, that I learned when I was an employee, for breaking a large vision into specific goals, or milestones, that you can work toward one step at a time. Each letter of the acronym directs you to one of the key elements of creating successful goals, thus giving you a better chance of a positive end result.

If you're new to creating structured goals, using the S.M.A.R.T. system *will* help you. As you become more familiar with incorporating these rules into your goal writing, you'll no longer need to follow the chart because these principles will have become second nature.

The table below shows the acronym, along with a short explanation for each letter.

Table 3: S.M.A.R.T. Goals.
(Note: Attribution S.M.A.R.T. The first known uses of the term occurred in the November 1981 issue of Management Review by George T. Doran.[1] http://en.wikipedia.org/wiki/SMART_criteria. Thanks to Susan Birkenshaw for expanding S.M.A.R.T. to S.M.A.R.T.E.R.)

Letter	Meaning	Action
S	Specific	Set your intention and describe precisely what you will do.
M	Measurable	Decide what success is for this goal. How will you measure it?
A	Actionable and Attainable	Stretch past your comfort zone but not so far that you scare yourself.
R	Realistic	Assess whether you have the skills and the resources required.
T	Timed	Set a time frame to take these actions and review your results.

Let's look more closely at the meaning for each letter and use some art-related examples to illustrate how you can use this method.

"S" Stands for "Specific"
Set your intention and state exactly what you want to accomplish. A goal to "improve your art skills" isn't very specific, but a goal to "improve the balance in your compositions" or "increase the contrast in your color values" is much more clearly defined. Provide enough detail in your goal descriptions to make clear what your desired results are and what actions you'll take to obtain them.

For example:

- I will create a signature style of art that is recognizable by my brush strokes, composition and color values.

- I will set up all my business structures so that I am in compliance with all government regulations (starting with my business entity, business license, bank account and accounting system.)
- I will find out what criteria I must meet to qualify for the XYZ juried show.

"M" Stands for "Measurable"

Decide how you'll know when you've completed the goal. Again, you want to be as specific as possible by listing finite quantities for your goal. Avoid using vague words like "more," "better" or "some." Don't say, "I'm going to paint more often." Instead, say, "I'm going to paint for three hours every Tuesday and Thursday night, and for four hours on Saturdays."

You need clear milestones by which you can track your progress. Setting goals that are measurable provides motivation to keep your actions on task and to continue moving forward. It also offers you the opportunity to celebrate your achievement by providing a clearly defined end point.

Some examples:

- I will practice three times a week to learn how to improve my brush strokes, composition and color values, then have my teachers review my work and give me feedback to improve my art skills in these areas.
- I will ask my accountant to indicate any urgent government requirements that apply to my business, put them into plain language and have a bookkeeper help me adjust my business structures so that I am in compliance with new government regulations.
- I will ask my accountant to review all my business structures so that I am in compliance with all government regulations.
- I will ask my art teacher to review my submission for the XYZ juried show to verify that I am ready to properly submit my qualifications and documents.

"A" Stands for "Actionable and Attainable"

Is it possible to achieve your goal with actions that you take yourself? Your goal not only has to be possible, but it has to be attainable through your own actions — meaning that it doesn't depend on luck, fate, or the actions of others. If you need a big "lucky break" just to achieve your goal, then it's not attainable. Similarly, if getting to your goal is dependent on someone else's performance, instead of just your own, you may be wasting your time.

Structure your goal so that *you* are the key player in the outcome, and so that *you* can achieve it with your current abilities and resources. Setting a goal to stretch 20 new canvases by the end of the month might be fine, but not if you're dependent on someone else to assemble the frames first, or if you've never used the tools before.

Any goal that requires hefty contributions by another person or mastery of a skill set you're just developing may not be actionable and achievable.

Here are a few good examples:

- I will take workshops to learn to improve my brush strokes, composition and color values; and then produce one 4' x 4' painting, one 3' x 3' painting and one 4' x 8' painting. I will also have my teachers review my progress and give me feedback to improve my art skills in these areas.
- I will ask my accountant to show me any relevant government documents that apply to my business, so that going forward I can learn to set all my business structures in compliance with all government regulations.
- I will ask my art mentor to provide a reference for my submission for the XYZ juried show, so I can show that my qualifications are endorsed by others.
- I will produce a body of work that consists of four 4' x 4' paintings, eight 3' x 3' paintings and two 4' x 8' paintings; then have my critique group review a piece from each group and give me feedback to improve my brush strokes, composition and color values.
- I will ask my art mentor to advise me on how to prepare a submission for the regional (or national) signature membership in Oil Painters of America.

R" Stands for "Relevant"

Make sure your goal is meaningful and significant. Is your goal aligned with your overall vision? Is it a necessary step toward your dream future? It's all well and good to make grand statements of what you want to achieve in your art career, but unless you can break those statements into meaningful, significant goals related to your future vision, you'll find it hard to maintain your commitment level long enough to achieve them. Make sure your goals are relevant to your vision, and not sidetracking you from them.

Some possible examples might be:

- I will practice three times a week to learn how to improve my brush strokes, composition and color values, then have my teachers review my work and give me feedback to improve my art skills in these areas.
- I will ask my accountant to indicate any urgent government requirements that apply to my business, put them into plain language and have a bookkeeper help me set all my business structures so that I am in compliance with all government regulations.
- I will ask my art mentor to help me prepare a submission for the XYZ juried show coming up soon.

"T" Stands for "Timed"

Give yourself a deadline for a successful and timely completion. Putting an end point on your goal makes you accountable — without one, your commitment has no urgency to drive you forward — so setting a time frame will help spur you to action. Having a deadline also establishes a guide for how you should be progressing, allowing you to monitor your progress regularly and "step up your game" if you're not on track.

Examples:

- By <month, date, year> I will produce a body of work that consists of four 4' x 4' paintings, eight 3' x 3' paintings and two 4' x 8' paintings. Each month I will have my monthly critique group review a piece from each group and give me feedback to improve my brush strokes, composition and color values. I will rework the art work within a week with the feedback I accept.
- I will ask my accountant to review all my business structures by the end of the month so that I am always in compliance with all government regulations.
- I will ask my art mentor to review my submission for the regional (or national) signature membership in Oil Painters of America by <month, date, year> to verify if I am ready to properly submit my qualifications and documents.

Make Your Goals Even "S.M.A.R.T.E.R."

While the S.M.A.R.T. Goals system has been in use since the early 1980's, I love the expansion by my friend and photographer Susan Birkenshaw, which includes categories that address energy commitment and rewards. Simply put, the goals have gotten "S.M.A.R.T.E.R."

Take a look at these additions below to boost your goal writing one step further.

E	Energetic Expansion	Resolve to focus your energy to take enthusiastic action on your goals.
R	Rewards for Results	Decide on the rewards for achieving your goals.

"E" Stands for "Energetic Expansion"

Choose goals that energize you as you work on them, or structure your goals in such a way that you can motivate yourself to complete them.

This means taking note of your energy levels. Focus on actions that expand your feelings of well-being rather than leave you feeling depleted. Notice which tasks make you feel better, and resolve to do more of that kind of activity. Also notice which tasks "take" energy, and find ways to break them down into smaller pieces or ask someone else to do them for you.

Examples:

- Three times each week I will practice improving my brush strokes, composition and color values for as long as I am enjoying the painting process. I will write down any positive feedback I get from my teachers on those subjects and post it in my studio where I can see it.
- I will have a bookkeeper set up all my business structures so I can be confident that I am in compliance with all government regulations and be free to focus on my painting.
- I will ask my art mentor to help me choose the right level of juried show for my art skills, and also show me how to prepare a submission for the next one coming up.

"R" Stands for "Rewards for Results"

Give yourself a reward for persevering and achieving your goal, and acknowledge what you did to get there. The result of reaching your goal is already an intrinsic reward for your hard work, diligence and willpower, but you'll reinforce your feelings of confidence even more if you reward yourself in other ways, too.

To keep yourself motivated, write a list of what you will do to celebrate the successful accomplishment of your goal. Your list could contain items as simple as doing a "happy dance", calling a friend, or as big as getting a larger studio space.

Here are a few other examples:

- I will put on an open studio event for my family and friends to show them the results of my time and effort practicing brush strokes, composition and color values.
- I will take my bookkeeper out to lunch to celebrate setting up all my business structures.
- I will take a picture with my art mentor in front of the work I submitted for my first juried exhibit submission.

Putting All the Elements Together
Okay, you've built each element. Now it's time to combine them into a full goal statement.

Here are a few sample S.M.A.R.T.E.R. goals:

- I will create a signature style of art (something that is enjoyable and unique to me) by painting daily with my art buddy. I will complete a body of twenty pieces of work to exhibit in my home at a party for my favorite art friends by December 31st 2xxx.
- I will set up all my business structures with a business license, bank account, filing, inventory system and accounting system (hiring an assistant to make sure it's done properly) so that everything is in place and ready to operate by the end of January 2xxx, and so that I will be able to submit my quarterly and yearly taxes with ease.
- I will produce a body of work that consists of four 4' x 4' paintings, eight 3' x 3' paintings and two 4' x 8' paintings in iridescent acrylic glazes by June 30th 2xxx. I will do this by working in my studio by myself three days a week for five hours and two days a week for three hours. When I have completed each piece to my satisfaction, I will buy something new for my studio.
- I will research ten different venues that are appropriate for the current stage of my career. I will find out what kind of work they show and meet the owners when I attend shows there. From those venues, I will decide on three where I want to show my work and find out what criteria I have to meet to show there. I will have this completed by September of next year before I go on my trip to New York to visit galleries.

Always Get Support When You Get Stuck

An artist's life is often a solitary one, so when it comes to reaching your goals, you will need the help of other people — particularly when you get "stuck." If a goal is feeling unachievable, sometimes the worst thing you can do is try to struggle on alone.

Naturally, you might weather the occasional roadblock just fine without assistance, but if it feels as though you've been unsuccessfully addressing the same issue time and time again, it may be that you need a little outside assistance.

Here are a few ways to do that:

1. Get a goal buddy
Find another local artist you trust who is also working with goals, and decide to meet regularly to review each other's progress and results. Just having the accountability of another pair of eyes and ears will help you get things done and find solutions to problems that you might not have realized by yourself. In the process of helping someone else, you will probably see new solutions for your own progress, too — and besides, it always feels good to help others.

2. Join or create a mastermind group
This is like having a whole crew of buddies. You just multiply the process of feedback and accountability, and have more help when you need it.

To give you an idea of how helpful support systems can be, a trio of artists who were part of a goals program I started in 2003 is *still* meeting weekly (by e-mail and phone) today. I hear from them regularly, and they tell me their mutual "reflection and support" process continues to help them stay on track and meet their art career goals over a decade later.

Acting on Your Goals and Tracking Your Progress

Most artists have an art career that is more like a marathon than a sprint. A slower pace may not be as exciting as a "rocket ship ride", but it creates a stronger foundation and allows you the opportunity to re-fuel and correct your course as you go.

Some artists do experience big breaks that propel their careers forward at an unprecedented rate, and yet, this isn't always good. Getting "discovered" doesn't automatically increase your self-confidence and competence in making your art — in other words, even if you did make it big overnight, you might not believe your work worthy of the acclaim or that you are, finally, a "real" artist.

Yet the fantasy of being "discovered" perseveres, despite its inherent problems, and it's something that many artists spend a lot of time dreaming about.

The important thing to realize is that while your dream life won't happen by magic, it *can* happen by determination and persistent application. Yes, you have to want your imagined future with great passion and intensity... but you also have to work hard to translate your dream-life into an actual, living existence. And yes, you *can* achieve it.

How can I say this with such certainty? Because I know that the reason MOST professional artists succeed is not due to the depth of their talent or the strength of their desire.

Progress is born from the actions you take, each day, in the relentless pursuit of your goals.

Of course, this takes extraordinary commitment, not to mention tremendous focus and clarity on the actions you'll need to take to achieve those goals. You've got to be able to apply your passion in pre-determined, measured steps to keep moving toward your dream. Perhaps an illustration here will be helpful:

Imagine that it's a Saturday morning and you assign your teenage kids the task of "cleaning and straightening up" while you're out running errands (feel free to substitute a spouse or roommate in this scenario). The goal seems straightforward enough: a clean house, with everyone's personal belongings put away. So how do things look when you get home? Probably the house will look a bit better than before, but it's just as likely that you'll end up asking them to do a few more things, or doing them yourself, before you're fully satisfied.

Why? Let's get past the fact that they're teenagers or they have a higher threshold for living with disorder —the real culprit is that your goal of "a clean house" was not broken down into the specific actions needed to achieve it. If you had listed the cleaning chores as item-by-item actions, the instructions would have been clear.

"Dust the furniture, vacuum the carpet, do the dishes, and clean the cat box" are all clearly identified actions that make the goal attainable. (Of course, if your house is anything like mine, it may take something more than clarity — like direct involvement.)

In other words, goals alone are not enough. They must be broken down into actions — specific steps taken day-by-day that will move you toward your stated desire. The number of action steps needed to complete each goal will vary depending on the complexity of the goal, so you'll need to tailor them appropriately. Keep in mind, also, that you'll likely be working on multiple goals (and thus multiple action items) simultaneously.

Identify Your Action Items

For many visual people, drafting long lists of tasks and then referencing those to-do lists daily holds varying degrees of appeal. Fortunately there are a lot of ways you can make this process more attractive, and even some are fun. I've outlined a few of them below to help you get started.

Many of these techniques will look familiar, so feel free to adapt them in any way you wish to create a balance between structure and inspiration that works for you.

1. Written lists

The simplest, most direct method is to write an actual list of the tasks required to get from point A to point B. You can include less or more detail depending on your preference.

For example, if your goal is "complete ten paintings measuring at least 4' x 3' for my show in six months," a summary of the action steps required may be:

- Determine the specific sizes.
- Buy/order the materials.
- Apply the base coat.
- Paint the image.
- Do the edging.
- Sign, photograph and inventory.
- Frame or wire.

You might find it helpful to draft your lists in more detail. By listing every action separately, you will know exactly what needs to be done and can estimate how long each action might take.

- Request a list of preferred sizes from the gallery.
- Buy Masonite boards in each size.
- Check gesso on hand; purchase additional if necessary.
- Prepare Masonite surfaces: apply a thin layer of gesso then sand lightly when dry.
- Repeat for four coats.
- While gesso coats are drying, determine images for each painting
- Re-size or reprint images as necessary.
- Determine paint colors needed for each image and check inventory.
- Purchase any paints, brushes, lacquers or thinners needed.
- Block out image for first painting.
- Etc.

The amount of detail in your list is entirely up to you. While this much detail might be daunting, it *can* have its advantages. In addition to simplifying time estimates for each task, it will highlight overlapping tasks, such as supply runs, which will help you work more efficiently. (It can also provide a ready list of jobs to hand off to an intern or studio assistant.) There can be a psychological benefit to regularly crossing items off the list as well, which provides a consistent feeling of progress and accomplishment.

And of course, you can still feed your need for visual stimulation by organizing your lists into different colors according to the nature of the goal: business goals in one color, marketing goals in another, studio goals in a third and so on.

2. Image "lists"

For some artists, a descending list of bulleted tasks simply won't do. They prefer more visual stimulation and need to be able to free-associate their action items rather than focusing on only one goal per list. If this describes you, try documenting your action items on a large dry-erase or illustration board. Begin by locating action areas for each goal in different regions of the board. This can be done either in words or pictures, whatever suits you best.

For example, if your goal is to organize your studio you might have action topics like "supply storage," "inventory storage" and "work areas" represented by colorful images of paint tubes, stacked boxes and a work apron. As you think of tasks related to each topic, simply jot it down in the space around it. In this way you can let your thoughts develop naturally while building your action steps, rather than imposing a particular order.

When completed, these boards will not only be colorful documentations of your goals and action items, but they'll probably clarify your priorities as well. By working in a creative format like this, the importance each item holds winds up being expressed intrinsically by its size, boldness, colors and quantity of surrounding symbols, squiggles and stars.

Your action image boards can be displayed wherever is most relevant and useful for you. You may want to hang business-related image boards in your office, art-related boards in your studio and so forth. Just keep a supply of colored pens and Post-It notes nearby so you can add to your boards and mark on them to reflect a goal's completion.

3. Calendar "lists"

If you are truly "deadline" oriented you may want to write down your action items list on an over-sized calendar. This method combines some of the elements of written lists with the colorful display of image lists — and since it exists directly on your calendar, it will automatically prepare you to complete your tasks each day.

To create a calendar list you'll need to start with a large wall-style calendar which you can find online or through your local office supply store — the larger the better! Take the calendar and write down each of your major goal deadlines in their appropriate squares, using a different color for each goal (you may also want to use all capital letters to signify that it is a final goal). Then simply work backwards from each deadline, writing down all the actions you need to take, and when, in reverse order until you reach your current date.

You may want to use Post-It Notes for your entries when initially drafting your calendar so that it's easier to adjust deadlines forward and back as your "big picture" emerges. You may also want to use lines of color, drawn across multiple calendar squares, to indicate actions that will consume your focus for several days running, such as workshops or travel.

While a "calendar list" is one of the more complicated action tools to assemble, it can also be one of the most useful, telling you at a glance what you must accomplish (and in what time-frame) to meet your goals. If it feels too complex to create directly, consider using a written or image list first, then transferring the action items to calendar form.

Chart Your Progress

Each action you take toward your goal is like a single frame in a movie. It takes an enormous number of these individual frames (or actions) day after day in a logical order to achieve the complete picture that you envision. Just as a film director monitors each day's filming, so too do you, as an artist, need to monitor your progress day-by-day to ensure that you're "on track" to reach your goals.

If all of this planning and action is new to you, or if you want to make a long list more manageable, it may help to break larger action-steps down into 15-minute "chunks" of time. You'll be amazed at how much you can get done in such a short period, and if the task is one you dislike, you'll only have to "hold your nose" briefly before moving on to something you like more. I have suggested this to hundreds of artists — and it works.

Some tasks obviously take longer than fifteen minutes. Assign these to days when you have more time available, and "reward" yourself with a more pleasurable task at the end. You could also "bribe" yourself, and undertake the pleasant parts of the task first, as long as you make sure to complete the less fun parts later.

People with the best intentions won't hesitate to go out and invest in the tools of organization — a plethora of color-coordinated boxes, bins and clips that allow them to *believe* they're working toward their goal, but until they actually sort the materials and *fill* the containers all they've done is gone shopping. Go past that stage.

At the same time, don't let your "chores become bores" or you might just kill your passion in the process. You need to be disciplined, yes — but just as you wouldn't force a piece of art, don't force your art career either. Like Edison with the light bulb or the chemists who created cleaning Formula 409 (because 408 "formulas" preceded it), stay on track with your goals, taking some action every day, and you're destined to arrive at your goal.

The following tracking tools can assist you:

1. Project files
I have a desktop box full of clear plastic file folders labeled for daily, weekly or monthly deadlines for key projects. They have multiple pockets so I can separate different aspects of each project, like people, places, tasks and communications.

I also put work-in-progress drafts and correspondences from project partners in here so I can instantly refer to the latest update about a project when I need to.

I converted a closet with shelving units for ongoing projects. I use binders with index dividers to store key documents for each project. If I run out of index tabs I use Post-It flags to mark each section and book binding tape to label each binder. Again, I color code each one for quick and easy scanning.

2. Photo records
Consider using photographic evidence to keep you abreast of your progress. Whether you take photos to document your mastery of a new art technique or to monitor your progress toward an organized business office, sometimes being able to look again at "where you've been" can be incredibly motivating, particularly when faced with the reality of "where you are." Take daily, weekly or monthly shots of your progression. Even if you're the only one who ever views these albums, the images will keep you on track and invigorated.

3. Outside input
Unless you have a partner, an agent or a gallery dealer who's taken a very strong interest in your career, you may not receive periodic, helpful observations from others. But just as you've employed "art buddies" to critique your art style, you can also use these artist friends to give you encouraging, uplifting feedback on your progress. When you work alone, a kind voice and fresh eye can do wonders to maintain your motivation and remind you how far you've come.

4. Goal review/renewal

While it might seem obvious at first, reviewing your goals is an often-overlooked means of monitoring your progress toward achieving them. Periodically stepping off the "treadmill" of your action-items lists to stand on the "reflective path" of your goals can be beneficial in a multitude of ways.

First, it will confirm how far you've come — information that's both practical and reaffirming. Secondly, it will allow you to revitalize your approach to your action-items by renewing your connection to your goals. Finally, it will give you regular opportunities to "check-in" with your goals, the driving forces behind your daily tasks.

What you find there may surprise you… if your motivation is waning, it may be because your goals have shifted without your notice. Read the next section to see if what you need is a simple goal renewal or more complex goal *revision*.

Of course you don't have to use *all* of the tools mentioned above, but hopefully some of them will appeal to you. Use my list as a menu; take what you need and then add your own creative touches!

Remain Flexible

Thomas Edison constructed over 3,000 non-working light bulbs before he finally crafted one that worked. If he'd been inflexible in his goals, or unreasonably tied to a list of failed action-items, we might still be sitting in the dark. But thanks to his persistence, he was granted 1,093 U.S. patents over his lifetime — one of which was for the light bulb.

Our goals are *projections* of what we'd like to see happen, the dreams from our mind's eye that we wish upon our world. Unfortunately, your projections may not always be accurate, and the world won't always "live up" to your expectations. Despite your best efforts, circumstances occasionally may not allow for your dream to move forward as planned. When "life" happens to you, it will help to have flexible standards. Adapting to what the situation demands, rather than demanding that the situation adapt to you, will help you be much more productive in achieving your goals (and a lot less stressed, too).

If your situation has changed since the time you wrote down your goals, it may be time to reassess. You do this when you create your art by standing back to take stock of how it's going — checking the piece against your "mental picture" to see if the values, composition and quality are as they should be. Do the same for your career goals. Any large life changes like a new house, a new spouse or a new baby are all good reasons to reconsider your goals (or at least adjust their time-frames).

Don't get in the habit of changing your goals too often, however. If changing your goals becomes like changing your socks — something you do daily — it's either a sign that you're not taking enough care when drafting your goals in the first place, or that you're not following through on your action-items and are downsizing your goals to compensate for poor performance. If you're adjusting your goals because you neglected to work on your plan, it's time to re-check your motivation.

On the other hand, it's true that disciplined work doesn't always bring about the results you desire. When you experience disappointments it's important not to let it "get you down" for long. Give yourself permission to lament briefly, and then prepare to move on.

One of the best ways to re-summon your strength in the face of a disheartening outcome is to assess what it was that happened differently than you expected. This will put you back in the driver's seat with new knowledge and new confidence that will (hopefully) prevent similar misfortune in the future.

To move from judgment to action, and to get the negatives out of your head, consider what you learned from your experience.

Are you objective enough to evaluate the situation yourself, or do you need to find someone else who can shed some light on the problem? Did you misinterpret what was happening? What should you stop doing, start doing, or do differently?

A friend of mine who is a brilliant linguist once pointed out to me a curious feature of the word *mistakes*, which forever altered the way I look at my "failures." If you split the word into two halves, what you get are *miss-takes* — essentially, things that happened not quite as we intended, until we *do them again*. This small shift within the word takes the importance away from the error, and charmingly places the emphasis on its future correction.

When things are not going according to plan, try looking at your mistakes as "miss-takes," so you can get back on your feet and back on toward your goal.

Incorporating Art Professionals into Your Career

The concept of art professionals (such as art critics, dealers, etc.) is a fairly recent cultural invention. Talented artists received commissions directly from churches and royalty during the middle ages, and private patronage emerged in the fourteenth century in wealthy families like the de' Medici, but there were no other players in the "art game" until much later.

Education was different too. Throughout the sixteenth century, guilds were the primary training system for professions such as fine art. They were the early form of "technical schools" mostly for boys whose parents paid to have on-the-job training through apprenticeships with master painters and sculptors.

The rise of industrialism in the eighteenth century changed all of that, however. Suddenly there were "private" wealthy art collectors, and the atelier system. With this transition came the demise of guilds and patronage, and there was no longer any system to indicate which artists were masters and what artwork was worth buying. Art critics, appraisers and dealers filled the vacuum, giving their "expert" stamp of approval to the work they deemed excellent. Then, galleries and museums rose to prominence and made the system more efficient by displaying the work of more than one artist at a time.

By the nineteenth and early twentieth centuries, galleries took artists under their wing, developed their careers and handled most (if not all) of the aspects of showing and selling their work. In exchange for their services they expected loyalty and took a small commission on each sale. Many artists today still long for the security and career development once offered by this type of representation — even though, unfortunately, it no longer exists.

As the world embraced new entrepreneurial and individualistic approaches to commerce, the art world naturally followed. Now, galleries come and go, their commissions are larger and dealers do less for you. The burden of career management and promotion has shifted to the artist.

Many artists still *hope* that all they need to do is create their art for success to follow. But successful artists know that creating great art is not enough — and they also know that they can't do it all alone.

The mechanics of the twenty-first century art world are too important to not understand. Once you know exactly how it all fits together, you can shape your career to make the most of the opportunities that have arisen with these changes.

Understanding the Roles of Art Professionals

I am often asked: "Do I *have* to do all these planning and business tasks myself? Can't I just hire an agent who will sell whatever I paint and handle the negotiations, details and paperwork?"

In short, no. Art professionals are people who can provide help for artists and art collectors, but they do not "take over." Some of their services overlap but most have special talents and distinct specialties.

You must attract their attention by building a stellar career that indicates that you and your work are worth promoting. You cannot usually hire them.

And, while it is sometimes difficult to hold back (especially when you are enthusiastic about building your art career) the best first step is to develop a relationship and get to know them on a personal basis. Show up at their events, but do not approach them as an artist who wants representation. Be part of the audience so you can understand whom they serve and whether this audience would be a fit for your art.

> "If an artist is really ambitious, they have to ask themselves 'What is going to make me stand out?' The answer is always the same: great work.
>
> The Internet hasn't changed everything. To have a real career as an artist you still need to find your way into the very intense hierarchy of the art world, and critics, curators and collectors are still the gatekeepers to that world. They are going to find you if your work is outstanding."
>
> ~John Seed, art explainer

Titles can be confusing so here is a brief description of several different types of art professionals, as well as explanations of how they work and for whom:

1. Art advisors

Art advisors, also known as art consultants or art appraisers have in depth knowledge of art, art history and the art world.

Art advisors perform the following types of services for art collectors:

- Educate their clients about the current value of work in their collections and the prices of potential acquisitions.
- Make recommendations of art purchases (or leases) based on the client's preferences, needs and investment objectives.
- Manage their client's art collection, including updated appraisals, inventory, preservation, restoration and protection of the collector's works.
- Install new artwork according to best practices and their client's preferences.
- Rotate the client's collection if there is more art than space to display it, so that the collector can enjoy the variety of their collection.

2. Corporate art consultants

Some art consultants purchase or lease art for government departments, financial institutions, healthcare facilities and other business organizations in the public and private sectors.

Corporate art consultants provide the following services for their corporate clients:

- Advise their clients on the value of certain works and their appropriateness for specific locations.
- Acquire and manage corporate art collections, including commissioning and installing site-specific artworks.
- Curate art exhibitions and produce art events for corporate sponsors (and others).
- Develop educational activities with their client's art collection for employees, customers and the local community.

3. Art curators

Art curators advise private collectors, museums and sometimes galleries on acquisitions and loans of art. Art curators are similar to art advisors, but (like art appraisers) tend to have formal training and longer résumés.

Art curators provide the following services for their collectors, dealers and museum clients:

- Visit artist studios to see finished work and select pieces for exhibitions.

- Evaluate donated artwork to determine collection-worthiness and value.
- Select artwork to be displayed from their client's vast collection.
- Organize traveling exhibitions showcasing selections of their client's collection.
- Write about art for catalogs, brochures, magazines, books or blogs.

4. Art licensing agents

Art licensing agents represent artists whose work is leased by manufacturers for use on products. Art licensing agents may do some or all of the following tasks:

- Select work that is appropriate for licensing.
- Identify the appropriate retail channels.
- Create a sales and marketing plan to promote the artwork.
- Promote the art to their contacts in the market.
- Negotiate licensing contracts and royalty payments.
- Administer contracts for licenses.
- Keep up to date on current licensing trends and themes.

5. Artist representatives

Artist representatives are private dealers who represent artists (similar to how a music agent would represent a popular singer) by creating opportunities to sell artwork in exchange for a commission from the artist for each sale.

Artist representatives provide the following services for their artist clients and collector base:

- Promote the artist to individual collectors and set up meetings where the artist can meet their collectors.
- Advise collectors on the suitability of the artist's work for their collection and on the value (and potential value) of the artist's work.
- Arrange and produce exhibits for the artist.
- Work with the artist to place their art in galleries and museums.
- Develop relationships with other art professionals, gallery managers and owners, and use these relationships to promote the artist.
- Work with big names in the art industry to sponsor and hold significant events.
- Advise the artist on public relations, coordinate public relations for events and ensure that the artist participates in public relations as part of their marketing strategy.
- Provide marketing services for the artist, issuing press releases or writing about the artist and their work.

- Arrange promotional support and put together promotional materials that feature the artist and their work.

6. Gallery dealers

Gallery dealers are retailers who present quality works of art while guaranteeing its authenticity and archival quality. Dealers cultivate collections usually for a particular type of art. Their connections and relationships are as important as the art they collect. Dealers vary widely in how active a role they take in promoting individual artists and helping to develop their careers.

Gallery dealers and their staff provide the following services to their collector clients:

- Share their expert knowledge with collectors.
- Exhibit and store an inventory of specific artists or art periods.
- Seek out and exhibit the work of artists whose art fits a specific niche audience.
- Use a fixed exhibit space or a "pop up" temporary space to demonstrate their expertise and exhibit their art inventory in exchange for a commission percentage of each sale (typically 50%).
- Promote selected artists' work in order to attract new collectors to the gallery and increase sales.

Note: Be very careful of offers to represent your work for a fee. There are many enterprising "vanity representatives" who charge an upfront fee for exhibits, online galleries and collector publications. This is certainly a valid retail business model but is not always guided by an experienced art professional. The value you receive from such an agreement may vary, but remember that most legitimate art professionals make their money through commissions on work sold, not shown.

Hiring an Artist Advisor or Art Business Coach

Unlike the six types of art professionals listed above, at any stage of your art career you can hire an artist advisor or coach to help you grow your business and get the attention of some or all of the art professionals described earlier.

Artist advisors, art business coaches and art marketing specialists advise visual artists on how to make a living from making art, usually by helping to figure out what kind of marketing would work best for the artist, their artwork, their personality and budget.

Artist advisors may provide some or all of the following services for their artist clients:

- Appraise individual artists' career stages and determine how to best position their art business for success.
- Help artists gain clarity on what makes art unique and desirable as well as an understanding of how to improve that in their own art.
- Help artists determine what they want from their art, then help to create a pathway of goals and action steps that match up with their available time, energy and resources.
- Recommend schedules and methods to continue to produce artwork and assess possible improvements to current production methods.
- Evaluate and improve existing art business and art marketing plans, or help build plans from scratch.
- Review art marketing strategies to assess what's working and suggest ways to get more exposure through activities that fit the level of artwork and career stage.
- Help figure out pricing strategies, and put together a structured pricing system and art purchase policy.
- Explore past sales results and offer advice on how to increase art sales and revenue.
- Review website, blog and social media interactions and suggest ways to improve Internet presence.
- Give advice for how to deal with collectors and other art professionals.

Unlike the other art professionals described in this chapter, artist advisors do not sell or represent your work — instead, they advise you on how to sell your work yourself and how to get representation.

Creating Your Signature Style

When I say Vincent van Gogh, Pollack, or Monet, there's a very good chance that you see an example of their distinctive artwork — their signature style — in your mind.

The same goes if you think about a fellow artist whose work you're familiar with, or that of your teacher. Whether you are a hobbyist, an amateur or a professional artist, your signature style is the way that *only you* create your work, regardless of training or similarity to other artists.

Every time you create a piece of art, you are making hundreds of decisions, the simplest among them being color, form, texture and perspective. You will find tendencies to make certain decisions again and again... and as these decisions persist, you will begin to discover the foundations of your signature style.

In the same way that you can't force a plant to flower, you can't force your signature style to appear before its time. Be patient with yourself — and enjoy the unfolding. Choose your favorite elements and use them consistently for six months to a year. You will notice that some disappear while others hold your attention enough for you to develop them further into something that is uniquely yours.

"I have become more aware of my own process over the last few years -- how my mind thinks of new ideas, how I formulate them, how I work in my studio. It has been trial and error, as well as a lot of mindfulness in noticing what works and what does not. I often need to ruminate on ideas and turn them over and over in the back of my head, almost in the deep, dark recesses of my sub-conscious before they are ready to be put down into artwork. Sometimes in dreams, sometimes while driving or doing dishes.

So, when I'm feeling stuck in the studio, I might need to do bunches of quick, unrelated sketches; a different kind of creative project; just quit for a few days and rest my head by watching a movie or reading. There is something going on in the depths of my mind, though, sorting through all my emotions, thoughts and ideas on what I'm trying to convey through artwork, and that will eventually be solidified into something I can understand and articulate visually. It feels frustrating to be in the middle of it, but is just part of your natural creative cycle, like barren winter and lush spring are all part of the same landscape." ~Amy Ventura, wood burning artist

Your signature style is not static — because, after all, neither is your creativity. As you get better at making art and have more pieces to show for your efforts, you will start to see patterns emerge that develop into a specific signature style. If you make enough of this kind of art, people will be able to recognize this work as yours. Even as your art career spans multiple decades, your signature style will continue to evolve.

> *"My art is recognized as being mine, even before my name signature is read. The themes, the style, the colors and the quality of my work retain their distinctiveness, so that regardless of subject matter, my paintings continue to be recognized as mine.*
>
> *My retail customers come back looking for new pieces that will continue to complement the ones they've already purchased, so for them my work needs to develop. This is also very important to my wholesale customers who know that they can count on my art to sell.*
>
> *My signature work helps define me to my audience. For this reason, and in order to stand out in a crowd, there is great value in having a signature body of work, and then to continuously hone that body of work."*
>
> *~Patrice Federspiel, watercolor artist*

A signature style is the tangible result of consistently creating high-quality, recognizable artwork that is worthy of being purchased by collectors, represented by galleries and featured by arts writers.

To create your signature style, you need to consciously hone your vision, master your medium and uniquely combine the elements of your own visual language. In the following sections we'll explore exactly how to do that.

What Makes Up a Signature Style?

There are many different visual elements that you can combine to create your very own signature style. Not all of these apply to every artist's work, and you may find that you describe the elements in your work differently. That's okay — the concepts behind the words are what matter most here.

(If you're not familiar with all of the terms below, an Internet search for "art terms" will give you a basic overview of these elements, as well as other ways to describe them.)

Composition: The arrangement, balance, rhythm, connections and variety of visual expression in a piece of art.

Design elements: The colors, values, contrast, textures, surface, forms, lines, shape, scale, proportions, focal points, perspective and use of space in a visual work.

Image style: The overarching style of a particular image, referencing abstract, conceptual, expressionist, figurative, impressionist, realistic or surrealistic influences (or a mix of these).

Light: A use of direct or indirect light, a predominance of reflections and shadows, or some other distinguishable characteristic of light within a work of art.

Media: The materials you use to create your art, such as paint, paper, ephemera, etc.

Substrate: The surfaces on which you create your art, like canvas, clayboard, glass, paper, vinyl, wood and so on.

Techniques: The methods that you use to create your art, which may include leaving visible marks of the tools you use (think brushstrokes versus palette knife).

Themes and motifs: Repeated symbols which inherently act as a visual shorthand for specific ideas, people or places.

Subject matter: The ideas, people, animals, objects, buildings, topics in the literal, visible images or forms that appear in a work of art.

Presentation of finished work: The materials used (and specific details of) armatures, frames, joins, mountings, stands, supporting devices or any other item integral to the presentation of the work itself.

Some artists take a lifetime to fully explore a certain signature style. They may depict the same subject from many different angles or use the same color palette and brush stroke for many different subjects. Other artists might vary their subject matter, but keep their media and style consistent. The permutations and combinations are endless. You can choose your own, and there is no "right way." There is only "your way."

Why You Need a Signature Style

If you want to build a name for yourself, collectors and art professionals must come to distinguish your work from any other artists who create work that is similar. This happens when you have something that makes your work stand out from the crowd, and is especially important if your subject matter is fairly common among artists, like landscapes or still life.

Here are six reasons why it's important to have a signature style:

1. It is inherently easier for viewers to remember your art.
Memory depends on a part of our brain that records patterns and relationships between visual elements. Ideally your audience experiences a feeling of familiarity when they see your work, so that your art becomes a "friend" they trust and recognize.

2. You demonstrate your control.
A distinctive signature style shows that you are in charge of your creative resources and have the ability to create a consistent record of your artistic vision and style.

3. You can work more efficiently.
Producing art within specific parameters allows you to focus on similar imagery and make use of similar materials, creating greater efficiency and economy in your workflow.

4. You develop greater expertise, more quickly.
Repetition and focus are great teachers. Maintaining a signature style will help you become adept at making your distinctive elements perform.

5. You can branch out into other price points and products.
With a successful signature style, you can easily create additional versions of your work to appeal to different segments of your audience. If your originals sell well, you can create giclées, prints, posters and notecards. Different versions at different price points will make your work accessible to buyers with different budgets, different exhibit spaces or varying amounts of room to display their art.

6. You can market your work more easily.
It is much easier to market an overriding theme or style rather than a cluster of disparate works. Once you have your signature style, you can define your audience and direct your marketing efforts to them rather than "everybody."

A signature style also makes it easier for art professionals to decide if your work is a match for the art preferences of their clients. Most commercial galleries have a niche market and represent a certain kind of work to a certain kind of client — they're looking for artists with a consistent, repeated style that they can rely on.

As an collector myself, I've seen how a consistent signature style has influenced my own art-buying decisions.

I followed one particular artist for years, and was eventually able to buy a piece that was stylistically similar to some of the larger ones I liked. Because the artist produced a signature style in a variety of sizes, I was able to fit a purchase into my budget.

Another artist whose work I collect began creating several small studies in a similar style that I liked. I couldn't decide which ones to buy, so I bought the entire series.

You might feel that an eclectic approach is the whole point of being an artist, and in some respects that is true. A certain amount of trial and error will help you find your true artistic "voice" and give you the time to learn to express it consistently and identifiably. Until you make a lot of art, you won't know the breadth and depth of your talent. (And having lots of creative, exploratory ideas is fundamental to establishing a career that lasts a lifetime.)

I know many talented artists who have not yet developed a signature style. Though highly skilled in the technicalities of art, their collected works lack a distinctive, coherent personality. For some of them, creating a signature style was never the point — they equate similarity to being stuck in a rut. These artists simply enjoy their creative explorations and are less concerned with commercial success.

I also worked with an artist who admitted to having a rather short attention span. After working on a particular style for a while, and getting bored with it, the artist would move on to something completely different. As a result, the artist's website showed seven different bodies of work.

Some were good, but a few were clearly not as developed or successful. I suggested narrowing down to no more than three collections of well-developed work with a common thread. Focusing in this manner increased the artist's motivation, led to better quality art, more consistent production and more effective marketing.

Having a signature style may sound confining, but it's actually quite the opposite. As you grow your creative talents (and your vision develops and matures) you will naturally eliminate a lot of "chatter" from your work and strip away the echoes of other artists' work.

The signature style you develop will be an expression of your viewpoint and your artistic aesthetic in your way, freed as much as possible from outside influences. It is the truest form of how you express your own creative individuality.

Developing Your Signature Style Over Time

Your signature style will develop only as you master your media, technique, subject matter and presentation — it is constant work over time that distills your authentic visual communication into something recognizably yours. As you grow ever more confident in your materials and talent, you will discover consistent elements that connect the pieces of your art into one greater theme.

> *"One thing all my paintings have in common is texture and many layers. I get in a zone and work on several pieces at a time with series of works. My first series of 'vessels' morphed into planets, which became 'Rhythm of the Universe.' Both the vessel and the circle used in the planets are female symbols. The planet series is now morphing into a more 'organic' state, using more found materials, i.e. coffee, tea, alcohol, salt, as well as inks, paints and collage. I continually try new materials and experiment with more organic shapes."*
>
> *~Vickie Martin, mixed media artist*

I've personally tried many different media and taken classes with many different instructors. Sometimes I tried to incorporate their ideas into my work for a few years. Eventually I either absorbed aspects of what I learned into my own style, or abandoned my efforts to do so. Throughout this process, my signature style of layered art emerged.

I create layered art with a variety of materials and methods and a few consistent themes. Much of my work is two-dimensional, made on canvas with archival paper and fabric, or with paint on plate glass. I also work on large three-dimensional wall pieces with copper, metal wires and fixtures.

Recently I've discovered book art, a natural extension of the work I've created to date, where I can combine my two-dimensional and three-dimensional techniques. Regardless of form, what distinguishes my work is a unifying "leitmotif" expressed in textures, a palette of multi-colored surfaces and bindings.

To create signature work, you must fully explore the possibilities of expressing your artistic ideas, from your first thoughts all the way to the tangible objects representing those thoughts.

You will need to turn those ideas over in your head, talk about them with your muse or other artists, make sketches of what the finished work might look like, and do studies that might be a "first draft" of what you want to create.

Discovering the factors that make your work truly unique will almost always involve much more experimentation, evaluation of subject matter, creative technique and media than most people imagine.

Other artists often ask me how long it takes to create a signature style, but there's really no answer to this question since each artist differs in so many ways. Even when you get clarity about the particular elements of your style, it still takes time to refine those elements into work that is unified in meaning and technically proficient. You will always start out with a few pieces that are unified in some way, and those together will exemplify your first signature style.

The time it takes and the relative ease or struggle you experience will depend on your skills, training, determination, creative energy, what sizes you create, whether you create originals or multiples, whether or not you work continuously and whether you make art full time, part time or overtime — in other words, it all depends on who YOU are as an artist and your life context.

Artists with a signature style know their limits and preferences. Signature style is defined as much by knowing what you can't (or won't or shouldn't) do as much as by knowing what you can and will do. For example if you admire figurative work but can't draw well-proportioned figures, you have a choice to make. You can either take classes until you master the technique, or you can switch to something that comes more naturally which you already do well.

Another possible route is to take those odd proportions and make them into your signature style, as did Botera, Giacommetti and Modigliani.

Your role as an artist is not separate from the rest of your life. Your signature style reflects your uniqueness in character and talent, as well as the circumstances that continually shape your life and art career. Changes in your life circumstances will act as a stimulus to alter or deepen your creativity. You may move, your family may grow or get smaller, or you might gain other employment. All of these life changes influence your state of mind, your resources, your time, your inspiration and your influences — all of which affect your art.

I have lived all over the world, on my own, with a family, employed by others and self-employed — all clearly influenced my life and art. The way I express myself visually has also changed over the past twenty years through my interactions with other artists, mentors and teachers. My art was shaped significantly by a health crisis, by selling my studio and gallery, by expanding my family, by studying chaos and complexity theory, and recently, by learning to play the electric bass.

I encourage you to honor all of your experiences because they may lead to surprising and important elements in your art. Once of the strongest (and most unexpected) influences in my own art is the change in the amount of space I've had to create, and the light available to do so. I adjusted the sizes, the tones, qualities and the surface treatments.

Throughout these changes my love of patterns and relationships in strong lines, vibrant metallic colors, textures, dimension and topography has remained constant in my work.

Your current work is often an outgrowth of past work. For example, if you started out as a California landscape artist and now focus on California oak trees, there is probably a good reason. You may have been attracted to doing landscapes but found that what really interested you was the trees. Then as you focused on specific trees, you found so much to explore and depict that you no longer needed to include their surrounding landscapes. Eventually you discovered nuances in each season and each year that you viewed a particular tree. Now you paint tree portraits, from saplings to mature giants, and your signature style is highly recognizable.

A combination of gut instinct, feedback and support will tell you when you have arrived at a signature style. Here are some of the indicators to help you recognize this moment:

- You feel a confidence that improves your competence in making your art.
- You can easily describe your current work and how you see it evolving.
- You can distill the essence of what you do into a ten to twelve word description of your art style.
- People will describe you in shorthand as "the xyz artist."

Your audience recognizes your work and is able to remember the main message of your work. Your art has come to represent a specific and distinct style to them.

Showing Multiple Styles: Good or Bad?

With so much talk about distilling down to one style, it's important to recognize that some established artists are skilled in a variety of art methods and media, and have succeeded in exhibiting and selling work in more than one medium. These artists tend to be well-established in their first medium and style before embarking on others, and have a proven track record and a following which helps them succeed. At a glance, it may seem as though they can create any kind of art they want, but if you study their careers, you'll see that they are actually producing *multiple series* of cohesive signature works.

Toni Scott is an excellent example of that type of professional. As a third-generation artist who has been exhibiting for many years in galleries, museums and powerful alternative spaces, Toni's art signature is unmistakable. Almost all of her work is about women, primarily the African and Native-American experience, but that doesn't mean that all of her work looks the same or gives the impression that she creates identical art over and over again. On the contrary, each piece brings its own vital and individualized exploration of the pride and strength of Toni's mixed heritage, whether it's through her photography, her sculptures or her paintings. Picasso went through many phases over his long career as well, but he stuck with each phase long enough to develop those periods into unique, stand-alone bodies of work. Whatever style or genre you eventually choose, make sure it is something that you are passionate about. If you truly love it, that passion will come through to your viewers — both in your work and in the way you talk about it — and you will *want* to stick with it until your talent and inspiration reach their fullest expression.

That being said, never underestimate the power of having an alternative medium to explore even as you focus on your signature style. Sculptors and ceramicists often have another medium to work in (photography or painting, for example) while they are waiting for various stages of their sculptures and vessels to be finished.

Ceramicist Mitch Lyons took this one step further. He was intrigued by the reverse images he found on the rice papers used to blot colors from his flat ceramic pieces. Over a thirty-year period, Mitch experimented and consulted with chemists to develop the techniques and materials of a totally new art form called clay monoprint.

The takeaway? You can never quite guess where inspiration may come from next. That's why I encourage artists to explore *every* avenue of their potential signature style.

Techniques to Explore Your Signature Style

When you first discover your love of making art, almost everything gives you joy. After all (and possibly for the first time) you've finally found something that resonates with your very soul. However, until you make a lot *more* art, you won't know the depth and breadth of your talents.

The same is true for identifying your signature style — you'll first need to produce a "fair" volume of work, and then you can assess it as a whole and discover any continuous elements that are the hallmark of your style.

As you work persistently to master your medium and materials, you'll develop the technical skills to produce the art you see in your head, or feel in your hands and body. Like great musicians who must master their instruments by practicing endless hours playing scales and compositions, so, too, must artists practice and improve. Along the way, you will most likely develop your own visual language with previously unexplored tools, techniques or applications, making your artistic expression just as unique as your mental vision.

Whether you're a newer artist just beginning your quest for a signature style, or you've been producing artwork for years but are still uncertain what your style is, try jump-starting your exploratory journey with one of more of the following techniques:

1. Experimentation

Experimentation is incredibly important while you are working on your signature style because it keeps you interested — *and* leads to discoveries. As you start out making art, let your influences, inspirations and methods have a "lot of room." Explore, observe and experiment with ideas for subject matter, materials, techniques, surfaces, reflections or whatever else your mind can conjure up. Notice what keeps your attention and explore more there, or, conversely, what bores or irritates you (avoid it like the plague).

Try buying new, unfamiliar materials to use, or experiment with your usual materials and tools in new ways. Shop in non-art stores and see what you can find for your art. (Home improvement stores have become the catalyst for many new techniques and styles in my own work.) Repurposing materials is exciting and stimulating, and often leads to the development of a look that's unique, fresh and worthy of a signature style.

Another method of discovery is to use another artist's work as a "jumping off" point. Do you admire the work of someone else, but have no idea how they accomplished it? By working to recreate it yourself while using only your current selection of tools and knowledge, you'll often stumble upon an entirely new look to incorporate in your own style.

Remember, it's okay to experiment without expecting that you will exhibit *all* the work you create. The result of your artistic play and experimentation are invaluable stepping-stones on your path to a new series or new signature style, and some of this work will be for your personal collection only. In fact, I recommend that you simply plan to put away a number of these transitional pieces — they are part of your process, and for you alone.

For my more ambitious artist clients, I often challenge them to keep reaching for that next level by saying, "If you are serious about your art career as a lifetime pursuit, work towards the goal of one day having a retrospective exhibition. You'll need a range of art that shows the work you've done throughout your art career, so you may as well start now!"

2. Study and research

One of the best classes I've ever taken was an art history class. I thought it was going to be boring, and that the exam would require lots of memorization. Instead, as the instructor showed us his research and images of the masters, he was full of enthusiasm about why he liked or disliked their work.

One of our assignments was to take what they did and not copy it, but use the masters' work and techniques as inspiration to make a piece in our own style. That assignment helped me understand these artists from the inside out, and I was able to "see" a lot more when I viewed their work in museums. This class stretched my art talents and my thought process about how to represent themes that interested me.

You don't have to limit yourself to art lectures or books. Make a point of getting out of your studio and exploring art fairs, galleries and museums. Study the work of artists online — those you admire as well as those whose work you don't like, because you can certainly learn from both. See what's available near where you live, and go on city art tours with guides or museum art tours with docents.

Use your study and research to do the following:

- Identify what you like and don't like. How would you use what you see in your own work or change it so that you *would* like it?
- Describe how a particular work or experience inspired you. Try incorporating your insights into an experimental piece of art.
- What common factors do you recognize in all the artists you have chosen to study? How is their work different from yours? How can you use these common factors and differences to improve your work?

3. Capture random thoughts
Some days you might not have the time or energy to make art, but you can prime the pump as you go about your daily business. I get some of my best ideas on my daily walk or in the shower. I don't want to lose these ideas but I know I may not remember all the details later, so I always have a pen and paper nearby.

Use these next several questions to fuel your exploration and help you expand the ideas you jot down while you are living your life:

- What catches your attention, and what details do you observe about it?
- What amuses or inspires you?
- What emotions are triggered?
- What intrigues you enough to suggest concepts, subjects or themes?
- What do you want to say to the world about it, and how do you want to say it?
- What do you want viewers to see about the idea?

- Who else has expressed the idea and how is your message the same or different?
- What materials and techniques will best help you express your intention?

4. Go "deep and wide" with a theme

One of my teachers at The Toronto School of Art assigned us two challenges that initially seemed to be impossible.

The first exercise was to create sixty sketches, all on one idea, in one hour. A timer went off after each minute — when we heard the bell, it was time to move on to the next drawing (whether or not we were finished with the last one). We were forced to let the ideas spill out, without judging them. It was like training for a sprint. We had to try not to think, and instead just "charge out of the blocks" every time we heard that timer go off.

I chose to see how much I could wring out of my love of trees. I selected one variety so that I had a limited scope and color palette. Then I painted the tree sixty different ways. I tried different perspectives, sizes, buds, leaves and trunk until I had squeezed every last aspect of "tree-ness" from the species I had selected.

In comparison, the second challenge was more like training for a marathon. Our assignment was to create sixty drawings in sixty days. There were no time restriction or requirements, just one per day, for two months. Just as a runner learns to put in the miles, I learned "to show up for work at a certain time every day" whether or not I felt like making art. I chose a theme and basic shape, and the end result always surprised me. I often did not like the piece at various stages throughout, but I trusted the process and I was never disappointed — in fact, once I got started it was usually very enjoyable. When the project was over, I even missed it. Now I work on a sketchbook or piece of art almost daily when I am at home, and I periodically review these studies to see what they suggest for the direction of my future work.

Give this a try for yourself: simply choose a subject that interests you and undertake my teacher's challenges. Use these studies to discover what is most compelling for you about the subject you chose — most likely your results will help inspire future pieces as well.

5. Trust yourself and the process

Like many other artists, I can be my own worst critic. I do realize that having high standards for what I make is partially responsible for my results. But on the other hand, those same high standards can quickly become impossible hurdles to overcome. There is a fine line between learning from critical thoughts and taking them too seriously.

> *"I was taking an art workshop when the instructor told me to 'quiet the inner critic.' I never said anything to anyone in the class about this voice in my head screaming at me telling me my art was awful but I guess she could tell by my facial expressions and the work that I wasn't doing. The inner voice was telling me that I was crazy for thinking that I could actually make a living making art despite my very strong desire to create.*
>
> *Getting in the studio everyday has really been the strongest strategy I've used against the inner critic. The more work I do, the more the volume on the inner voice is turned down."*
>
> *~ Robin Jorgensen, emerging artist*

Whether you love every single one of the pieces you create or not, you are *not* failing. There is no such thing as creative failure. Accept that those pieces are transitional for you, and view them as necessary steps in the journey of getting from where you are (or where you don't want to be) to where you want to be.

Don't worry if you are still looking for "your style" or still building on your skills. You may not be completely sure of your media, your subject matter or your signature style, and you are no less of an artist. In fact, to master your art, you must *always* be engaged in some search for what's next.

> *"I'd been working as a graphic designer for ten years and when I started to paint, my paintings had a distinctively graphic style to them. For the first month or two I felt I was 'doing it all wrong' because my paintings weren't turning out like anyone else's. Once I'd finished about eight pieces and laid them side by side, I could see a theme developing. It was then that I realized I had a distinctive style."*
>
> *~Patrice Federspiel, watercolor artist*

Finding a signature style and creating a few bodies of work is not an end point — you will continue to hone your signature style for the rest of your art career. Your work might always contain the same recognizable elements, or you may decide to make significant changes and establish a new signature style sometime down the road. The good news is, you can make a lot of refinements on your own with the techniques I've already described above.

As artists we often over-identify with our own artwork. It's not easy being objective about a subjective process like making art. It's almost as though you have to be two-headed to be somewhat objective... in other words, you have to simultaneously look at the work both from *your* point of view *and* from the viewer's point of view. To get the full benefit of this practice, you have to check your ego at the door and take a good hard look at your art.

How to Assess Your Own Signature Style

The ability to curate your own work is essential for artists. The more finely you can hone your ability to self-critique, the better you can realistically assess each piece and determine whether or not it's good enough to show.

I have worked with many emerging artists who needed a simple way to assess their current work, so they could see where and how to "raise the bar" on their art skills.

Here are two simple exercises to use:

1. Be your own "art curator"
Hang all of the art you've completed so far in order of creation. Look at your work as if you were looking at someone else's work for the first time. Record voice notes on your mobile telephone, or take photos or short videos, as you ask yourself the following:

- What specific materials and techniques do you use with skill and finesse?
- How do you apply design elements with your own particular "touch"?
- Which of your compositions to expresses your ideas best, and why did you choose it?
- How do you share your ideas through your own unique interpretations?
- How do you pay attention to detail from creation through finishing?
- What stands out, what works, and what could work better?

2. Become an "arts reporter"

Now take on the role of an arts reporter. Describe your work in detail, including your intentions, materials, subject matter, methods, style, presentation and impact. Write about what you see in the development of your signature.

Once you've completed that exercise, ask yourself these questions and summarize your answers in writing:

- What do I think about the quality and technical maturity of my work now?
- Where and how can I improve my work?
- What common elements do I see in my pieces? What makes my art uniquely my style?
- How would I describe my current style? Is my signature style crystal clear or only a suggested direction?
- How does my body of work "show?" What would improve the presentation?

After doing these exercises, an artist I worked with said she had not seen the progression of her style so clearly before. Previously, when she had finished a piece of art, she just put it away and started on the next, so she had no sense of how they all fit together. By looking at your work from beginning to end, your improvements and style will come across loud and clear.

Ways to Learn How Others View Your Style

Before seeking outside perspectives about your work, I recommend that you formulate your own opinions. Once you have gained a little skill and confidence through self-assessment, *then* it's time to gather information and feedback from others. The goal is not to simply change your work based on what you hear, but to help you understand the impact of your work on your audience, and give yourself a framework of ideas for how you might improve it.

It is *always* up to you to decide whether or not to accept the opinions and advice you get. Getting feedback from viewers is a bit like going in for a job interview. You must be able to separate yourself from what you hear, not take it personally and, somehow, learn to rise above the comments that hurt. Remember, art appreciation is simply a matter of taste. The goal is to produce the best possible art you can, which will stand the ultimate test of being seen by people you don't know.

Try one or more of these six practices below as you work on your signature style and develop new bodies of work:

1. Peer viewer assessment

I have looked at hundreds of group shows where the work is hung salon style on the wall. Often these shows are created around similar themes, textures, and/or media. Even with the large number of works to look at, I always notice that some of them (even not hung together) jump out as being created by the same artist.

Use this simple test with a group of artist friends, or at your local arts organization:

Display ten pieces of your work among ten pieces of several other artists' work. Try to find art in the same medium, size and subject matter as your own, and put them all up without adding names or titles beside them. If someone unfamiliar with your work can pick out at least eight of your ten pieces, you have a strong signature style.

2. Artist critique groups

Being part of a critique group improves your artistic eye, your communications skills and your critique skills, both for your own work and for the work of other artists. A critique group is a great forum for fellow artists to give each other feedback, because there are usually as many opinions as there are artists in the group. This mirrors the variety of audience reactions you'll experience everywhere.

To make the feedback usable, use the suggestions below to take charge so that you don't get overly generalized or unhelpful input that you cannot use:

- Describe to the group what your intent was in creating the piece. Then ask for feedback on how successful you were in fulfilling that intention.
- Request comments about specific aspects of your work that you are curious about improving, such as composition, values, perspective and etc.
- If someone says that your work needs "more development," ask what that means to them, and how you can accomplish what they're suggesting.
- Ask specific follow-up questions about each comment. For example, find out who teaches the skills that your critique groups thinks you need to develop, or what artist's work would be relevant to study in order to improve a specific technique.

Take in all the information that is given and try to suspend your reactions until the end of the critique. If you are defensive about any feedback, you may end up ignoring an important piece of useful information, or discouraging the group from being honest with you.

Listen to your internal response while you do the following:

- Look for the elements that "ring true" for you, even though you may not like what you heard. What resonated?
- Identify what you can learn from the comments. Consider every comment carefully before tossing it in your mental garbage can. What new ideas were presented? Did your viewers understand what you wanted to express? What did they feel worked well? What didn't work so well, in their opinion?

A critique is not a "final exam." All of this information is simply preparation for the true test of exhibiting your work to non-artists. Use the critique as an exercise to improve yourself as a professional artist — both in your art and in the presentation of your work. If you have chosen your group well, they will be rooting for you. Accept their support as well as their critique.

3. Juried exhibitions

Every juried exhibition is a great opportunity to get feedback on your work and to meet artists and art professionals, so make sure to attend the award ceremony. You will be able to hear comments people make as they view your work, you can compare notes with other artists about the competition, and of course, you can also meet the jurors who decided the outcome.

Jurors usually give reasons for their decisions when they announce the winning entries, so if you won an award you'll hear why directly. If you don't win, ask for feedback. You won't always get a reply or the answer you hoped for, but it's worth asking.

You'll certainly increase your chances of getting feedback, if you pay attention to your timing and how you submit your request to the juror. Make sure to select an appropriate time for the conversation. Don't ask in the middle of the award ceremony or with others around. Find a private moment when the juror is more likely to be open to your request. If you don't see an opportunity at the award ceremony, a telephone call or e-mail may be your best option.

Let the juror or organizer know that you appreciate the extra time they have devoted to doing this for you. Remember that most jurors are volunteers and have already given many hours to the job of reviewing all of the submissions and making their selections.

Once you are communicating with the juror, ask these questions:

- What were the key characteristics of the winning entries?
- How was my work different from the winners?
- What would you suggest I change in order to meet the standards you used?

Whether or not you get a response that helps, always remember to thank the juror and organization for their time and for participating in the competition.

4. Apprenticeships or internships

Atelier-based instruction is a longstanding tradition in the arts community. An established master artist will take on apprentices or interns to pass on their skills to the next generation of artists. Apprentices and interns take part in the daily life of the artist, through a practical, hands-on approach, sharing in preparation, cleaning, maintenance and any other tasks required by the master artist.

Not all master artists want apprentices or are good at working with interns. Looking for one is like a cross between finding a job and finding a temporary life mate. You need to find a master artist who is willing to devote enough of their time and energy to take a budding artist under their wing. I suggest that you have a written agreement about what you will do, and what you would like to learn from the experience.

It's important to choose someone that you believe you can get along with, since you will be working side by side with them for an extended period of time. You will be working to help the artist meet *their* goals, not yours, and you will be intimately involved in their work. You may or may not earn anything monetarily from the arrangement (in some cases you may need to pay for the materials and overhead *you* use) but if you pay close attention, you can learn a lot.

You might consider joining an apprenticeship program for one or more of the following reasons:

- You want to learn highly specialized skills or techniques developed by only a few artists who do not teach their skills in workshops.
- You want to learn skills that require special equipment or a team of specialist workers.
- You especially like the work of one particular master artist and want to develop a professional relationship.
- You would like to take your signature style in a new direction and want an experience that will stimulate your thinking.

Apprenticeships are not as common as they once were, but they can still provide an excellent developmental experience. Look for an apprenticeship that will last long enough to provide you with the skills you want to develop. Make sure your résumé reflects prior experience in your art form, significant promise and a serious long-term commitment to practicing art.

Connect with other artists who have completed their own apprenticeships to locate good opportunities and hear some real stories of their experience. I've heard about good apprenticeships and horrid ones, so do your research before you jump into anything.

Of course the best match benefits both the master and the apprentice. The master artist gives up time and energy to accommodate your learning process, and in exchange, you give back an extra pair of hands and energy.

5. Artists' residencies

Also called artists' communities, colonies, retreats, workspaces and studio collectives, these retreats offer a dedicated time and space for creative work away from the pressures and habits of everyday life. Residencies also offer their art experiences within a specific geographic and cultural context.

It's hard to give a simple description of how residencies work since there are many variables. There are quite a number of colleges, foundations, national parks, museums and even master artists who host artist in residence programs. Programs run for varying periods of time, from a week to a semester, or even for several months. Some programs host one artist at a time, while "artist colonies" may have up to twenty-five participants.

A few residencies are fully funded or pay an honorarium, but most of them require the artist to pay all transportation fees, and some of them ask artists to pay for room and board as well. In funded residencies, the artist will often interact with the public by offering a class or presenting a talk.

These creative communities are a diverse group, and help to provide artists of all disciplines with many different styles and models of support. If you like to learn in the company of other artists, then residencies are a great way to add practical skills and useful knowledge to what you already know. While you network with other artists, you may also find out about places to exhibit your work — and of course, your expenses there can also be a tax deduction.

If you're looking for a residency, start by doing a web search using the keywords "artist-in-residence" to see what's available. Review each of the residencies you find against your criteria. Most artists look at location, timing, which artists are guiding the program, the number of artists selected, stipends or fees and scholarships or funding.

Make a short list of the ones you like and look for blog posts by any artists who have been involved in those residencies to learn more about their experiences. Like anything, it's a good idea to do your research *before* you spend time and money going anywhere. Read the submission and acceptance requirements to make sure that you can deliver what they want in return. For example, if you don't like to demonstrate or teach your art form, it doesn't make sense to apply to residencies that require you to offer public classes.

One other option, similar to residencies, are "retreat programs" which are not competitive. These are more like an artist-run vacation spots where you can seclude yourself and focus on making art. If you can pay the fees, you can easily reserve a space and time — that's the only application process required.

6. Mentors

Mentoring benefits both people involved. Unlike apprenticeships, there's no money changing hands in a mentor relationship.

> *"Creative processes are about who we are inside, how we view the world and the method we find to express it. When a mentor connects to that life on the inside of us to the extent that they can respond to it with enhancing guidance... well, there is no greater satisfaction.*
>
> *Mentoring is a synergistic event that has the potential to multiply for both people involved."*
>
> *~ Barbara Riche, mixed media artist*

The ideal mentor is creative, flexible, interested in helping artists learn more about their art form, comfortable with their role and committed to serving as a mentor. Their own careers serve as inspiration — they have high standards for their work, and they demonstrate their professionalism through a long track record of making, exhibiting and selling art.

Mentors can be a great help when you're unsure about your next move, when you want a safe place to ask questions, or if you simply need an "ear." Building relationships with mentors opens doors that you would not be able to unlock on your own. Good mentors are willing to share access to people and resources as well as provide you with feedback about the art world and the issues you face.

Most mentors have a deep love for their work and have been the recipients of mentoring themselves. They usually mentor for free because they love to teach others for the pure joy of it, or they feel an obligation to "pay it forward." Many mentors say that they learn as much from the process as the artists they mentor.

To find a mentor, you can either approach a businessperson you admire or an artist who has succeeded on a level that you want to reach. Seeking out art instructors who you already know or talking with people on arts associations or councils are also good ways to find mentors.

It's very important that you and your mentor be a good fit for each other. Both of you must be able to identify what you want from the relationship. When both benefit, it makes for a much richer experience all around.

Early in his art career, Bruce K. Haley Jr. approached fine art nature photographers he admired to become his mentors. One mentor eventually fired him for "knowing too much" and they became friends and co-teachers:

> "My mentor, noted nature photographer Jim Clark, was all that and more as my mentor. Actually, he still promotes me whenever he can. His friendship is one that I will always treasure.
> It isn't all about the creative process. It's also about the people that we meet along the way who have an effect on our lives. 'Passing it on...' is one of the most rewarding things you can do as an artist."
>
> ~B.K. Haley, Jr., fine artist photographer

Mentorships provide an excellent developmental experience. To find a mentor, or to become one, start with a little self-reflection:

- What is working well in your art career?
- What is not working well in your art career?
- Can you take direction and criticism designed to help you develop?

Your answers to these questions will tell you what you are ready to pass on to others, and what areas you will need to explore with them.

Next, prepare for action:

- Who do you know who has a mentor? Can you ask them for a referral?
- Write out what you want from the mentor relationship, including the why and how. That way when you meet, or are referred, you know what to say.
- Like any relationship, "chemistry" is often a deciding factor.

Once you find a mentor:

- Thank all of the people who helped you find this person.
- Remember to thank the mentor, as well as reciprocate your mentor's generosity.
- If you are serious about staying sharp and focused on art, plan on becoming a mentor. It's a great way to pay it forward while constantly refining what you know.

How to Handle Rejection

No discussion of art criticism and feedback would be complete without addressing the prospect of rejection.

Artists often tell me that they don't want to enter juried shows, seek gallery representation or apply to any number of other "qualified" art events because they fear rejection. Quite truthfully, that's just human nature. We put a lot of care into creating our art, and want that care to be noticed and respected. But instead of running the other way to avoid any and all kinds of feedback, we need to redefine what "rejection" really is.

Rejection by a show or gallery doesn't necessarily mean that the quality of your art is lacking (although quality *may* be an issue at times). More often, rejection simply means that your work isn't compatible with a given show's — or judge's — aesthetic. Or, it may mean that your work doesn't meet the requirements of the competition.

Oil painter Eric Armusik gives this wise counsel about handling rejection:

> *"You will deal with rejections from juried shows, art galleries, and commissions. The key is to not take it personally. MOST times it has NOTHING to do with your art or your abilities. There are so many people in this profession all fighting for the same results. You have to keep honing your abilities at what you do, stay focused, stay professional and continue to work at it everyday. In the end you WILL succeed."*

Every time you enter a show, approach a gallery or have an exhibition, you're going to face the prospect of rejection.

Consider your own taste in art: you probably *dislike* just as many styles as you like. Some people highly regard the skills of a certain artist or genre, but know emphatically they would never want to live with it in their own home. So it's just as understandable that jurists and gallerists not only have their own personal preferences, but also feel entitled to "weed out" artwork that doesn't fall within their show's specific scope. So what's a sensitive artist to do?

To again quote painter Eric Armusik:

> *"Obstacles are everywhere in this profession. You have to understand that early on. The sooner you get a thick skin the better. You will fail, but you have to get back up and forge ahead. It is a law of averages. Over time, if you continue to fight, and you are vigilant, you will succeed. You have to keep pushing and pushing until people have heard your name so much that you become a staple in your regional or worldwide art community."*

Acceptance largely follows a "law of averages." So, enter multiple shows, apply to multiple galleries and submit to multiple competitions at the same time. Your odds of being successful are higher, you'll develop your "thick skin" faster and you won't be as heavily invested emotionally in any one specific venue. Just imagine: how would it feel to enter your work *so often* that the experience and feedback, positive or negative, simply becomes part of your routine.

The very first time I entered a juried show for a gallery exhibition, I also was an assistant for the jurying process. I thought it would be a great way to get an "inside view" of how the system worked. I imagined there would be a printed document with several listed criteria that the jurors would use to make independent assessments. Then, I assumed, the group would come together to discuss their opinions and find a consensus.

Some juries are like that. This one was not. This particular show was being juried by *one* person: a well-known art representative. She looked at five works at a time, and took a total of thirty minutes to review sixty pieces — an astonishing pace of roughly thirty seconds per piece.

My job as the volunteer was to help the gallery owner bring each new group of paintings in for review. Half a minute later I'd pull the "rejects" from the room, then scramble to assemble the next five works "for the chopping block."

Eventually I was tasked with carrying my own artwork in before the judge, and it was hard to keep my face neutral. Having seen what I considered to be "lesser works" kept in the stack for final review throughout the afternoon, I felt relatively certain of acceptance. But with a casual flick of the wrist, my piece was taken out of the running. I was shocked, crestfallen and heartbroken.

As I continued to watch the juror make her selections, I thought there might be a pattern to the rejection at hand. If I could only identify what criteria the judge was using, or determine what she felt was "missing" from my work, I could make adjustments and stand a better chance in the future. Taking my best guess, I inquired of the gallery manager, "Was my message too obscure? Did she not understand what I was trying to achieve?"

"No," came the reply, followed by an explanation. The judge completely understood my intention… it just didn't match her tastes, which ran more to realism than abstraction.

In speaking with jurors over the years, they usually mention many of the same aspects of what makes a good signature style: color balance, composition, emotional or decorative appeal, technique, unique subject matter and expression of ideas. How they interpret the "best" in each of these areas comes down to personal taste and comparison with other entries. My advice is to do the best you can, and submit only your best work. The rest is out of your hands.

Of course, you can research jurors before you enter a competition, but you won't necessarily know how they will respond to your work. Sometimes all the jurors will be from within the organization sponsoring the event. As such, they may have developed certain similar preferences in the jury process and for certain artists, styles or subject matter. Other times, outside panels are created, mixing local art jurors with some guest jurors.

I applaud jurors who both publish their criteria and are willing to give specific artists feedback on their artwork. Just being a juror is a lot of work already; when they go the extra mile, make sure to thank them.

Looking Beyond Awards and Prizes

Despite the fact that the jury process is subjective, and the chance of receiving constructive criticism from judges is small, I am still recommending that artists regularly apply to artist alliances, juried shows, residencies, "calls for art" and galleries.

Why? The reasons are surprisingly plentiful.

> "My initial goal was to gain 'Signature Membership' in the Georgia Watercolor Society, at their National Exhibition in April, 2008 (which I did). But through my diligence and persistence, with that and with other shows, I accumulated lots of experience (as both entrant and juror in more than sixty shows over five years). As a result, my success took a huge leap."
>
> ~Pat Fiorello, painter

While it's great to gain entry, win awards and see growth and success, in the "here and now" of juried shows and competitions it helps to have a larger purpose.

Here are four good reasons to think about entering juried competitions as a means to an end:

1. You'll build your credibility

Being accepted into a prestigious show or winning a "best in show" award does wonders for your credibility. "Prestigious" means a few are chosen where many apply, so if you aspire to be among the elite you had better get used to being part of the masses first. Be prepared to enter more than once, and follow the submission instructions to the letter – it shows that you're a professional and it makes the jury's job easier when you respect their system.

You may not win, but those important decision-makers (who might not otherwise have had the chance to be exposed to your art) will see your work and qualifications.

2. You'll build your visibility

Entering juried shows keeps your name and your work in front of collectors, publishers and arts representatives. Whenever possible, choose shows and sites that are heavily promoted and have a track record of good sales, but also find locales that fit with your travel budget and preferences. If it's an online show, take a close look at the fine print to make sure the opportunity is genuine — not just a promotional strategy that benefits only the sponsoring site.

3. You'll see how you "stack up"

While feedback from jurors might be rare, self-assessment is *always* an option. Attend the event once it opens and evaluate the work that was selected. Be as honest and objective as possible. Even in the case of prejudicial judges there will always be a lesson available. If you can't see these lessons, you may need to bring more realism to your self-evaluations.

4. You'll keep yourself current

Having an entry deadline will push you to get those photos done, those frames ordered and your résumé updated. Get into the habit of updating your professional portfolio whenever you have something valuable to add to it, so that you're always ready for any "call to artists." You never know when a gallery might come across your résumé and want to know what you have done that merits recognition.

So, don't worry about what's out of your control — gaining entry and winning awards aren't the only benefits of entering shows and competitions. Instead, focus on making and presenting your best work in a way that is uniquely yours, and taking every opportunity to let the world know about it.

A Quick Note on Signing Your Work

Besides creating a signature style for your art, you will also need to develop a consistent *name signature* for your work.

My art mentor advised me early on to be "loud and proud" about my art by signing, naming and dating it. This simple act declared that I was finished and that the work was ready to move from my studio into my inventory.

There are certain questions that only you can answer about how you will sign your work.

Will you use your initials, first initial and last name, full name or pseudonym? What media will you use? If you are a painter, you will probably use paint, but it's up to you. If you sculpt or make ceramics, you may scratch or engrave your signature, or find another solution. Whatever method you choose, make sure that it is as archival as your art itself.

You will need to choose where you will sign. When I painted mid- to large-sized works on paper and canvas, I signed on the bottom right. My more recent book art and some of my paper works on canvas are miniatures, so I don't want my signature to dominate. Since my art extends around the edges and covers the back of the canvas or books, I prefer to sign on the bottom edge or the inside back cover.

Finally, you will need to decide whether or not you will include a date. The debate about including dates on art came about with the consumer notion of "sell by dates" on consumable products. Art does not go stale or deteriorate (unless you do not use archival materials) but our culture has an obsession with "new and improved" when it comes to contemporary art. If you choose not to include a date on the actual piece of art, make sure that you keep good records for when it was created, and have paperwork — like a certificate of authenticity — to accompany the art when it is sold.

Producing a Body of Signature Work

I've described a body of signature work as a cohesive group of artworks created by a single artist. Each piece should be typical of that artist's vision, style, approach, media and techniques at a specific point in time, allowing the artist's signature style to be instantly recognizable.

You've learned that a completed body of work demonstrates that you are capable of giving physical form to an idea, and can do so repeatedly using your mastery of specific art-making techniques. When you see a group of your art pieces together, and they look like they belong together like a harmonious family, you have created a body of signature work.

Artists often ask me, "How big should a body of signature work be?"

Unfortunately, there really is no blanket answer to this question. However, artists who create two-dimensional works should have at least fifteen to twenty mid-sized signature works ready for each solo exhibit, and slightly fewer for group shows.

For a successful and financially viable art career you will need a large inventory of quality signature work in order to attract a sizeable group of collectors and art representatives (at least, if you want to be able to offer them choices). As your career progresses, eventually that will mean creating several bodies of work that may seem like siblings or distant cousins. Galleries need to know that you can create distinctive work of high quality which stands apart from other artists' work, and that you can create more similarly recognizable work as demand for your art grows.

> *"Three major bodies of work have emerged repetitively throughout my career: human figures, sea life sculptures and outer space themed artwork.*
>
> *My figurative work examines not just the outer surface of a person's skin, but the inner warp and weaves that make up character and experience - the metaphorical 'skin.' In my 'Ocean of my Mind' series, water symbolizes the subconscious and at times also has sculpted imagery from my dreams. I interpret rock and earth in glass, the contrast between the solidity and the innate fragility of glass. My 'Cosmos' series combines orbs and nebula to create installations with the feeling of being in outer space."*
>
> *~B.J. Katz, glass artist.*

165

I challenge my clients to produce 100 pieces each year of mid-sized two-dimensional work. These artists may make more or fewer pieces, but my challenge gives them a number to aim for until they arrive at the size of body of work that makes sense for their goals and the type of work they create.

Over the lifetime of your career, you will create an "oeuvre" (the French word for a collection) of several bodies of signature work.

> *"What I hope to leave as a legacy is an ambitious large collection of work with a very high value for my children and their children. I believe I will continue to be a major player in this movement of contemporary realism. I don't aspire to simply paint a figure; I paint a moment, a human experience, and an emotional dialogue that transcends culture, religion and time."*
>
> *~Eric Armusik, oil painter*

Keep in mind, the development of each new body of work does not have to be linear — many established artists return to themes from earlier in their careers. These pieces can greatly expand their offering and even help them reach new collectors.

> *"My art continues to evolve. For a number of years the work I'd shown had been predominantly abstract, but my love of the figure kept calling me back. So, three years ago, I began combining the two, introducing highly expressive, loosely painted figures into my abstract canvases. The response from collectors was phenomenal! Since then, I've expanded the line even further, adding abstracted landscapes into the mix this past year.*
>
> *I've also begun playing with sculpture once again, first in cast bronze figures installed within an abstract painting, and now slowly moving into stand-alone figurative sculpture, but still very abstracted... it's as if one of my painted figures 'hopped off' the canvas and into 3-D. I love to constantly grow and explore as an artist."*
>
> *~Bruce Marion, painter and sculptor*

As you create your first body of signature work, you'll notice that your creative process has its own rhythms. There may be days when it's hard to get started in the studio, or when your confidence is down — about your art, or life in general. Some days, nothing may turn out the way you think it will. Sometimes your muse will come when you call; other times you may have to wade through the muck to find her.

Whenever possible, try to figure out what interrupted your creative flow. Remember, it may have nothing to do with the art you're working on: it could be physical or emotional stress, money worries or other problems swirling around in your head. Solve these issues first if they are more than temporary worries and your artistic doldrums keep persisting. It's simply too hard to be creative when your mind is fretting about something else.

If you discover that your block is specifically art-related, then locate the source. A lack of skill or materials can easily be handled by joining a class to gain the skill or buying the right materials. If the problem is more elusive, you need a way to get to the bottom of what's troubling your muse. You have to understand what's holding you back.

Accessing Your Creative Muse

Initially, it might seem counterintuitive that artists can benefit from understanding the process of creativity, but getting inside "how" you create will most likely help you manage your muse and troubleshoot those creative blocks.

One of the creative techniques I used when recovering from two strokes many years ago was Chris Welsh's "Six Stages of Creativity." My recovery process had not been going fast enough for me and I wanted to get my brain working again, so I took Chris's course Mastery of Learning® to speed my process and discovered "The Six Stages" which I adopted and still use today.

These six steps help by getting the worries out of your head and down on paper (where they are usually smaller than they seemed in your thoughts). If you have anything clouding your mind and limiting your creativity, try the following steps — you may choose to do one stage at a time, or do several passes through all of them until you get the clarity you need to move forward again.

1. Identify what you really want to create or accomplish

Describe your work of art or your goal in as much detail as you know right now. Add sketches to illustrate what you want to produce, whether it is a painting or an office area. Write and draw until you clarify exactly what you want.

2. Write down what you need to reach your endpoint

Make lists of materials, skills, techniques and steps — again in vivid detail. What comes first, second and third? Draw a flowchart to make sure that you have not left anything out. Ask other artists or do a search online to learn what others have done in cases like this.

3. Notice what is "calling" you right now

Are you in a creative state, or would you be better off cleaning your studio? Sometimes you just need to take a break and do something different. Trust your instincts and stay in motion. After a break, you may get that flash of insight that opens up new opportunities or solves your creative problem.

4. Stay curious and be open to any ideas

At some point you *will* get the inspiration and motivation that you have been waiting for. You can't force creativity — your muse comes in its own time. Your brain keeps processing the problem, even while you are doing other things, and will come up with an idea which will move you to action. Even if the idea seems "wild," accept and use what comes. Your first idea may not be the final solution, but it will probably lead you one step closer to something that will work.

5. Figure out how to make the idea work

The idea is there — now comes the specific planning. Write notes on the steps you need to take, make drawings and create samples or models to try out your new idea. Your initial notes about what you want to achieve may help you to flesh this step out more fully.

6. Experiment with producing your idea

Take your time and be really present to what is happening in your mind and through the tactile sensations in your hands as you create. Notice what works and pleases you, as well as what doesn't. You may need to do a series of experiments to decide if this idea is worth pursuing.

I've added a seventh step –

7. Persist or desist

When it isn't going well, move past the point of "get me out of here please," and take a hard look at the idea you were working on. Sometimes you'll come to the conclusion that the idea wasn't as good as you thought. If that's the case, it's okay to discard what you were working on and move on to something else more interesting and productive. On the other hand, sometimes you'll have a breakthrough simply by persevering past those "get me out of here" feelings.

If you find yourself resisting any of these steps, take a look at your underlying attitude so that you can give yourself an "attitude adjustment" if needed. Sometimes the assumptions you have going into a project make it easy to resist change — when that happens, recognize it, let go, and trust the process instead.

Making Use of Your Creative Flow

Everything ebbs and flows — even creativity. I would love it if all of my work happened easily in that rich feeling of artistic flow. If you've been making art for even a little while, however, you probably know that's not always the way it works. There are times when a few "tricks up your sleeves" will help you to move out of the ebb and back into the flow.

Try these:

1. Pay attention to your energy

Whenever you are freshest, do the most important projects or the tasks that demand the highest level of creativity. All artists have different times of day (or night) when they produce best. Sense your rhythms and respect them. When your "inner bell" goes off, it's time to move on to something else which requires a different kind of energy. Instead of working late to finish a piece while you're tired, you might switch over to preparing a new one. It's all part of production, so save the mundane tasks for when your creative "tank is empty."

2. Chunk the project into smaller bits

Break your art projects down into small bites: it's usually easier to maintain your enthusiasm with smaller pieces than one massive task. In the same way, don't set yourself up to be overwhelmed by expecting to produce too much during a single work session. You'll enjoy the work better and have a more consistent experience of satisfaction if you spread things out.

3. Change art projects that bore you or sap your energy

When you're just "not feeling it," find other art projects to work on, or look for the kernel of excitement that provoked you to begin the project in the first place. Look for even the smallest speck of interest in what you have created, and then start another piece of art with that speck. Remove yourself temporarily from *making* the art and see if you can recapture your excitement in the project. If you can't get enthused, put the project away or throw it out and move on.

4. Change the result you envisioned

Maybe you created something that doesn't feel like the final version of what you envisioned. Consider it a "practice piece," and remove the pressure of it being the finished product.

5. Find other artists and teachers to help you

Isolation can make ordinary problems seem bigger and scarier. Other artists go through the same experiences, so they can always empathize with what you're dealing with — connect with those artists whenever possible.

> *"You can't create art in a vacuum. It is important to continue learning and seeing what is being done out in the art world and what trends are popular."*
>
> *~Vickie Martin, collage artist*

Growing Your Creativity

Whether you are naturally creative or you've developed your talents through training, it's important to build good habits that will help you nurture your creativity.

Here are a few of the techniques that I recommend to my clients:

1. Keep an art ideas journal

Buy a notebook and keep it with you at all times to capture ideas, sketches and references. These entries will prevent you from wasting time rediscovering things you have already worked through, and give you a wellspring of ideas when your creativity seems to run dry. Date the ideas and give each a clear title so you can easily sort through them later.

2. Pin ideas to your art board

Post pictures, quotations, advertisements or anything you find through Internet searches to stimulate your thinking. I have a board in my art studio for art ideas, and another one in my office for business thoughts. I never know what will come from these artifacts, and more than once I've been glad I kept them around.

3. Fill an ideas treasure chest

If wall space is at a premium or you want a more portable means of inspiration, get a box or two to collect images and artifacts. Save anything that will stimulate ideas for future work and store them in such a way that makes them easy to get at. (I like clear plastic boxes so I can browse before even selecting a box.)

When you have actual things that you can pick up and handle in your treasure box, it's a lot easier than trying to recall ideas or start from scratch. You will remember why you chose the objects in the first place, and you'll also see new connections. It's like opening a gift from a loving friend who really "gets" you and what your art is about.

Any of these techniques can work, and do work, for many artists. The important thing is to pick one or two methods and be consistent. Developing good creative habits *now* will stand you in good stead for the rest of your art career.

Managing Your Ongoing Art Production

Art is what you "manufacture" — which means, literally, to *make with your hands*. Your art drives your business, so the art you produce needs to be consistently good, and you will need to be consistent at producing it.

Fortunately, producing art is less like a factory assembly line (where each task is rigidly defined and controlled by routines and machines) and more like gardening. If you control the materials and the methods, your creative nature will do the rest.

Commit to Creating on a Schedule

To be a successful professional artist, you have to love making art even when it doesn't come easily. It's a myth that artists simply go into the studio whenever inspiration strikes, or when they "feel like it."

Exhibits and commissions come with deadlines that don't recognize the ebb and flow of your creative impulses, so professional artists must produce quality art even when they don't want to, or they feel that their muse is nowhere to be found. Curiously, the muse tends to return once the bait has been set, like putting out art materials, intention or a deadline.

In order to have an art business that is financially viable, you *must* master the art of production. This means committing to significant studio time and consistently producing marketable art inventory. Without that production flow, there is no chance for income flow.

Respect Your Art Production Deadlines

All businesses have deadlines and you will too, but remember that deadlines are also a matter of choice. If an exhibit is coming up or a commission is due by a certain date, you can decide to say yes or no. If you say yes, you must have your work ready to deliver by the agreed deadline.

As soon as you have a deadline, mark it on your calendar. Then, work backwards and mark in the dates when you need to have each stage of the project done. It may help to double or triple your time estimates, because you can never anticipate everything that will come up.

Whatever you do, don't wait until the last minute to start working. You are much better off having extra time left over than being rushed to finish (and showing inferior quality work) or being embarrassed by not finishing at all. Instead of being known for apologies, start on your projects right away, give yourself plenty of time to finish and get a reputation for being reliable.

I know several artists who believe that they create best "under pressure," and I've worked with some very talented artists who admit that they often leave things to the last minute. This is always risky, though. If you got away with this once or twice you were lucky, but repeating this behavior won't always work.

"Tone Up" Your Art Business with Healthy Work Habits

In elementary school I was the kid who avoided gym class whenever I could. We had to wear funny uniforms called "bloomers." (The name alone tells you how unattractive they were.) Back then, exercise was mostly a way to get us to expend some of our wound-up energy so we could pay more attention in English class.

As my body has aged, my attitude and approach to exercise have changed significantly. Now I want to exercise to keep my heart healthy and prevent gravity from completely taking over any soft body parts. I have the motivation, but I know from experience that without action, nothing changes — a body at rest stays at rest. Likewise, a body in motion tends to stay in motion. I have learned that the key to fitness is to develop a habit of working out, and over time that good habit brings healthy rewards.

Developing the habit of making art is a lot like building muscles. You will need space, time, motivation, the right methods and the ability to stick to a schedule. You may sometimes feel like quitting, but if you want a healthy business you must learn to press on. Make a plan and decide on incentives that will help keep you on schedule. Continue to raise the bar with additional training and repetition. You will see steady improvements by changing your behavior, developing consistent habits and maintaining a regular schedule.

Eventually, your habit of continually making art will feel as natural and enjoyable as breathing, and your portfolio (and saleable inventory) will grow because of it.

To build good art production habits, I always recommend the following training program:

- Organize your creative work space.
- Set your sights on the results you want.
- Create and follow a schedule to build your art production habit.
- Motivate yourself to continue your daily habit.
- Reinforce the art production habit.

Let's take a closer look at each one:

1. Organize your creative work space
Your first task is to prepare and organize your art making space. Your goal should be to create a space that is *always* ready for you to go to work — that way you won't squander precious minutes, resources and creative energy getting set up each time.

If you haven't already done so, visit other artists' studios and see how they organize their space. Think about what you see that you like, and decide whether or not a similar set-up would work for you. Even if you only have part of a room devoted to your art, you can make that work too.

I suggest that you arrange your space into two areas. One space is for making your art, where you create and have all of your supplies, and the other space is for storing completed work. You'll be able to step into your art space and immediately produce art without any interruptions if you make sure to take the following precautions:

- Get the supplies you need ahead of time, so your work will never be interrupted when you run out of something.
- Put together a permanent art supply storage area with re-usable containers, and get rid of junk. This will eliminate the need to search for materials or move them around every time you want to work on your art.
- Set up racks or shelves to efficiently store your finished work so that you can easily find what you need when it's time to exhibit.

2. Set your sights on the results you want
In order to build a large enough portfolio for future exhibits, you will need an idea of how many pieces you can produce each month. Initially you might have no idea, so start by keeping track of how long it takes you to make each piece. Some pieces will take longer than others, but after a while you will have a realistic idea.

Now you are ready to estimate how many pieces you would like to finish this month. Set a goal for a reasonable number. As you learn from experience what you are capable of, adjust the number of hours or the number of completed works in your monthly goal.

3. Build the habit of art production

Many experts say it takes twenty-one days to make behavior into a habit. Whether or not that's true or works for you depends on many things. You may be able to change tiny habits in a matter of a few days but it may take years to replace habits you've had for a lifetime.

Still, it helps to have a plan to change your habits, so for the sake of a place to start, select a period when you can carve out the time to build your art production habit in a consistent way. Every artist is different, so you can decide what "consistent" means to you, depending on the other things you do in life in addition to creating art. It could be daily, weekly, monthly or on every full moon.

For the purpose of building this habit, try to set aside fifteen minutes a day at first, or an hour a day for five days a week or three hours once a week. Choose a recurring block of time that fits your lifestyle so that you will stick to a regular schedule. That consistency is a very important part of creating habits that produce results. It does not mean that you will get into a rut. It means that once you develop the habit, you can decide how to incorporate it into the rest of your habits.

Mentally prepare yourself to add in this new habit into your schedule. You might have to adjust your attitude about doing things you don't always enjoy, or eliminate some activities from your current schedule. Also, make sure to discuss your plans with the people who share your life.

Create a small area where you can log your activities, schedule your studio time and plan future work efforts. This is the "brain center" of your art business. Do your logging, scheduling and planning in this space so that you associate your progress with your new workspace and habit.

Decide on the date that you will start to build your art-making habit. Write this date on your calendar as an important appointment and draw a big star beside it. It's common to set unrealistic timelines as part of our imaginative nature, so resolve to pick a realistic start date and set yourself up for success. Otherwise, if you miss it, you'll end up feeling bad about not meeting your target, even if it was unrealistic to begin with.

When you reach your start day, commit to building your new habit of art production for the next period. If you choose other ways, count ahead twenty-one days and mark that date down on your calendar. (Draw another big star beside it, or add an image that reminds you of celebration.)

Whatever work-habit schedule you've decided upon, mark the start and end times as appointments with yourself on your calendar. Make these time slots unwavering commitments to your present and future as a productive artist. Keep these commitments sacrosanct. Don't let them "slide" or allow other things impinge on your studio time.

Remember, the amount of time is not as important as the consistency. If you can work only fifteen minutes a day, do that. You can always increase the amount of time, the frequency or both, once you develop momentum.

Start Your Own "21-Day" Schedule

You know the basics for creating a good art production habit. Now adjust the sample 21-day schedule below to suit, the time period you've chosen, as well as your current lifestyle and shape of organization.

Make sure to track your progress daily by adding a checkmark on your calendar each time you follow your schedule. Then in the margins, or in a separate notebook, write down what's working well and what could work better.

If I miss my daily allotment of studio time, I keep track and catch up the next day (or within a few days if necessary). You may need to start your 21-day schedule over again if you aren't able to catch up in a few days. That's normal — I've sometimes had to restart important new habits as many as half a dozen times.

Here's a sample schedule:

Day 1. Clean and organize your "studio" so that you have one space for making art and another for storing it.

Day 2. Decide what you need to do to make your studio space work better so that you can step into it and simply enjoy making art.

Day 3. Order supplies and equipment online or go into town to buy them. (This is one time when shopping equals work.)

Day 4. Put away your supplies, set up new equipment and admire your progress.

Day 5. Fine-tune your studio space so that you can step into it tomorrow to make art without any further setup. Take a photograph of your handiwork.

Day 6. Work on a piece of art. Enjoy the flow. There should be no distractions. If you want maximum time and space for creativity, tidy your studio before you leave it and set out the materials you will use the next day so you can step right into creating again. If tidy isn't your style, at least arrange the studio so you don't have to climb over too many things to get to work tomorrow.

Day 7-20. If you are new to making art, work on your current piece for at least fifteen minutes each day. If you have been making art for a while, increase your time accordingly.

Day 21. Look over the log of your experience for the last twenty days. What worked well? What didn't work so well? What do you need to stop, start or do differently to improve your level of art production? Reward yourself in some way for sticking with the schedule the entire twenty-one days.

As you build your art making habit, you may find yourself losing track of time. As long as you don't have any other appointments, that's fine. I use a timer to let me know when the creative period I set aside is up, because for me, time in the studio bears no relation to "clock time."

If this is your first attempt at developing better production habits, it might feel nearly impossible to complete all three weeks. Or, maybe the entire experience will be much easier than you ever expected! Either way, the three steps below should help you complete your "test run" with flying colors.

1. Motivate yourself to continue your daily habit
Unless you have a "studio supervisor" you will have to motivate yourself to keep up with your new schedule. Here are a few ways to do that:

- Think about the positive outcomes and write down in specific terms how this habit improves your art life. Review this list any time your enthusiasm flags.
- Keep a daily log of how each day went. Describe what was good, what was bad and what was horrible about the time you spent. No one else needs to see your daily log. At the end of "21 days" your notes will help you figure out how to adapt your schedule into one that you can sustain.

- Review your daily log at least once a week and look for patterns. What is helping you build your habit? What is distracting you? Write down ways to reinforce what's working and change the things that are getting in the way.

2. Make lists of the steps needed to create each piece

Some days I go into the studio and my creativity needs a jumpstart. It may sound counter-intuitive and uncreative, but lists help me more than anything on those days. All I do is grab the list for the day's major art-making activity so that I don't have to think about it. I simply consult the list and do the next task.

If I haven't done a particular kind of work for a while, or it's a new project, the list makes sure I don't miss any steps which could cause me to waste time (or worse, materials) or get frustrated doing things over.

These lists also come in handy to teach other artists, or to train studio assistants. Here's mine for making layered paper paintings on canvas:

- Make notes about my theme for the series.
- Prepare canvasses with gesso.
- Sketch the initial layout of the piece.
- Select papers, paints and glues.
- Glue first layer of paper for background.
- Cut or tear paper for creating the image.
- Glue paper pieces to build the texture and image.
- Photograph work in progress.
- Make notes about what I worked on, how it felt and what I will do next.
- Clean up my workspace and lay out materials I think I'll use next time.

3. Reinforce the art production habit

New habits don't always come easily, so be gentle with yourself and take one day at a time. When you are building a habit, the occasional slip is natural. Expect to slip, forgive yourself, decide what to do next time, pick yourself up and get going again.

Try the following techniques to reinforce your intentions:

- Imagine what it will feel like to succeed. Use all of your senses and put yourself into a mental movie of having achieved your production goal.

- Decide what you want to get done in the time you have, and set realistic expectations for what you will accomplish. A work of art takes time to mature in your mind as well as emerge from your hands.
- Give yourself pep talks. Describe the progress you've made towards your goal and forgive yourself when you miss a day, or when you feel that the time was wasted. Then, see what got you off track and decide how to handle that in the future.
- Get "cheerleaders." Ask friends, family and other artists for support. Tell them when your art is going well and ask for support when you need some. Only choose people who fully support your efforts, and avoid people who would bring you down.
- Reward yourself daily with a "pat on the back" or something more tangible, like new art materials.

Above all, **remember that developing the habit is the point.** Be patient if you're not completing the amount of artwork you hoped for. As your daily art production becomes habitual for you, you'll naturally produce more art, faster. Keep your emphasis on developing workable habits and the artwork will follow.

Achieving a Balance between "Life" and "Art"

If you stick to a production schedule without fail, and let either your personal life or your business tasks slide, you'll have art but you won't have a life or a business. It's better to examine the pros and cons of each decision you make, and consciously choose to be "present" in all the parts of your life.

Consider the cost of your choices, versus what you gain. Do you get up early to fit in extra studio time at the cost of enough sleep? Do you spend less time with your friends in order to grow your business in the evenings or on weekends? Which choice will get you the best results for the least pain?

One problem that many artists have is how to make enough art. A common solution is to get up early and spend two hours a day in the studio before going off to work, or to stay up after the rest of the family is asleep and do it then. If you can maintain those hours, in two years you'll accumulate a lot of valuable experience and a much larger inventory than if you hadn't. Of course it also means that for two years you are taking that time away from other activities.

The "opportunity cost" of making more art is less sleep and more exhaustion. If you choose to sleep longer, however, the opportunity cost could be not having enough inventory to do the shows you've planned for.

We often trade short-term advantages for long-term results. Some artists drink too much coffee, neglect their physical needs or stop having a social life to create more art. I don't recommend this for anyone over twenty. It works for some artists for very short periods of time, but recovering from these bad habits can eat up precious time or damage your health later.

Sample Schedules from Working Artists

In my monthly interviews with members of the Artist Career Training community, I ask artists to describe their typical day, week and month. As you read their answers, you will see that there is no "one size fits all" artist schedule (phew!) Maybe you will be inspired by some of their answers:

"A typical day right now is generally split between my spiritual practice, my to-do list, my study time, and my creative exploration. Basically it's meditate, write, be productive, learn something, create something. I pretty much make art daily — or it makes me. It's not really a choice sometimes the way it unfolds."

~Peter Bragino, painter

"Discipline is important to me. I do not rely on inspiration to work. I do paint everyday if I can. On days that I do not feel like painting, I still sketch or work on things that get the creative juices flowing. I do not have set times of the day or night to paint and I like that spontaneity. Sometimes I break through the night working. Other times I start early in the morning."

~Frank de Las Mercedes, painter

"Three mornings of each week you can find me at hotels painting, making contacts with new people and selling prints at the galleries there. One night each week I teach a watercolor class to a local adult-education class. The other three days (yes it's a six-day work week for me) I'm in my studio, starting new paintings, writing my e-zine, prepping for my classes or workshops, doing paperwork, and planning.

~Patrice Federspiel, watercolor artist

"I work in a very organic way. I have a general list of what needs to get done by when, and I'll tackle different parts of it each day. Unless I'm on deadline, I don't 'force' myself to do a particular thing at a particular time.

I usually have 3 or 4 paintings going at a time. I give myself permission not to paint for a few days if I don't want to... the work I've produced while trying to adhere to a formal, structured schedule winds up feeling, well, formal and structured.

My typical day starts about 6 a.m. I'll check emails, then head to the gym for an hour. Most often I'll end up doing office/computer work until lunch, then hit the studio to work on commissions, pieces for my galleries, or artwork for licensing in the afternoon. I like to go out to lunch most every day. It gives me a necessary change of energy, and allows me to keep up on my art magazine and book reading. I try to wrap things up at the studio by 5 or 6 p.m., to get home for dinner and family time."

~Bruce Marion, abstract painter and sculptor

"I've had a full-time job for 21 years, which has afforded me plenty of vacation time. I take off a minimum of one Monday a month to devote myself totally to art. I generally paint at least one day a weekend, and several nights during the week for a few hours. I make the time to document the work I'm doing, because potential buyers always like a story about the work. When I'm just too exhausted to actually paint, I will read about art and artists."

~Vickie Martin, mixed media artist

"During the week I generally wake up, check in with my kids and pets, and then I pour myself a cup of hot tea and cozy up next to my computer. I check my emails, update my Twitter and Facebook accounts and catch up on my other art business.

Then, I am off to the gym for an hour class, or out hiking a mountain trail with my dogs... during the winter you can find me out skate skiing. An hour of exercise clears my head and I seem to produce better paintings this way. It's time to get into my studio and paint! I usually take an hour to two-hour lunch break (depending on if I am painting for a show or not) and use this time to run my errands in town.

The afternoon is generally devoted to painting. (I check in with my social media sites a few times during the afternoon too!) I usually stop painting around 5:30 and start working on dinner. I am a night owl and I sometimes get my best work done late at night. Depending on my art show schedule, I either paint or catch up on art business. In fact, right now it is 11:45 pm... and I usually have a nice cup of tea before bed."

~Lori McNee, painter

"A typical day begins with my wife, enjoying a cup of coffee, looking out over Clam Bay and the Gulf of Mexico, watching the sunrise and the birds fishing.

I then clear my desk of business and turn towards my easel in preparation for the day's work. When I am painting it is pure concentration and focus.

There are, of course, days I have scheduled for errands or varnishing a painting. Some days I will paint late into the evening but I try to wrap it up by 7 pm. I try to get in a minimum of 5 hours a day, 5 or 6 days a week."

~Nicholas Petrucci, realist painter

"I get up some time between 10 and noon, have coffee and deal with e-mail and Twitter while I'm waking up. For the rest of the business day it's mostly phone calls and e-mail or time out in the studio. Around 6 or 7 my wife and I have dinner and we set aside 4 to 6 hours that is really just our time. Then later I may do more e-mail or project work. Obviously there are times when I might take a whole day or two in the studio.

Most of my work is 'on demand' so I get the order, make it and go back to other tasks. I actually take downtime now, which is something I never used to do. I've decided that I should enjoy some of this too."

~John T. Unger, metal artist

"Each of the last five years has been dramatically different. This year I have trimmed down my schedule to just two shows. This has given me a lot of time to finish several small commissions and to create new ideas for next year.

I have also had time to promote my work to potential buyers and compete for the commission opportunities that always seems to take a back seat to everything else.

I typically work 6.5 days per week, 9:00 a.m. to 6:30 p.m. and take only 'working' vacations. When I have no available cash to build new sculptures, I build models for new projects and organize my studio and image files."

~Bilhenry Walker, metal and light sculptor

All of these artists have a terrific production record. Rather than see other roles or duties as obstacles to making art, they simply set a schedule that includes these responsibilities. They are among the most prolific and successful artists I know.

Section 3: The Basics of an Art Business

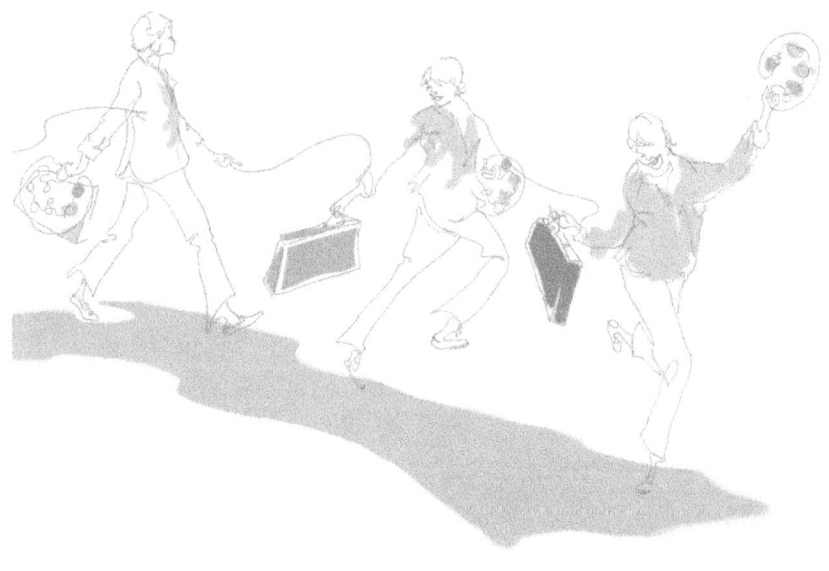

Section 3: The Basics of an Art Business

Build a Foundation for Your Future

Before we get into the details of how to create a solid foundation for your art business, take a minute to visualize your future.

Perhaps for you it's the image of entering your studio early in the morning with a mug of steaming coffee in your hand. As you slip across the beautiful hardwood floor to your easel, a flash of movement beyond the French doors draws your gaze outside. There, in the morning's hazy light, a deer and her fawn graze beneath a tree before making their way to the edge of the creek for their morning drink.

Or maybe you prefer to imagine yourself at an opening night reception in the trendy art district, where you receive accolades by the dozens from your delighted collectors and share a wink with the gallery owner who pastes yet another red dot next to one of your gorgeous works of art.

These are lovely images, and whatever yours are, I want you to have them as well. But they are only a *part* of a successful art business.

If you can also visualize getting all of your filing done, finishing the updates to your contact list after your recent show or finding a less-expensive resource for canvases that will ship to a residential address, you'll be a whole lot closer to achieving your dreams.

For many artists, one of the most challenging aspects of creating a successful art business is accepting that it *is* a business, with all the work that entails. You *are* an artist-entrepreneur… and just like a business entrepreneur in any other field, you will need to spend a great deal of your time on business aspects unrelated to "making your product."

Perhaps it will help if you think of it this way: to have a successful art business, you need to master the art *of* business. That's what this section is all about.

Please note: these next steps are ones you need to take **before** you start to market your art. For some of you, this means you'll need to put in some extra effort to get "up to speed." If you've already discovered a market for your work, scan this section and make sure that you have a solid business structure in place to support your current art business. If there are areas that are lacking, take some notes on any scaffolding you could use.

If you follow the guidelines in the coming pages to comply with common business practices and government regulation, and make a habit of consulting professionals (such as lawyers or tax accountants) when needed, you'll be well-equipped to manage your art business and avoid the pitfalls and problems that can plague the ill-prepared.

> *"'An ounce of prevention is worth a pound of cure.' Trite? Yes, but it's true. And it's very true when it comes to business and law. Lawyers don't do "cure" well. The whole legal system is terrible about solving problems. But business lawyers do* prevention *very well. A little planning can avoid problems very well. Tempting as it may be to ignore things that sound thoroughly unpleasant like business structure and regulations, spending a little time to arm yourself with information can ensure that you protect your legal rights, and that when all is said and done, that you will own what you want to own, get paid for what you want to get paid for, and keep as much money after taxes as possible."*
>
> ~ Nina Yablok, business attorney

I am not a lawyer or an accountant. I am an entrepreneur who follows these guidelines and have helped artists to implement them. The information here is based on laws and business practices in the United States, but is not intended as legal advice or replacement for individual research into the specific legislation governing your geographic location.

In addition to local, regional, national and international differences, laws and practices change over time. Use this information as a research guide for your own locality, and to get legal and financial counsel on the specifics for your business.

Setting Up Your Business Structure

For a hobbyist or amateur artist, focusing on developing business skills or setting up a good business structure is unnecessary. However, since you've read this far, I'm guessing you've already committed yourself to (or are at least still seriously considering) making a living from creating art.

So let's make sure you have the best business foundation you can — one that will help you grow your business into the art career you want.

Choosing Your Business Name

Your very first task as a new business owner is to decide on a name for your art business. You'll need a business name before you can get a business license or set up your business bank account.

Choose a name that is memorable, easy to spell, and one that people will immediately associate with you and your work. The simplest solution is to use your own name, combined with a reference to art. Be careful not to select a name that could limit your future work, however. For example, the name "Lee Jones Watercolor Florals" gives a clear, immediate idea of the artwork, but if Lee Jones ever wanted to change media or branch out into other subject matter, the name could become a problem.

By selecting something more neutral like "Lee Jones Art" or "Pat Smith Studios," you'll have more options down the road. If those sound too generic to you, you might try something slightly more specific such as "Lee Jones Paintings" or "Pat Smith Sculpture Studio," which offer a bit more information without limiting materials or styles.

Here are a few additional points to consider:

- Does the name of your business show your creativity while still sounding professional?
- Is this name being used by anyone else? Would adding a middle initial help distinguish you from another artist?
- Is the name easy to understand, spell and remember?

Registering a Domain Name

Once you've chosen your business name, you will need to register a domain name — this is the series of letters and numbers that will serve as an address for your website (for example, mine is http://www.artistcareertraining.com).

Resist the temptation to be clever or tricky with your domain selection. While your creation might make sense to you, oftentimes these intentionally misspelled or unusual words within a web address are confusing to everyone else. Usually the simplest, most memorable domain name is a repeat of your business name, so savvy entrepreneurs will always check the "availability" of a potential domain name before committing to using that business name. If possible, try to get a .com extension because that indicates a commercial site (in the U.S.)

Once you've chosen a domain name, make sure to do the following:

1. Check for trademarks
Take the time to do Internet searches for your business name to ensure that it does not infringe on another business's legal trademark.

2. Check domain availability
A surprising number of domain names have already been taken by other people. Even names that you've carefully crafted to specifically reference yourself or your art may already be "owned" by someone else. Luckily, there are many sites you can use to verify a domain name's availability. Two common ones are GoDaddy (http://godaddy.com) and Register.com (http://register.com).

3. Buy the domain name
Once you've found an available domain name that's appropriately tied to your business name, *register it!* Even if you don't plan to launch your website right away, you need to secure that name now — don't assume it will still be available later, when you need it.

The cost to register an available domain name is a nominal fee, and is *much* more affordable than building your business around a domain name that legally belongs to someone else. There are companies that intentionally buy up promising business domain names — by the thousands — with no intention of ever using them. They make their money by "renting" the names to legitimate businesses that need them "down the road." Avoid that scenario!

Unfortunately, the world of Internet domain names is riddled with regulations, loopholes, rip-offs and fine print which can be confusing and tricky to navigate. Do yourself a favor and do a little research before selecting an entity through which you'll register your name. Avoid any "bargain basement" pricing lures, as well. The largest, most reputable domain registration sites (like GoDaddy) typically charge less than ten dollars per year — a figure so affordable that taking a risk with an unknown entity who charges less truly isn't worth it.

If you're using a webmaster or hosting site to assist you with attaining a name and building your website, be sure to clarify who will "own" the rights to your domain name. Many webmasters use their own names when registering domains for their clients in order to simplify their transactions. However, this could cause problems if you ever decide to transfer your site to another website builder or host. Even though it's "your" website, if their name is on the registration document they are the only legal entity with rights of transfer.

How would this affect you? Say, for example, that you were to become dissatisfied with their service or need additional features for your website which their business can't support. They could delay the release of your domain, or refuse it completely, unless you "agree" to pay a fee. In other words, they could hold your domain name hostage and demand a ransom. Imagine facing the choice of either buying your domain name back from your host (who you've already paid once) or being forced to rename your business and start over from scratch. This happens! As in all things business-related, be careful, ask questions and do your homework.

Selecting a Business Entity

A business entity describes how you set up your company for tax purposes. Types of business entities include the following:

- Sole Proprietorship/DBA
- Partnership/Limited Partnership
- Limited Liability Company (LLC)
- Incorporated Company (Inc.)

For many working artists, the two most common entities are the DBA and the LLC. Let's look more closely at the pros and cons of these two business structures.

The DBA

Your simplest choice for a business entity is the Sole Proprietor/DBA (also known as a "Sole Proprietorship," "Doing Business As" or "Fictitious Name"). This business type is not considered a separate legal entity from its owner, and still allows you to choose a name under which the business will operate.

Choosing a Sole Proprietor/DBA for your business bypasses the complication of setting up a separate legal entity, making it easier (and less expensive) for you to establish and manage. All business income is simply added onto the owner(s) personal tax returns, which is known as "pass-through taxation." If there is more than one owner then the business is classified as a "General Partnership" but the same rules apply.

The drawback to a DBA is that the owner has *full financial liability* for their business and debts. However, if revenue and expenses are small, and potential liability issues are negligible, there is probably little or no need for the legal protection of a more complex business structure — making a sole proprietorship the most sensible option for the majority of emerging artists.

Since DBAs are typically not recognized at the state level, check your local city or county website to find out their specific requirements for filing a DBA in your area.

PROS: Easy and inexpensive to set up and maintain.

CONS: Because the owner is personally liable for the company and its debt, there is a risk of losing house, cars, personal assets, etc. in the event of a lawsuit. There is also no corporate prestige of having "Inc." or "LLC" attached to your business name.

The LLC

A Limited Liability Company can best be described as a hybrid between a Corporation and a Sole Proprietorship. It provides easy management and "pass-through" taxation (profits and losses are added to the owner's personal tax returns just like a Sole Proprietorship) yet it has the liability protection of a Corporation (because, like a corporation, it is considered a separate legal entity).

The heart of a Limited Liability Company is the "Operating Agreement." This document sets the rules for operating the company and can be modified as the business grows and changes.

Operating an LLC is less formal than a Corporation and has fewer compliance requirements — usually you will just need to have an Annual Members' Meeting, and show Members' approval of changes to the Operating Agreement (in an LLC, the owners are referred to as Members).

Limiting your personal liability is the most common reason for choosing a more complex business entity like an LLC. Established and profitable artists who have multiple employees, multiple studio locations, an international business presence or a six-figure (or larger) income may wish to consider limiting their financial risk in this way.

And, while incorporating as an LLC requires a bit more paperwork and carries some additional expenses, many feel these negatives are offset by the lessened liability, potential tax benefits and increased prestige and presence in the business community.

PROS: Provides the liability protection of a corporation without extra levels of management or corporate formalities (such as board meetings, shareholder meetings, minutes, etc.) Taxes are also handled the same way as a Sole Proprietorship.

CONS: More expensive to form than a DBA, while requiring slightly more paperwork and formal behavior.

Applying for Licenses and Permits

Do you need a business license in order to sell your artwork?

There's a lot of confusion about this issue, so let me put many of your questions quickly to rest. If you want to be a professional artist, you will need the proper licenses because they will affect how the government and the general public regard your art business. And, so you know, simply being *incorporated* as a business is not the same legal process as being *licensed* to do business.

Licenses are permits issued by government agencies that allow individuals or companies to conduct business within a geographical area. While in certain instances a generic "Business Registration Permit" will suffice, you may need multiple licenses, registrations and/or certifications to conduct your art business where you live.

Typically the *type* of business you run, as well as its physical location, will determine your licensing requirements. Other determining factors may include the number of workers you employ and the business structure you chose for your business. Government agencies can fine or close a business operating without the required business licenses.

In the United States, each state has its own business registration and licensing requirements, but there may be additional licenses required by individual cities or counties as well. The Small Business Administration has a list of links to state websites for licensing requirements along with other helpful information for business start-ups. Visit www.business.usa.gov to get an overview of your state and county requirements (just follow the prompts under the "Start a Small Business" category, then enter your zip code for specific links to your area). This is an official business link to the U.S. Government, managed by the U.S. Small Business Administration, and in many cases includes online application opportunities for the various forms and permits as well as information explaining why they're required.

Keep in mind, unless you have a valid business license the Internal Revenue Service (IRS) will not consider you a legitimate business and can label you as a "hobby" instead. This means all of your business expenses could be disallowed. Without a business license, the general public might also view you as a "hobbyist," making it more difficult to command premium, professional prices.

Let's take a brief look at some of the typical situations artists find themselves in, when a license or permit may be required:

Selling art in galleries

Galleries accept work on a consignment basis, which means they sell to the customer and then reimburse the artist based on a pre-agreed percentage. In these instances, the gallery doesn't actually "own" the artwork… the artist does. Once the sale is made, however, the ownership transfers from the artist to the gallery (since it's illegal for them to sell something they don't own). Still, since the artist isn't selling directly to the public, a Sales Privilege License typically isn't necessary.

Selling at arts and craft shows

If you set up a booth and sell your artwork directly to the public, you need both a Business License and a Sales Privilege License. You may also need a license from the city where the arts and craft show takes place. The show promoter should be able to tell you if you do, but contact the city directly to be certain.

The exception to this rule occurs when each artist has his or her own booth, but all monies for sales are collected by the show promoter at a central office, in which case the license requirement falls to the promoter. Make sure you understand these requirements beforehand.

Many cities require each vendor to display the license within their booth space. If you don't have one in your booth you could be fined, and any excuses involving ignorance of the law won't save you from the financial penalty. When in doubt, do your own research rather than taking another person's word on the issue.

Wholesaling

You don't need a Sales Privilege License as a wholesaler because you're not selling directly to the public and collecting sales tax. Instead, you're selling to a store (or other entity) which then sells directly to the public. Many online sites that sell artwork are a combination of a wholesaler and a gallery. They don't take physical possession of the artwork, but they do take payment for it. The customer buys the artwork from the online site and pays them directly. The online site then notifies you to ship the artwork and pays you for it (less a processing fee). You determine the price for the artwork and know what the fees are before the sale is made, but are otherwise uninvolved in the transaction so a Sales Privilege License isn't usually necessary.

Commissioned art sales

Commissioned artwork is work that you create specifically for someone else, based on their direction. That direction can be general, relying on your artistic abilities, or extremely detailed, with extensive notes as to shape, color and subject. The artwork belongs to the person that has paid you to create it, so from a tax standpoint you're not selling them something — rather, they're hiring you to create it.

This is known as "Work for Hire" and can be a tricky area for artists. In these circumstances, if you've been hired as an "employee" to create the art, you don't need a business license. However it may also mean you don't own the rights to the original, so be careful if you are tempted to avoid licensing fees by "commissioning" your work. Not owning the copyright for your art might prove far more expensive in the long run.

Selling from home

In addition to permits and licensing concerns, artists who operate out of their homes also need to abide by regulations and restrictions governing the development and use of property. All property is designated for residential, commercial or industrial use, within a defined area.

Generally speaking, if you merely have an in-home studio where you produce your art and an in-home office where you conduct your business transactions via telephone, you won't have any problems. However, if you occasionally use your home as a "gallery" space (inviting multiple potential clients in for a viewing) or if you teach classes within your home (with multiple students regularly coming "on-site") you may encounter some space use issues.

An artist with whom I worked ran afoul of her local zoning laws when neighbors complained about the increased traffic and parking each time she held a workshop in her backyard. Similarly, local HOAs (Home Owner Associations) frequently have their own regulations regarding the number of acceptable guests and the frequency of their visits which might prohibit your home-based art business. In cases like this, pre-emptive action to get on the "good side" of your neighbors may be enough to circumvent future problems.

Tattoo and body art

The final regulatory area of concern regards county health permits. This is a highly specialized area, however, and typically only affects tattoo and body artists. If you are a tattoo artist and/or create body art, especially at fairs, fund-raisers or other public events, you'll need additional Certificates of Registration and health permits that signify you comply with all hygiene regulations. If operating from your home, you may also need to obtain a land use permit from your local zoning office.

Managing Your Money

Managing finances, keeping records and preparing accounting statements typically have little appeal for those of us with artistic temperaments — myself included. Nonetheless, these tasks must be done. Remember, you're not just the CEO and President of Design and Manufacturing for your art business, you're also the Chief Financial Officer... at least during the early years of your business. Deal with these monetary realities early on and you'll find it much easier to realize your dream of supporting yourself with your art and ensure that you have a profitable, sustainable business from "day one."

According to Statistic Brain, the trusted research provider to Forbes, CNN, The New York Times and other highly-regarded news and information media, 46% of business failures are due to one or more of the following: no experience in record keeping, no knowledge of pricing or emotional pricing, no knowledge of financing or the inability to pay taxes. This is a frightening statistic all by itself, but to make the importance of money management even more clear, let's apply those numbers directly to a fledgling art business. Even if you're extremely talented and produce consistent, high-quality work, *one out of every two art businesses* fail simply because the owners didn't take the time to learn how to manage money.

I don't want you to be part of that fifty percent!

Opening a Business Bank Account

We've all heard the warning, "Don't mix business with pleasure." Not surprisingly, this axiom applies to your finances as well. It's a bad idea to mix your business expenses with your personal expenses, for a number of reasons:

First, if your supply expenses are co-mingled with your personal charges, you won't have an accurate idea of how much it actually costs you to make each piece of art. Amateur and emerging artists are often so excited that someone wants to buy their work that they don't realize their low asking price is losing them money on the sale.

In the same way, if your personal income and expenses are mixed with your business ones, you'll have unclear information on your overall profitability. You won't know how much you are really investing in your art business compared to the income you're generating. Just because they so strongly want to believe in their work, it's not uncommon for artists to focus on the dollars coming in, and mentally "weed out" the dollars "going out."

Lastly, to be considered a "business" by the American government (and thus be able to deduct expenses from your business revenue) you must maintain a separate business bank account. Your business tax returns will be much simpler when you handle all your business finances from a single, dedicated account, and you'll also have documentation that is acceptable by the IRS for tax submissions and audits.

Not all banks are created equal, however. When you choose a bank for your art business, consider these four things:

1. Convenience
Since most artists set up their businesses as a DBA or LLC, they regularly need to transfer funds between their business and personal accounts. Will it be more convenient for you to use the same bank for both? Many times it will.

2. Access
An artist's show schedule often requires a fair amount of travel — does the bank have branches nationwide? Do they have weekend hours and online management services?

3. Service
Is the bank known for being particularly helpful to businesses, with employees and services specifically dedicated to their business clientele? As a sole proprietor your time is extremely valuable. If your bank branch provides designated tellers and account managers for their business clients, the time you save by banking with them could be significant.

4. Fees
Does the bank require minimum deposits and/or charge service fees? These requirements may seem inconsequential, but when you're trying to build a business every dollar counts. Choose a fee-free bank if at all possible, as long as all the other considerations I've listed are met.

The information needed to set up a bank account will vary by institution, so save yourself some time by calling the bank beforehand and asking specifically what you need to bring with you. Usually, at minimum, you'll need your business license, but depending on your business entity (Sole Proprietorship, LLC, LTD, etc.) you may also need an EIN (Employer Identification Number) and photo ID.

Many banks have someone who specializes in helping business owners, and it's often worthwhile to begin a relationship with this banker. As your business grows, this person will usually be the one to help you get a merchant account so you can accept credit card purchases for your art. He or she can also assist you in getting a credit card for your business and will be your guide to the many other services your bank provides to merchants.

Creating a Filing System for Your Business Records

The earlier that you establish your filing system, the better — and it needn't be complicated. A box or two of hanging file folders, a box of manila folders and a single file cabinet (or several portable file boxes) are all you need to set up storage for every category of your business income and expenses.

Of course, if you prefer, you can purchase a scanner and file everything digitally. Take extra care to make sure that each file has a clear name and date (for example, Art Sales Receipts — June 2013) which you can readily recall. If you decide to just keep digital files, you'll need to be especially conscientious about creating timely back-ups of your data. I strongly recommend duplicating all important files at home on an external drive, as well as online with a backup service or "cloud" provider.

The newest innovation in record-keeping and filing are smartphone applications (like "Expensify") which allow you to upload transactions from your bank account into a user-friendly database before adding notes or "tagging" your expenses with keywords. These on-the-go filing aids are rapidly growing in popularity, and many banks and financial service companies are adding them to their own online banking systems. I suggest that you do this in a secure environment so no one else can pick up your transmissions.

> "I ALWAYS record my sales receipts in my excel spreadsheet the day they come in (okay, sometimes it's the next day). This spreadsheet automatically computes my GE tax (that's similar to a sales tax to those of you not living in Hawai'i), and keeps a running tally of it so I know how much to pay when it's due. I ALWAYS deposit my income on the first available bank day…this includes any charge card sales I accept… In addition, I file receipts regularly, in preparation for filing year's tax returns."
>
> ~Patrice Federspiel, watercolor artist

Some of the most difficult aspects of establishing a filing system are determining which documents and receipts you need to keep, how long you need to keep them and how to organize them.

To determine what will work best for you, consider the primary reason for keeping business records in the first place — for most of us, that's taxes. You want your filing system to help you make the most of the deductions on your business tax return, as well as justify those deductions if the IRS auditors challenge your claim.

If you're using a bookkeeping or accounting firm, or a software program such as "Quicken" to keep your books, you may not need to separate your receipts by category. That task is likely being done for you as you record your transactions. If so, a filing system divided by month should suffice. You'll simply use two folders each month, one for revenue and one for expenses.

With this simple method, at the end of each year you will transfer the 24 files (12 for revenue, 12 for expenses) from your current filing cabinet (containing "active files") to a banker's box (containing "inactive files") which can then be moved into storage for as long as you might need to have those records available.

As a general rule, records should be kept in storage for seven years, although certain items such as mortgage or home sale records should be maintained indefinitely. As with all things tax-related, check with your legal advisor or tax preparer for guidance.

Now, if your bookkeeping system does *not* help you separate your expenses into different categories (which is important for figuring your tax deductions), you may be better served by setting up your filing system according to category. If you do this, each of your file folders should contain the entire year's receipts for one category of expenses. For example, one folder would contain all receipts for "Supplies," another would contain receipts for "Postage," and so forth.

One of the simplest ways to know which filing categories you might need is to look at the expense categories on your tax form. This also makes future tax filing very simple. Here's a sample of the types of file categories needed by most artists (again, please consult your tax advisor or accountant for assistance before setting up any system):

- Advertising
- Bank charges
- Bank statements
- Books and magazines
- Car and truck expenses
- Computer hardware
- Computer software
- Courier
- Credit cards
- Education or training
- Finance charges
- Internet
- Legal and professional services (accountants and attorneys)
- Licenses (license and regulatory fees paid to state or local governments)
- Medical and dental insurance
- Office expenses
- Postage
- Professional associations
- Repairs and maintenance
- Sales tax (state and local sales tax imposed on goods sold)
- Supplies
- Telephone
- Utilities

Hiring a Bookkeeper or Accountant

The question most artists ask when it comes to financial management is, "Can I afford to hire someone to handle my bookkeeping and accounting?" The best answer I have for you is, "Can you afford *not* to?"

You've already seen the statistics on how money management principles can make or break your art business — I believe very strongly that this is the one area where every artists should "splurge," if at all possible, and hire professional help.

Mistakes in money management, tax preparation and planning are simply too expensive to risk, and learning the skills required to handle them personally is often too time-consuming to make it a viable option for most artists. Besides, a good, attentive accountant will frequently *save* you enough money to offset most, if not all, of the cost of the services.

The exception, naturally, is when you have direct experience and/or training in these skills from a previous career. But assuming you don't, who should you hire?

Many people use the terms "bookkeeping" and "accounting" interchangeably, but there *are* significant differences in the type of services offered by bookkeepers and accountants.

Bookkeepers record transactions, making sure all of your income and expenses are properly documented to give you an accurate look at the fiscal health of your business.

Accountants, on the other hand, are trained to analyze and interpret those numbers in order to guide you toward profitability while assisting with tax preparation, reports and payments. A CPA, or Certified Public Accountant, has also passed a rigorous state licensing examination.

So do you need a bookkeeper, an accountant, or both?

The answer will depend largely on your personal knowledge base. If you have a good grasp of accounting principles (based on your previous work experience or training) you may do very well on your own with no need for additional help.

If you have no previous experience or training, but have a fair handle on cash flow and profit/loss, you might want to employ a bookkeeper part-time for data entry only, and use a CPA for tax preparation. (While CPAs typically charge higher fees, they are the only preparers eligible to represent you before the IRS in the event of a tax audit.)

And, if you have little-to-no knowledge of accounting principles, you may need to hire both, at least at the outset, to get your "books" set up, your record keeping on track and your pricing on target to turn a profit. Luckily, many CPA firms include bookkeepers and non-certified accountants on staff so that routine financial tasks can be handled at less expense while still under the supervision of a CPA.

In the end, whether you "go it alone" or hire out some or all of your bookkeeping and accounting needs, I still recommend that you familiarize yourself with the key concepts of business accounting discussed in the following sections — after all it's your money!

Keeping a Profit and Loss Statement

A Profit and Loss Statement (P & L) is the easiest, simplest and most visual way to manage your cash flow and ensure that you have a profitable business. As the name implies, a P & L will let you know whether you're making money or losing it — and you don't have to be a math genius or accounting whiz to use one. At any time, you can use your P & L to calculate:

- Gross income (how much money your business has taken in).
- Expenses (how much money you've spent to generate that income).
- Gross profit (your income minus labor and manufacturing expenses).
- Net profit (gross profit minus business expenses and taxes).

If you're doing your business bookkeeping with a software program like Quicken or QuickBooks you can easily generate a Profit and Loss Statement at any time just clicking a button — the program will create it for you.

If you're not using one of these programs, you or your bookkeeper can create a spreadsheet through Excel (or something similar) for your P & L. Setting up the spreadsheet is the hardest part, so if you haven't worked with Excel or you are unsure of your accounting skills you may want to get some help with this step. Once your spreadsheet has been created, however, it will be fairly simple for you to keep it up-to-date each month by yourself.

A Profit and Loss statement is set up in columns and rows. To build yours, at the top of your spreadsheet establish 13 columns. Skipping the first column, enter the 12 months, in order, of your fiscal year. Then, on the far left side, running down the side of the page in the first column, list every source of income for your business. Use a separate entry for each different source (such as gallery sales, art fairs, commissions, web sales and so on).

ABC ART COMPANY
FISCAL YEAR 2015-2016 - Profit and Loss

INCOME	January	February	March	April	May	June	July	August	September	October	November	December
Gallery Sales												
Jones Gallery	$ 3,450.27	$ 4,023.08	$ 999.67	$ 2,631.76	$ 4,003.80	$ 4,212.60	$ 3,134.00	$ 4,138.51	$ 4,291.80	$ 3,453.76	$ 3,935.49	$ 330.36
Smith Gallery	$ 225.04	$ 2,124.08	$ 3,737.58	$ 1,226.64	$ 3,676.55	$ 1,496.20	$ 4,971.26	$ 1,547.99	$ 1,573.28	$ 4,582.58	$ 892.43	$ 1,993.03
Gallery of Art, SF	$ 1,267.90	$ 3,446.91	$ 4,931.97	$ 1,390.00	$ 1,943.54	$ 2,194.28	$ 2,350.53	$ 3,253.94	$ 1,117.57	$ 4,439.60	$ 4,620.38	$ 3,897.42
Art Fairs												
Treasure Island Fair	$ 544.89	$ 4,112.61	$ 2,559.72	$ 3,718.01	$ 2,969.77	$ 4,749.80	$ 4,539.47	$ 2,875.27	$ 2,479.83	$ 4,294.62	$ 141.76	$ 3,634.13
Fort Mason Fair	$ 227.54	$ 1,230.16	$ 3,508.30	$ 1,029.24	$ 2,734.94	$ 4,261.15	$ 1,618.93	$ 1,341.13	$ 1,199.57	$ 4,706.13	$ 3,196.70	$ 1,780.90
Nob Hill Fair	$ 400.62	$ 398.23	$ 2,546.99	$ 449.39	$ 748.26	$ 3,791.28	$ 1,298.48	$ 569.28	$ 351.48	$ 3,921.96	$ 4,871.59	$ 814.34
Commissions	$ 1,290.65	$ 2,085.85	$ 248.72	$ 3,988.86	$ 1,500.75	$ 1,936.45	$ 4,840.12	$ 4,359.12	$ 2,412.37	$ 4,127.92	$ 260.24	$ 2,146.26
Websales												
My Website	$ 700.98	$ 1,703.63	$ 904.40	$ 297.83	$ 803.63	$ 2,187.27	$ 753.48	$ 2,444.54	$ 3,200.39	$ 1,289.23	$ 3,214.04	$ 4,434.62
Amazon.com	$ 897.23	$ 867.88	$ 1,280.62	$ 3,517.20	$ 2,999.60	$ 4,128.87	$ 3,907.44	$ 1,807.75	$ 535.05	$ 2,575.67	$ 2,286.18	$ 4,075.65
eBay.com	$ 265.12	$ 733.88	$ 2,877.38	$ 1,913.22	$ 706.41	$ 1,982.34	$ 731.65	$ 3,142.88	$ 3,753.10	$ 287.39	$ 64.80	$ 2,732.50
NET INCOME	$ 9,270.24	$20,726.31	$23,595.36	$20,162.15	$22,087.26	$30,940.25	$28,145.35	$25,480.41	$20,914.44	$33,678.85	$23,483.59	$25,839.22
GROSS INCOME	$284,323.43											

EXPENSES	January	February	March	April	May	June	July	August	September	October	November	December
General Business												
Website	$25.00	$25.00	$25.00	$25.00	$25.00	$25.00	$25.00	$25.00	$25.00	$25.00	$25.00	$25.00
Phone	$150.00	$150.00	$150.00	$150.00	$150.00	$150.00	$150.00	$150.00	$150.00	$150.00	$150.00	$150.00
Office Supplies	$75.88	$28.50	$128.20	$147.06	$146.13	$123.36	$14.59	$36.64	$12.21	$120.61	$103.06	$132.42
Travel/Transportation	$641.96	$906.44	$708.57	$513.34	$173.70	$524.27	$748.41	$685.00	$519.31	$504.20	$122.30	$860.10
Virtual Assistant	$600.00	$600.00	$600.00	$600.00	$600.00	$600.00	$600.00	$600.00	$600.00	$600.00	$600.00	$600.00
Studio Rental	$950.00	$950.00	$950.00	$950.00	$950.00	$950.00	$950.00	$950.00	$950.00	$950.00	$950.00	$950.00
Net Business Expense	$2,442.85	$2,659.95	$2,561.76	$2,385.41	$2,044.83	$2,372.63	$2,488.00	$2,446.65	$2,256.52	$2,349.81	$1,950.36	$2,717.52
Art Production												
Paint	$364.09	$119.10	$14.67	$282.09	$202.24	$168.88	$133.71	$172.07	$217.64	$292.77	$80.30	$215.31
Canvas	$320.56	$204.94	$271.11	$77.03	$297.81	$343.79	$155.48	$164.73	$134.22	$51.11	$323.39	$412.65
Brushes	$52.67	$36.60	$99.59	$98.98	$32.33	$65.59	$80.83	$11.39	$87.23	$40.67	$3.12	$53.21
Frames	$947.98	$1,481.94	$1,226.15	$1,219.79	$1,389.78	$124.29	$428.14	$541.37	$370.48	$434.81	$1,185.44	$13.32
Net Art Expense	$1,685.30	$1,842.58	$1,611.53	$1,677.89	$1,922.16	$702.55	$798.15	$889.56	$809.56	$819.37	$1,592.25	$694.49
NET EXPENSES	$6,570.99	$7,162.47	$6,735.06	$6,448.71	$6,011.82	$5,447.81	$5,774.16	$5,782.85	$5,322.61	$5,518.99	$5,492.98	$6,129.54
EXPENSES	$72,397.98											

NET PROFIT	$ 2,699.25	$13,563.83	$16,860.31	$13,713.44	$16,075.44	$25,492.44	$22,371.19	$19,697.56	$15,591.83	$28,159.86	$17,990.61	$19,709.68
GROSS PROFIT	$269,278.02											

Note: a fiscal year does not always begin in January and end in December... it may run over any period of 12 months, and is referred to by the date on which it ends. For example, if a company's fiscal year ends October 31, 2012, then everything between November 1, 2011 and October 31, 2012 would be referred to as FY 2012. Your fiscal year will have a direct impact on the amount of net profit you claim on your tax form, and keeping meticulous records can reduce the tax you pay — because, as long as you are a sole proprietor, you can deduct the Cost of Goods Sold on your Schedule C tax form.

You may want to be even more specific and use these income source listings as headings, under which you list each gallery and each fair individually. Doing so will allow you to compare each gallery's sales trends month-to-month, as well as their total productivity compared to each other for the entire year. This additional level of detail will help you determine which of these sources are most effective so you know where to focus your energies. Once your sub-groups are complete, add one more row underneath everything where you'll add each column to get your monthly income totals. At the end of the year, you can add up all of these monthly totals to see your yearly total — this is your *Gross Income.*

Now, underneath all of that income data, you will need to repeat the entire process for expenses. You'll want to see your income and expenses on the same spreadsheet, so just scroll down and start listing all of your business expenses, by category, considering carefully where you need to be more specific by creating sub-groups within the categories.

For example, you may want to have one group of expenses related to producing your art versus expenses that are part of general business overhead (such as office supplies, travel, etc.) This will allow you to calculate both *Gross Profit* and *Net Profit* (which is useful for evaluating your pricing structure, examining how much you're paying in overhead costs and determining the Cost of Goods Sold).

Record each expense category, then add up each monthly expense column. Now that the bulk of the data entry is done you'll be able to calculate your totals.

Below your entries, create a row of *Net Profit* totals by deducting your Expense totals from your *Net Income* totals. If you're also calculating your *Gross Profit* (the profit from your art alone, separate from your business overhead) then deduct your art production subtotal from your *Gross Income.*

Once you've completed your monthly calculations, do the same for your yearly totals to see the actual amount of money your business has earned. And here's a helpful hint: if you always tabulate your totals in both directions — up and down for months, side to side for years — you have a built-in safe-guard for errors. If the totals don't match, you've got an error to look for.

By keeping a "running" P & L, you'll know the facts of your business's fiscal health at all times. This will allow you to make smart decisions, in *real* time, about pricing and spending that can make a positive difference in your financial success.

Determining Cost of Goods Sold

Cost of Goods Sold (COGS) refers to the inventory costs of the goods that a business has sold during a particular time period. Let's say you want to know the Cost of Goods Sold over the last year — you would take the value of your inventory at the beginning of the year; you'd add the costs of any inventory purchased throughout the year; and then you'd subtract the value of your inventory at the end of the year. The number you're left with is the value of the goods that were sold during the year.

Of course, this process can be done at the end of each month, quarter or fiscal year depending on your business.

For IRS purposes, most artists are considered a "manufacturer," which means that you're taking in supplies and using labor and creativity to turn them into a finished "product." As such, the IRS requires that you put a value on your inventory (which includes all of your unsold art and unused materials) on the last day of your fiscal year, and then account for the change of that figure from the year before.

You may want get help from a bookkeeper or accountant when calculating your actual figures, but it will help if you develop your own understanding of COGS. Once you understand the information you'll need, you can track it throughout your fiscal year and avoid scrambling come tax time.

The IRS website gives a quick and simple overview of how to determine your cost of goods sold. Their directions and line-by-line explanations (reproduced below) explain how to fill out a "Schedule C" tax form, which is the standard COGS reporting form.

Figuring Cost of Goods Sold on Schedule C Lines 35 Through 42
(Note: http://www.irs.gov/publications/p334/ch06.html)

Line	Explanation
35	Inventory at beginning of year. If different from last year's closing inventory, attach explanation. i.e. How many art pieces did you have last year and how many do you have now? Where are the ones you do not have in your studio (sold, on loan, in an exhibit?)
36	Purchases less cost of items withdrawn for personal use (e.g. equipment).
37	Cost of labor (e.g. assistants) *Do not include any amounts paid to yourself.*
38	Materials and supplies (e.g. to make art and to market it).
39	Other costs (e.g. Internet, exhibit fees, etc.)
40	Add lines 35 through 39.
41	Inventory at end of year.
42	Cost of goods sold. Subtract line 41 from line 40. Enter the result here and on page 1, line 4.

Understanding Your Cash Flow

In the simplest terms, "Cash Flow" refers to the movement of money in and out of your business during a designated period of time, typically a month or year. In accounting terms, Cash Flow is determined by looking at "Accounts Receivable" (money owed to you) versus "Accounts Payable" (money you owe to others).

The clever expression, "Too much month left, at the end of the money," which was popularized by salaried workers having trouble making ends meet, perfectly encapsulates the concept of cash flow. If, during any given time period, you have more money going out than coming in, you've got a "cash flow" problem.

Keep in mind, *cash flow* is not the same as *profitability*. You can be enjoying tremendous sales with a very healthy profit margin but still see your business go under. How is that possible? If you're not receiving payment for the work you sell quickly enough to cover your immediate expenses, and don't have a savings account or credit line to tide you over, your cash flow will be in the red (even if your sales are in the green).

While it's simple enough for a salaried employee to monitor how much money is coming in each month, for the artist entrepreneur it can be anything but easy. Your income can vary widely from month-to-month, and even well-established artists with multiple galleries across the country must endure the ups-and-downs of monthly sales.

For the emerging artist who is trying to support an art business from show-to-show, keeping track of cash flow can be extremely challenging. In addition to the regular ebb-and-flow nature of retail sales, galleries and art shows are often seasonal in nature. Many galleries are located in destination spots and rely on tourist traffic during the "high" season for the majority of their business. During the low season the picture can get bleak for gallery owners and artists alike. Even when an artist has multiple galleries that perform well in-season, if the slow periods are all aligned during the same part of the year the artist's income could fluctuate wildly with the calendar.

Artists working the outdoor show circuit, for example, might have ample opportunities to sell their work during warm-weather months but find their income drying up once colder, damper weather sets in. Even at a typically productive show, a weekend of bad weather can curtail attendance and cause a major drop in income for the artist — who is still "out" any show fees and travel expenses.

A show circuit can also strain the artist's cash flow even when sales are strong. That's because, typically, show fees, booth rentals, advertising co-pays and shipping expenses must frequently be paid well in-advance of the show dates, necessitating that the artist use savings or credit to cover these "up-front" fees.

Similarly, providing new inventory to several galleries at once, in preparation for their high seasons, can drain cash reserves and make managing cash flow a tricky proposition. Not only must the artist cover the costs of materials and production services for their new inventory, but also the packing and shipping costs to deliver their new work. For sculptors with foundry fees along with "hefty" shipping weights this can be particularly costly.

So how best to weather these ups-and-downs of income? With proper planning, of course… in addition to carefully drafting projections, monitoring financial and sales performance and building a sizable "emergency" fund.

Keeping Your Own Books

If you *do* decide to "keep your own books," whether completely on your own or with the help of a spouse or family member, I recommend choosing one of the following methods for recording your financial information:

1. Columnar accounting books

This is the oldest method of bookkeeping, in which every record gets entered and tabulated by hand. While it may seem antiquated to some, and offers none of the perks of more current methods (like automatic calculations and chart generation), this manual system still works.

2. Excel spreadsheets

Using Excel on your computer to do your bookkeeping has a lot of similarities to the old-fashioned columnar-book method. The primary advantage is that it comes with a "built in" tabulation feature, allowing you to customize your spreadsheet to automatically add or subtract columns and generate totals.

Excel is fairly simple to set-up, and the ability to quickly check your running totals for monthly income, expenses, net profit and the like, makes this system very helpful for keeping an eye on the bottom line.

3. Bookkeeping software

Programs like "Quicken," "Quick Books" or "Bookkeeper" are great for the computer-savvy, do-it-yourself artist. With a wide range of styles, looks and "bells and whistles," these programs can generate reports, graphs and charts that give you innumerable ways to not only tabulate your numbers, but interpret them too. Naturally, such specialized software requires a higher learning curve, but if you or your helper already has that experience or can take the time to learn, these are the ultimate bookkeeping tools.

It really doesn't matter which option you choose, particularly when you're just starting out. However, as your business builds to half a dozen galleries (or more) and you find yourself managing multiple studios or employees, more detailed financial tracking will certainly make it easier to keep tabs on your accounts. Of course, by then you can hire a bookkeeper or accountant to fully handle the books for you, if you prefer.

At this point what matters most is that you don't delay getting started — and don't let weeks pass without recording your receipts! It's so much better to record as you go. Not only will you avoid those dreaded hours of data entry to get "caught up," but you'll also have much more accurate records than if you're constantly searching your memory trying to recall if a receipt was for art supplies, office supplies or personal use.

In addition to not procrastinating, here are several more tiny bookkeeping tips that will yield big results:

- Mark each receipt with the details of its origin, and try to err in favor of too much information. It's not enough to simply know the receipt is from your neighborhood postal service company — you also need to know if it was for shipping charges (and for what), for your P.O. Box, for stamps or for a postcard mailing. Once recorded, file the receipt or invoice.
- Create "revenue receipts" or "reverse invoices" to help you track any money you receive. A simple photocopy of a payment check, made before you deposit the original, will provide a helpful paper trail to support your bookkeeping records.
- Record your transactions by category *and* by month. This not only allows you more insight to your expense patterns, seasonal business, etc., but it also provides a quick accuracy check for your books. The totals for all expense categories should equal the totals for all months, just like when you balance your checkbook against your bank statements. If the numbers don't match, you know you've got an error to sort out.

Always keep back-ups of your bookkeeping files. If you use a columnar ledger, make photocopies of the pages at the end of each month and store them off-site or in a fireproof lockbox. If you manage your finances on the computer, make a backup digital file and a paper copy. Again, store both of these files off-site or in a secure, fireproof location.

Following all of these suggestions will leave a good "paper trail" of your transactions and make sure that every business purchase and expense, as well as every bit of income, is documented by a printed invoice or receipt. If the IRS should ever audit your business, you need to be able to support every figure on your tax return with physical proof of its legitimacy.

If you don't have a well-organized paper trail, you could be subject to multiple penalties and fees, not to mention innumerable, frustrating hours sifting through shoeboxes of paper scraps trying to find proofs of purchases and expenses for the IRS agent overseeing your case. I've been there in a couple of businesses and dreaded the outcome. I am glad to say that my well-organized system of documentation (along with a terrific accountant) made the audits relatively painless.

Lastly, don't ever assume you're "too small" to get audited. Recent reports show that over the last five years the IRS has increased its focus on the small-business sector by 33% while audit numbers for big businesses have fallen by 30%. Furthermore, one of the primary reasons that businesses are selected for audits is because they have a low (or negative) profit-to-expense margin — a financial status that describes many artists during their early years in business. Known as the "Hobby Loss" factor, if your business isn't regularly making enough money to turn a profit (in other words, it's always operating at a "loss") the IRS may determine that you *don't* have a business after all — just a hobby. Suddenly, under the Hobby Loss Law, you no longer qualify to take business deductions. With exceptional business records, though, and a "bullet-proof" paper trail, you can prove that you work hard to make your business profitable and come out on top with the IRS.

Recently, an artist I'd worked with called to thank me for insisting that she get her business records set up properly, including her paper trail. As luck would have it, she was selected for audit and a diligent IRS agent spent three days combing through every financial record and receipt — determined to find something suspicious.

On the third day the auditor emerged triumphant, brandishing a grocery receipt for a few pieces of fruit. "This receipt is marked as "art supplies," the auditor accused, "and you can't claim your lunch as a deduction!"

A bit unnerved, the artist looked carefully at the small slip of paper. In the lower left corner was another small notation — a series of numbers separated by dashes. A smile broke across her face as she recognized the code: it was an inventory number for one of her still life paintings of fruit. Pulling her database up on the computer, she showed the agent the corresponding numbers and then showed her the painting itself. There, item-for-item, were the same fruits listed on the receipt. With that, the audit was over.

> *The final result was a happy ending and a clear audit with no penalties or expenses (other than lost production time) as well as an enormous amount of satisfaction for the artist because of a detailed, cross-referenced paper trail. The auditor — not so much.*

Setting up your filing systems and keeping a thorough paper trail doesn't have to be an overwhelming task, and it will pay off in the long run. If it seems daunting, you might start by asking an artist mentor or friend who has already mastered money management to show you their system and recommend a trustworthy bookkeeper or accountant. One artist I know hired a small bookkeeping firm not only to set up her books and filing system, but to teach her how to maintain them. She is still using the same system now, twenty years later.

If you have no experience at all in business accounting (and many people don't) you might even consider taking a class or two at your local community college. While this does require a small time commitment, it's a minor sacrifice in light of your future business success and you'll have a *much* better chance of understanding the key concepts of your business finances.

Building Business Credit

If you're just starting out, you may not feel the need to do too much with your burgeoning art business — especially if you're still working a "day job.". However, operating as a sole proprietor and using credit cards to fund your business purchases is a simple and straightforward way to get started. Artists, like other entrepreneurs, are wise to build their business credit whenever possible.

Whether you plan to use credit to finance a new studio or merely to help "make ends meet" if your career hits a rough patch, a line of business credit can improve your company's image, protect your personal credit, limit your liability and increase your credit capacity.

A credit line can make the difference between expanding when you're ready versus waiting to accumulate sufficient savings. It can help you maintain a smooth production flow instead of laying off employees during a slow period (then having to hire and retrain new ones when sales return to normal). It can even allow you to stay at the cutting edge of your field, rather than working with limited supplies and outdated equipment. You get the idea.

So while it may not be *necessary* that every emerging artist immediately begins to build an art business structure that includes a line of accessible business credit, it's a consideration that shouldn't be placed too far back on the entrepreneurial "burner." With that in mind, here are the steps you'll need to take before you can start building your business credit rating:

1. Incorporate
The first thing you'll need to do is separate yourself from your business by incorporating, if you haven't already done so. For most artists, this will mean changing your business structure from a Sole Proprietorship or DBA to an LLC (consult your personal tax advisor to discuss your specific needs).

2. Get a tax ID number
As a corporation, your company is considered a separate entity. It has its own tax registration with the IRS and state agencies, which means that if you don't already have an Employer Identification Number (EIN) you'll need to obtain one. This allows your company to file a tax return separate from you, its owner, and to build a separate credit history as well.

3. Get a DUNS number
Just like those companies that track your personal credit history, there are also credit bureaus that rate your business credit profile using a number called a *D & B* or *DUNS*. This number is how lenders will determine your business credit worthiness. You can apply for a DUNS number for free online — go to the website for Dun & Bradstreet (the primary business credit bureau) once you've established your business entity and have obtained your EIN.

4. Transfer your commercial accounts
Put all of the business services and credit accounts you have — phone, Internet, bottled water, basically any company that currently bills you for their service — in the name of your business using your EIN and DUNS number for identification.

5. Get credit with vendors
Ask for payment terms from any vendors with whom you frequently do business (again using your EIN and DUNS numbers for identification). Many types of suppliers, including national chain stores, extend lines of credit to small businesses. Check with your office supply resource, your membership warehouse store and even your local art supply shop about billing services (terms are usually net 30 to net 60 days). Make a point of utilizing these credit lines regularly, *always* pay your invoices on time, and you'll quickly build credit history.

6. Get a business credit card

This can be a little difficult if you've just started managing your art business money in a separate account from your personal finances. If your accounts are both with the same bank, a loan officer may be willing to consider your *personal* credit and banking history when assessing your request for a *business* credit card. However, this may not help you if you have a poor personal credit history or use separate banks for your business and personal accounts.

If that's the case, you may need to start with what's known as a "secured" credit card. Essentially, you will be required to make a deposit with your financial institution for the full amount of the credit line being offered — these funds are not available to you for use, but are held by the bank the entire time you have the secured card. While this takes some funds out of cash flow for a period of time, once you've established a good payment history by using the secured card you can qualify for a traditional card and those funds will be released back to you.

While there are a number of companies that offer unsecured credit cards to those with little (or poor) credit history, these accounts usually have much higher fees and interest rates to compensate for what the company considers the additional "risk" in lending to you. Since building your credit history requires that you carry forward some of the balance each month, these higher fees and rates do start to add up. (While it may seem a little counter-intuitive, completely paying off the total due on your statement does *not* contribute to your credit history. Carrying forward some of the balance each month does.)

Even though some of these steps may seem burdensome or unnecessary, particularly in relation to the current size and scope of your business, don't overlook them. If your business grows quickly or the financial climate changes unexpectedly, having taken each of these steps early on may prove invaluable.

Because many small business owners choose to skip these steps, having corporate status and your EIN and DUNS numbers gives potential lenders immediate insight into your vision and determination to succeed — which translates as credibility and risk-worthiness.

Accepting Credit Card Payments

There are many advantages to being able to accept credit cards as a form of payment, not the least of which is that credit cards are very convenient for your collectors and enables them to make impulse purchases (which will increase your overall sales). They also add authenticity to your art business and allow instant verification of funds — unlike checks, which can be returned for insufficient funds.

Of course, there are trade-offs for these conveniences too. The process of obtaining credit services is often confusing and complicated, and deciphering the various fees and (often hidden) charges can be a nearly impossible task.

But don't despair! With the rise in popularity of e-commerce and small, home-based businesses there are now an increasing number of simple, straightforward options for obtaining merchant credit services. Whether you decide to work with a traditional merchant services provider, utilize a mobile "app" or accept payments strictly via PayPal (or other third-party provider) accepting credit card payments is becoming easier and more affordable than ever before.

The following options are three of the most common ways to accept credit cards:

1. Merchant account services

The way that most traditional businesses accept credit cards is through a merchant account services provider — typically a bank or other financial institution. These entities act as a secure conduit between the business, the customer and the credit-card company. They do this by establishing a "merchant account" for the business owner which serves as a "holding location" for debit- and credit-card payments while the card-issuing company verifies the cardholder's funds. Once the funds are approved, the merchant services provider transfers the money (minus a commission for facilitating the transaction) from the merchant account to the business owner's bank account.

The primary types of merchant accounts are retail, internet and MOTO (mail or telephone order) accounts. Here's a breakdown of their differences:

- Retail merchant accounts are typically for businesses with a "storefront" location — for example, any artist who has one or more galleries which are open to the public and staffed by employees.

- Internet merchant accounts are for online, or "e-commerce," transactions only. This merchant account option could be useful if you are planning on selling your work directly from your website.
- MOTO merchant accounts are for businesses that operate by taking payments via the telephone and/or direct mail.

When choosing a merchant account services provider, give careful consideration not just to your immediate needs but to your future needs as well. Not all of these companies offer every type of merchant account, which could complicate later efforts at expansion. On the other hand, some providers have developed account packages specifically geared toward the needs of small business owners. They do this by bundling retail and online access, and often include the physical equipment needed to accept debit and credit cards, like in-store point-of-sale (or "swipe" terminals), along with fraud and security protection.

Merchant account services were once the *only* way for a business to accept credit cards — but no longer. While they are still considered by many to provide the most secure transactions, they can be difficult to obtain and their fee structure is multi-layered and complicated with a lot of "fine print." Indeed, an article in Inc. Magazine quoted Stella Fayman, Marketing Ninja at FeeFighters, saying, "A lot of card processors make their money off of small businesses who don't read the fine print."

2. Online credit card processing

Small businesses owners who wish to bypass the effort and paperwork required to use merchant service providers have another option for accepting credit cards. These "third-party" processors (the most well-known of which is PayPal) are commonly referred to as "gateway" providers and can handle a business's online debit- and credit-card services without the need for a merchant account. At the same time, they will also usually provide the secure "shopping cart" feature on your website for online purchasing. Boasting lower setup costs and lower monthly fees, these services can be an attractive option, but don't bypass doing your research — in some cases, the per-transaction fees are higher with "gateway" providers and may negate the setup savings that are so enticing.

While any business can use these "gateway" providers, particularly now that many are offering mobile services, they're typically best-suited for businesses with a bad credit history or those that process very few credit transactions per month. Most third-party processors determine their charges based on a tiered system, in which transaction fees start out higher for smaller amounts of monthly sales and are reduced as monthly sales go up. For example, businesses using PayPal which take in less than $3,000 a month in credit-card payments currently pay a 2.9 percent commission, plus an additional 30 cents for each transaction. However, if those monthly sales increase to a point between $10,000 and $100,000, the transaction fee drops to a 2.2 percent commission.

Despite the simpler startup requirements, using online "gateway" providers also has its drawbacks. In addition to higher per-transaction fees, gateway services frequently re-route your customer away from your website onto theirs during the check-out process. This redirection can often confuse buyers and interrupt or delay their purchase. All it takes is an unresolved question about site security and a few extra minutes of contemplation for your buyer to click away.

3. Mobile credit card processing

Artists frequently need the flexibility to accept credit cards at multiple locations, anywhere they sell their art. Mobile credit-card processors are the newest players in the credit-card business, allowing you to accept credit cards at every show, exhibit and fair you attend. By using an "app" and a card-reader that plugs into your smartphone or tablet, these services allow you to accept charge payments "in the field" or, in other words, anywhere you get cellular service.

The current "standard bearer" for mobile processing services is Square, founded by Twitter creator Jack Dempsey. Frustrated by the quagmire of fee schedules and service packages offered by other merchant providers (mobile or traditional), Dempsey created Square, designed to provide flexible, transparent service for the small-business owner. There are no initiation fees, monthly fees, or charge minimums to meet. Instead, you pay a flat commission percentage (2.75 % at the time of this writing) on every charge processed.

When you enroll in a "square-type" account, you're given a free card reader — a small device that plugs into your smartphone (or tablet), and turns it into a portable "swipe style" credit card terminal. You can utilize the Square anywhere you get cellular service, making it very convenient for artists on the show circuit.

Of course, you can also use the Square in your studio or gallery, but keep in mind that if you are only using it for that purpose, the rate is somewhat higher than fixed-location merchant service charges would be. And naturally, if you don't already own a smartphone or tablet, you'll have to include the price of purchasing a "smart" device and paying for monthly cellular service to your start-up costs.

So now you know some of your options for accepting credit cards — but even with that knowledge, it's still a tremendously confusing field, with many hidden costs to be aware of. I recommend that you do additional research and consider the following questions before selecting a system for your personal use:

- Is there a minimum length-of-service contract or a minimum monthly fee?
- What are the transaction fees and how are they calculated? (Typically, there will be a percentage fee plus a flat fee per transaction. The percentage can vary wildly, so look for the lowest percentage and the lowest per-transaction fee that you can find.)
- What kind of support does the processor provide? Will you have a dedicated support person to help you with your account? Does the company provide 24/7 support?
- Are there additional fees if you make sales online? (Some processors make you pay a minimum monthly fee for your physical terminal and another minimum monthly fee for any online sales. Always find out if online transactions are included in the same minimum monthly fee.)
- How long does it take the credit card processor to deposit your funds in your account? (Some companies do this within twenty-four hours, but some take forty-eight hours or more. Ideally you want the shortest timeframe possible.)

For a more comprehensive look at the credit-card financing system (and the service provider options that make it available to small business owners) I recommend Paul Downs' NY Times series on the art of running a small business, "You're the Boss." Access the initial post, entitled "What You Need to Know about Credit Card Processing," is available at http://blogs.nytimes.com/2013/03/25/what-you-need-to-know-about-credit-card-processing/

Understanding Tax Laws

When first embarking on the career path of a full-time artist, you will most likely encounter a significant change in your taxes (and no, I don't mean because you'll be making less money).

Now that you are solely dependent on the sale of your work for your income, you are firmly in the ranks of the *self-employed* — which has a pronounced impact on the way you prepare and pay taxes. While being "self-employed" means different things to different people, to the Internal Revenue Service it means the following:

- You carry on a trade or business as a sole proprietor or an independent contractor.
- You are a member of a partnership that carries on a trade or business.
- You are otherwise in business for yourself (including part-time).

As a result, you have an increased level of responsibility to plan ahead for, and pay, your taxes. Take special note of the following topics and how they affect you.

Paying Self-Employment Taxes

As a self-employed person, you will be required to file an annual return on April 15th much like you've done in the past as an employee. However, you'll also need to pay "Self-Employment Taxes" in addition to your regular income tax. The "Self-Employment Tax" is a Social Security and Medicare tax for individuals who work for themselves which simply replaces the Social Security and Medicare taxes that are normally withheld from your paycheck when you work for someone else.

In addition, as long as your business shows a net profit (typically $400 or more per year) you'll need to make quarterly tax payments to the IRS based on what you estimate you'll earn throughout the year. (Since you are no longer traditionally employed, no one else is withholding your tax payments for you — so these quarterly payments ensure that the government still receives taxes from you throughout the year). Your estimate of what you will earn in the coming year is based solely on your earnings from the previous year. For your first year as a self-employed artist, you will only be able to estimate what you *expect* to earn.

As you might imagine, these estimates can easily be off the mark. If you find that you've overpaid, you will simply receive a tax refund like most people do, but if you underpay throughout the year, you'll need to make it up at the end of the year. This is another good reason to maintain a business savings fund, especially in the early stages of your art career. After an extraordinarily successful year where you've made quarterly payments based on a much lower income, you'll need those savings funds to pay the difference.

Paying your taxes each quarter may be the biggest adjustment you'll have to make, but your "annual" tax return will also change once you're a full-time artist depending on the type of business entity you've established (Sole Proprietorship, Partnership, LLC, etc.). In some states you may also be responsible for paying State Income Tax — another liability that didn't exist when you were an "employee."

Applying for Tax ID Numbers

In order to ensure that your tax payments are credited to your business and not to another business by mistake, you must have a Tax ID number. Sole proprietors can use their social security number as their Tax IDs, but because you'll be selling a product, you'll already need an Employer Identification Number (EIN) in order to apply for a sales tax permit and/or resale license. Your EIN can also be used for your Tax ID, and in many cases is preferable.

EINs are federal tax identification numbers, and are usually written in a nine digit series, for example: **"XX-XXXXXXX."** You can apply for an EIN in one of four ways:

1. Use the IRS's online application
You must already have a valid Taxpayer Identification Number (such as a Social Security Number, Employer Identification Number or Individual Taxpayer Identification Number) in order to use the online application.

2. Call the IRS Business and Specialty Tax Line
You can get an EIN immediately at (800) 829-4933. The hours of operation are 7:00 a.m. - 10:00 p.m. local time, Monday through Friday. An agent will take your information, assign an EIN and provide the number to you over the telephone.

3. Fax Form SS-4

You can fax the completed Form SS-4 application to your state fax number (found online at the website below). If you provide your fax number, a fax will be sent back with the EIN in about four business days.

4. Mail Form SS-4

Before you mail Form SS-4, ensure that it contains all of the required information to avoid delays. The processing timeframe for an EIN application by mail is about four weeks.

For other questions, the IRS (www.irs.gov/businesses/small/article/0,,id=102767,00.html) has all the information you will need to apply for an EIN. Of course, it goes without saying that you should always file your EIN paperwork immediately with your financial records for easy access.

In some cases you may also need a "state-version" of an EIN (it may be called an EIN, a State Business License, or something similar). Just like a federally-issued EIN, it's the number your state uses to identify your business entity. Without it, you can't ensure that your state tax payments will be properly credited to your business.

Collecting Sales Tax

Any sales of tangible personal property made to consumers for their own use are considered "retail sales" and are subject to a sales tax. A variety of *services* may also be defined by your locality as "retail sales activities" and are similarly subject to sales tax.

Since your art is meant to be sold to consumers for their own use, it too falls within this taxable category. This means that every time you sell your art, you are required to assess and collect sales tax, then report it and pass on the money you have collected to the appropriate governing authorities within a prescribed time (usually quarterly).

Sales tax rates (and laws) vary from state to state, county to county and city to city, causing many opportunities for confusion. E-commerce allows merchandise to be purchased online from one locale and shipped to another, further complicating matters. Whose tax rates apply to these transactions, the buyer's or the seller's? What if the sale is made by phone or in person? What if a buyer wants to hand-carry the item to her home in another state, as opposed to having it shipped?

Because the rules and regulations governing these different situations are so complex and change from area to area, it's best for you to research sales tax guidelines specific to your region and circumstances. A visit to the government's Small Business Administration website (www.sba.gov) is a good place to start, or you can do an Internet search for "How to collect, report and pay state sales taxes in [your city and state]" to get an overview for your location.

While collecting and reporting sales tax *will* add to your workload, consider the upside: as a "manufacturer" you're entitled to buy your supplies at wholesale price, without sales tax. This prevents double taxation (tax on your raw materials *and* tax on the finished product). All you need is a resale number, which in most jurisdictions is the same as your sales tax permit. I recommend doing an Internet search for "[Your state] resale permit" to make sure, however.

Deducting Business Expenses

As a small business owner you are allowed to deduct reasonable business expenses from your income, decreasing the overall amount of income tax that you owe. This doesn't mean, however, that you should deduct *everything* possible, or do so without careful study of the IRS rules and regulations. The last thing you want to do is trigger an audit.

Some deductions like studio rent and mileage are known to raise red flags with the IRS. Even if your deductions are perfectly legitimate and backed by a well-documented paper trail, an audit will require you to take time away from your art business while you prove the legitimacy of your deductions to the agent assigned to your case. Can you afford that time?

I don't mean to suggest what deductions you should or shouldn't take, only that you should be prepared to make an informed decision — it's up to you and your tax accountant to determine which deductions are worthwhile. Whatever your choices, follow the requirements carefully and make sure to always have proper documentation so you can back up your claims.

I *have* found that of the most confusing areas for artist entrepreneurs is the question of deducting studio or office space in your home as a business expense. If you're using part of your home exclusively for business purposes, and can *prove* it's never used for family purposes, you may be able to take expense deductions for that square footage.

Again, I emphasize that the space must be used *solely* for your art business. For example, if your dining room table doubles as your "desk," but your children occasionally sit there with their cereal bowls while you're doing filing, it won't meet the deduction requirements. Similarly, if it serves as "Command Central" for your business every day except for Thanksgiving (when you clear the file folders to make way for place settings), it's *not* eligible as a deduction.

Don't consider "fudging" on these restrictions when preparing your tax documents! A deduction for home office space is one of the key determinate factors for the IRS to initiate an audit. As a general rule, self-employed individuals are four times as likely to be audited as those with traditional employment. The primary difference? Misinterpretation or perceived "wiggle room" in deduction laws for small business owners.

If a guest room or utility shed has truly been dedicated to use exclusively by your small business, then of course you're eligible to deduct its square footage (as a percentage) of your mortgage, utility and insurance payments. To understand your potential for savings, divide the square footage of your home by the square footage of your designated work/studio space.

The problem with these deductions comes "if and when" you decide to sell your home. When you make a profit selling a residential property, you're not required to pay taxes on the first $250,000 of financial gain (more for joint filers). And if your profit is greater than this limit, you're taxed at the most favorable rate.

However, those favorable rates don't apply to a home office that's already been declared and deducted on your taxes. If you've depreciated the office portion of your home, the amount of that write-off reduces your property's "basis" (a term used in tax assessment that describes the starting value or cost of your home *minus* the square footage you've depreciated).

When you decide to sell your home, this lower basis translates to a higher profit on the sale, and if it pushes you over the $250,000 limit, your tax exclusion can vanish. One artist I know had to pay a substantial sum, for which she was entirely unprepared when she recently sold her home. Staying on top of changing tax laws — or having a tax preparer who does so — can save you money and heartache.

If you plan to sell your home within a few years of establishing your home studio and expect to realize a profit on the sale, it might be beneficial to forego deducting the workspace in favor of staying below the $250,000 limit or qualifying for the more advantageous tax rate on your gain.

If you've already deducted your studio space for a year or two when you decide to sell your home, you may still be able to reduce a negative financial impact by filing amended tax returns (without the studio deductions) for those years.

Always check with a tax professional to determine which option is best for you, but if you'd like more insight on the home office/studio deduction, I recommend journalist Kay Bell's article at Bankrate.com, "A Home Office Can Have Hidden Costs." (http://bankrate.com/finance/money-guides/home-office-can-have-hidden-tax-costs-1.aspx)

One final consideration regarding deductions (and an interesting aspect of owning and operating an art business) is that your business may not be profitable every year, particularly early on. If you are a sole proprietor, these losses can sometimes be deducted against other income you earn in order to reduce your total tax payment. However, you can't do this *every* year, and doing it at all can make you vulnerable to the "Hobby Loss" law. Under Hobby Loss, your business MUST make a profit three out the last five years, including the current year, to be considered a business. If the IRS notices that your business isn't making a profit and labels it as a "hobby" instead, you could be left with a huge tax bill.

Making Charitable Donations

As a professional artist, you may occasionally be approached by local charities to assist in their fundraising efforts by donating one of your works — either free of charge or "at cost" if you are a sculptor contributing foundry work. Donating a piece of your artwork to a charitable fundraising event is not only an admirable act of altruism for a cause you support, but also a great way to get your artwork in front of a specific (and typically wealthy) audience.

It is a mistaken belief, however, to think that such a donation will bring you a generous tax write-off. While the buyer of your work will typically be able to deduct the full-amount *they* paid, the artist cannot — whether the selling price is above or below the piece's true retail value.

Artists are only allowed to deduct the cost of the *materials* used to produce their donated art; they are not allowed to deduct the income potential which that artwork represents. While initially confounding, with a little contemplation it's easy to see the reason behind this regulation. Valuation of an artists' work is completely subjective, meaning that any artist, at any art show or fair, may price their work however she or he wishes.

While most "career track" artists are very careful with their pricing and strive for legitimate, justifiable price tags for their work, we've all encountered artists who simply don't subscribe to "the norm." These artists ask outrageous (to some minds) amounts for their work, regardless of the lack of substantiation — and, they sometimes get it!

Inflated valuations like these are the true target of the donation deduction limits, and when viewed as such seem quite reasonable. What does *not* seem reasonable — but is unavoidable under current law — is that the regulations penalize artists who practice legitimate pricing, and who can justify their value with a track record of gallery sales. Unfortunately, until our tax legislation can be changed to account for this, artists will be unfairly compensated for their generosity.

My best suggestion is to sell the art to a collector who then donates the art. You get income; the collector gets the full deduction. In the meantime, choose your charitable donations with care and follow your heart (not your tax return). Ultimately, this will bring the greatest reward, both for you *and* your charity.

Additional Information

There are a number of easily accessible and (surprisingly) understandable learning tools provided by the IRS for small business owners. The "Self-Employed Individuals Tax Center" online is a great place to start (http://www.irs.gov/Businesses/Small-Businesses-&-Self-Employed/Self-Employed-Individuals-Tax-Center). It contains *readable* answers to questions and topics like:

- What are my self-employed tax obligations?
- How do I make my quarterly payments?
- Understanding home office deductions.
- Husband and wife business — what is a qualified joint venture?
- When to consider a tax professional.

Another excellent resource, "Small Business Taxes: The Virtual Workshop," is comprised of nine interactive lessons designed to help new small business owners learn their tax rights and responsibilities (http://www.irsvideos.gov/SmallBusinessTaxpayer/virtualworkshop). You can also visit the entire *IRS Video Portal* (http://apps.irs.gov/app/scripts/exit.jsp?dest=http://www.irsvideos.gov/) for even more tax-related educational offerings.

Insuring Your Art Business

Do you need insurance for your art business, or, for that matter, your art? The answer to that question varies widely depending on your risk tolerance, the nature of your art business and the expense of producing (and replacing) your art.

Many artists don't feel they need business insurance, for a variety of reasons. Unfortunately, many of those reasons simply aren't true. Let's take a look at four of the main art business insurance fallacies, and the hard-core truths about these mistaken beliefs:

1. My home studio is already covered by my homeowner's policy

Unfortunately, most homeowner's policies provide little (typically $2,500 for business equipment) or no coverage for business related assets. Even worse, some homeowner's policies stipulate that should "any portion of the building (be) used as a business, no portion is covered." You may be able to add endorsements or riders to your homeowner's policy, but for adequate coverage most in-home businesses need a separate business insurance policy, particularly to cover liability.

2. I rent my studio space, so my landlord carries the insurance

False. Your landlord's insurance will certainly cover his asset (the building) but might not cover your assets (your equipment, tools and inventory). Even if the landlord's policy does extend to you, collecting on a claim could be very difficult. Proving you had no liability in the accident, proving the value of inventory lost or having compensation limited by a low coverage-cap could all cause extra grief.

3. I only show at weekend fairs, and they don't require insurance

It's true that not all show sponsors require that artists and craftspeople carry a commercial "general liability" policy, but as a general rule, exhibitors are held responsible for most accidents that occur within their display spaces or booths. This means that if something happens, you, the artist, may very well be held liable.

Furthermore, your contract with show organizers typically waives them of all liability, including accidents, theft or other damage of your property, which may occur during the show. The show organizers may have to accept liability if an accident occurs as a result of their negligence, but this would typically be in public spaces, not within an artist's booth.

4. I only show in reputable galleries so my work is protected by their insurance

Maybe. Some galleries do carry insurance on consigned artwork (usually for half its market value, which is the amount the artist would realize from a sale) but many only carry insurance on works they own outright, leaving most of their artists uncovered. An additional concern for artists is whether a gallery's policy extends to include "acts of God." If not, any damage due to earthquake, tornado, hurricane, flood and the like would similarly be uncovered.

In the event damage does occur, and is covered by the gallery's insurance policy, artists may still encounter difficulties. When artwork is damaged but not destroyed it is often the insurance company that determines and oversees the repair process, which may not be to the artist's satisfaction. An even worse issue may arise if a gallery files an insurance claim on a work deemed irreparable. Once the settlement is paid, the insurance company gains title to the damaged art and may decide to repair and sell it independently in an effort to recoup their loss. This could put sub-standard work on the market, reflecting poorly on the artist's reputation.

These four misconceptions aren't the only causes for worry. As an art business coach, I've heard far too many heartbreaking stories of uninsured loss. Whether it's an entire show's profit "lifted" from an untended cash drawer, a season's worth of inventory lost in a studio fire or a laptop computer (with an entire client-base of contact information on it) stolen from a van, all are equally disastrous.

Each of the scenarios I just listed falls under "Property" coverage, which insures against personal, material loss. Obtaining property insurance coverage protects you when these all too common tragedies occur. Without it, one or more seemingly random unfortunate events could mean that your entire art career plan gets thrown off-course.

The other major insurance category is "Liability" coverage, which insures you against the event that your property or your work causes injury to others (whether to their personal property or their physical well-being).

© 2015 Aletta de Wal, Artist Advisor, Artist Career Training
www.ArtistCareerTraining.com

The potential for ruination here is even more frightening. Whether it's a student slipping and falling during one of your classes, a panel from your public art installation injuring a passer-by or your kiln catching fire at an outdoor art show and causing damage both to the venue and your neighboring artists' work, lawsuits resulting from these types of calamities may not just impede your career plans — they could devastate your financial future.

Let's take a closer look at these two primary business insurance types, and the particular concerns related to your needs as an artist which you should clarify with your insuring agent:

Business Property Insurance

No matter the size of your art business, it's likely that you have both finished products (your inventory on hand) and equipment (the tools you use to make your art) which would be costly to replace. Generally speaking, property coverage is designed to protect your investment in these items. For the artist, property coverage considerations should always include the following:

Building
As might be expected, this covers the physical structure of your studio or workspace (the building itself).

Business personal property
This insures the contents of your studio, such as tools, equipment, raw materials, inventory in progress, finished products, valuable papers and records and electronic data processing.

Business interruption
This covers loss of business income incurred during the period of time you're unable to carry on your normal work because your studio/workspace is temporarily closed or non-functional due to an insured calamity (or its resultant repairs).

Inland marine
Despite its unusual (and somewhat misleading) name, this coverage insures your work while in transit to shows and galleries, when stored temporarily before being transported or in any other situation that requires your art to be out of your studio (a common occurrence for artists). This useful, versatile coverage can also include your booth materials, shelves, display cases and so on, when similarly in transit or off-site.

Personal property of others

This coverage is for artists who work on other people's property in their own studio. As an example, let's say you are commissioned to create a portrait for a client in the style and tone of one of their other paintings. If you keep that other painting in your studio for reference, it would need to be covered under "PPO" insurance.

General Liability Insurance

General liability insurance protects you from financial liability due to accidents, injuries or claims of negligence related to incidents that occur on your business property or within a space where you conduct business (a studio, art booth, etc.). It also covers you if your faulty product or workmanship causes injury or damage at another location (for example, if a portion of a large sculpture installation topples, injuring members of the public or damaging a building).

Typically, these policies cover costs related to bodily injury, property damage and medical expenses, as well as libel, slander, lawsuits, legal fee assessment and settlement bonds or judgments required during an appeal procedure.

For more financial protection beyond your liability coverage limits, you can also purchase umbrella insurance. Umbrella insurance "kicks in" when all other liability coverage is exhausted and is usually purchased in increments of $1 million.

Additional Insurance Coverage

Basic insurance policies cover risks to property like fire, lightning, explosion, water damage, theft, vandalism and so on. While it's frequently called "all-risk" coverage, that term may actually be a misnomer since most policies come with a wide range of exclusions. Casualties like flood, earthquake and acts of terrorism are often *not covered* in a standard insurance package, so make a point to review the exclusions in your policy with your agent and evaluate their potential risk factor. If your specific circumstances make you feel at risk for any of them, you may want to consider additional coverage.

These "Acts of God" policy riders should be of special importance for artists who are located (or show their work) in particularly vulnerable geographic regions. For instance, you may want earthquake insurance in California, Oregon, or Washington; hurricane coverage along the Gulf Coast or eastern seaboard; tornado coverage for locations in the tornado belt, etc. Ask your galleries in these areas about their specialized coverage (many don't carry any) and consider getting it yourself — particularly if your work is extremely valuable or costly to produce.

Also, be certain you know the "amount limits" of your coverage (for example, up to $25,000 for studio contents, $25,000 for work that's off-premise or in-transit, etc.). If the proposed limits leave you feeling exposed, you may want to increase your coverage.

Other common "add-on" business policy coverage types include:

Extended business income
This extends payments for loss of business income beyond the coverage time limits of Business Interruption insurance.

Extra expense
Just as it sounds, this insurance covers certain expenses that are outside the scope of more general property insurance. For example, it might pay for the relocation expenses of moving your studio, if necessary.

Volunteer accident
This insurance offers medical reimbursement for someone injured while working for you who is *not* getting paid for his or her help.

Employee dishonesty
This coverage insures losses due to dishonest acts of employees.

Theft Concerns and Precautions

> *"Art and cultural property crime — which includes theft, fraud, looting, and trafficking across state and international lines — is a looming criminal enterprise, with estimated losses running as high as $6 billion annually."*
>
> ~Federal Bureau of Investigation, Art Theft Program

Art theft is big business, and it's not just confined to expensive works by well-known artists that are housed in national museums and private collections. Theft affects gallery owners, dealers and artists from every sector of the career curve — from the highly successful international artist who has a cylinder of valuable giclées go missing from the studio, to the struggling emerging artist who returns from the bathroom to discover a small piece missing from a booth at a weekend fair.

Here are a few real-life examples from clients and friends of art-world robbery:

> Owner Margaret Danielak (Danielak Art) was stunned to suffer a loss from a show at her gallery in Pasadena's Historic Playhouse District. "We took down the Exhibition after I discovered that one of Julie Snyder's lovely paintings, entitled 'Bourbon Street Balcony,' had been stolen in broad daylight. We continue to work with the Pasadena Police Department to recover the stolen art, and remain hopeful of finding the piece."

> A San Francisco area gallery owner suffered an overnight break-in, during which three paintings were stolen. Luckily, the artwork was later recovered, when an honest citizen, seeing a news report about the theft, recognized the works as the same paintings he'd bought from a street vendor earlier in the week, and returned them to the gallery. A happy, but unfortunately uncommon, ending.

> An East Bay area jewelry artist was ecstatic about her success at a high-end outdoor show, having realized close to $100,000 in sales. Her celebratory mood was short-lived, however. Always careful to have someone guarding the valuable merchandise all through an event, including the set-up and take-down, somehow a van door was inadvertently left unlocked during the last load-out. When she returned just minutes later, her cash box, and her remaining stock worth $350,000, were gone.

Why include these tales of theft and loss? Hopefully to save you from similar misfortune.

Even though good luck (and good insurance) may keep you from experiencing a devastating loss due to theft, they may not completely protect you from its impact. Some artwork is simply irreplaceable, whether for tangible, physical reasons or emotional ones. And while an insurance company might compensate you for the cost of the artwork, that won't necessarily replace its personal value.

Furthermore, while insurance coverage may provide you peace of mind, the process of filing and settling a claim is frequently anything but peaceful and may take considerable time. Plus, due to contract exclusions and loopholes, your coverage may not be as comprehensive as you believe, leaving you and your artwork vulnerable and exposed.

The bottom line is this: insuring yourself against theft doesn't mean *just* buying a policy. It also means taking extra precautions to safeguard your work and equipment as a part of your daily business routine. Insurance coverage or no, it's up to you to protect your art, no matter where you show or how you sell — because, unfortunately, bad things can happen to even the most careful art professionals and artists. Below is a tale on this topic from artist Wm. Kelly Bailey, along with five lessons he learned the hard way:

> *"One Friday recently, I went to visit 'gallery row' in Houston in the early afternoon. This is in a rather well to do area of town. I parked right in front of a gallery... very close to a fairly busy intersection. While inside visiting the galleries, my truck was broken into (without setting off the alarm) and my attaché case and my big canvas art bag were stolen. My personal checkbook, two weeks' paycheck and thousands of dollars worth of artwork and art materials were all gone! One big hardbound sketchbook had over 120 finished pen & ink and wash drawings in it! Over two and a half years' worth of work!*
>
> *Please note that I did not have anything visible in the truck. It was all concealed so as to be invisible from outside. The truck was locked. The alarm was set. That is an automatic habit with me. However, evidently the thieves were nearby watching when I parked, saw me put my attaché case down behind the seat and under the back seat of the truck and they had a way to disable the electronic lock. I usually stop several blocks before my destination to move any visible items to the trunk. However, I had dropped by the galleries on a whim and so was not planning ahead... I did not see anyone nearby and so concealed the attaché after I parked and before I got out."*

Lesson one: Always conceal valuables before you arrive at your destination, in case potential thieves are in the area watching.

"Through this very grievous experience I have learned some other tough facts that most people are not aware of, so hopefully you, my fellow artists, can learn from my hard knocks.

"Your automobile insurance does NOT cover personal items in your car. If they are covered, it is through your homeowner's (or renter's) insurance. Therefore, instead of a typical $500 deductible, it is usually 1% (sometimes 2%) of your home's insured value, so it can be a deductible that is many times higher! In other words, usually much higher than the value of anything stolen, so insurance companies seldom have to pay on this type of loss!"

Lesson two: Assess your risk. When deciding whether you can afford to pay for insurance, consider what it would cost to replace all of your art inventory and supplies instead.

"After the huge deductible, there is also a 'cap' the insurance company puts on personal items stolen from a vehicle. . . usually 10% of what personal items are insured for in your home."

Lesson three: Read the fine print to make sure your fine art is covered.

"All of the valuable items stolen were my personal belongings... even the artwork stolen was my personal pen and ink and/or charcoal drawings and a few, small, personal plein air watercolors done on various vacations in a little Arches travel pad that I kept adding to. One was a plein air watercolor of the Art Students League Building in New York City, one was a plein air painting of some favorite mountains in my Arizona home town, another was a plein air watercolor of Big Beach in Maui from when I took my wife there for our 35th anniversary. This whole personal travel sketch 'kit' is entirely separate from the art supplies I do my 'formal' painting with in my studio at home. I do not show or sell my drawings or plein air paintings; they are done purely for personal enjoyment; it's my favorite form of recreation and relaxation. (I still have all my personal sketchbooks clear back to when I was a teenager! Not a single sheet out of any of them has been shown or sold.)"

Lesson four: Some things are priceless and irreplaceable. Care for them accordingly.

"However, since I am an artist and I have shown and sold my finished, 'formal' paintings before, and since I am represented by a gallery, the insurance company investigator ruled that the stolen items were all business property; and (proudly revealing this previously hidden loophole) he announced the policy does not cover business property in a vehicle! 'So I'm recommending we don't pay a penny on this claim!' he victoriously proclaimed. I was dumbfounded! I have paid this insurance company for over 30 years without a single theft claim only to find out that I wasn't in caring hands after all."

Lesson five: Build a relationship with an insurance agent who cares more about your art and ongoing business, than about saving the insurance company money.

"I sincerely hope no other artists have to go through this agony; truly it was like a huge mule kick in the gut.... twice! And the second time from people I mistakenly thought would be there to help! I sincerely want to prevent my fellow artists from going through anything like I did, and as the old saying goes: 'forewarned is forearmed.'"

~Wm. Kelly Bailey

Hard lessons to learn! So find an insurance broker who specializes in small businesses and is accustomed to helping clients (who are on a tight budget) evaluate their risks and needs. Ask other artists you know for the names of agents and providers they use, and what their experiences have been.

Remember, the agent's income is dependent on selling you insurance — don't waste their time, but don't feel that you must buy from them simply because they give you information. Your goal is not to *overspend* on insurance, but to spend *enough*. Saving a few dollars on cheap insurance is not worth putting yourself at risk of a major loss.

To determine your insurance needs, consider the dollar value of the assets you need to protect. If you have few or no assets, you're unlikely to be the target of lawsuits since there's little for a plaintiff to recover. You should also examine the ways you do business — are you extremely careful, conducting your business in such a way that you're unlikely to have problems? Or are you more casual or free-spirited when it comes to business management, leaving you with more exposure to risk?

Finally, analyze what the consequences could be for your business if the worst should happen and you have no insurance. What would happen if you suffered the loss of your workspace and all of your inventory and equipment? What if someone gets injured in your studio? What if a friend (or relative!) is crippled when an installation goes wrong, and neither of you has insurance? Tragedies like these do happen, and while insurance will not prevent them, it *can* provide much-needed financial support afterwards. When you really consider all the possibilities, good insurance can be a relatively inexpensive way to sleep better at night.

Using Legal Contracts

I've found that all too many artists ignore the need for legal documents and contracts in their businesses. Typically, they give me one (or more) of the following reasons:

- They find the "legalese" of contracts confusing to read and comprehend.
- They assume drafting a contract will be an expensive process, requiring an attorney.
- They believe contracts indicate distrust, and don't want to offend the people involved.

Contracts needn't be confusing, any more than they need be expensive. Contracts can (and should!) be written in simple, straightforward language that will be easily understood by anyone without legal training. They don't NEED to be drafted by attorneys, either.

While it's advisable that the person "drawing up" your contract be familiar with contract terminology and structure (historically this was the realm of lawyers) today there are many contract "blueprints" and forms available to everyone online — many of which are free-of-charge and created specifically for artists.

As for potentially "offending" someone by requesting a contract, remember that a contract is really nothing more than a written agreement — it should simply list the mutual understanding and promises between two people in a business relationship.

A contract describes what each person must "do" to start the relationship, what they will "do" while they're in it, and what they need to "do" to get out of it. Good contracts anticipate, and therefore avoid, unwanted outcomes for *either side*. This creates a clear roadmap leading to the results that both parties desire. There should be nothing offensive about stating mutually beneficial goals.

You can still establish a selling price for your art on the strength of a handshake, or write a commission agreement on the back of a napkin — in some cases, those actions may serve just as well as a formal document of sale or a commission agreement. But there always comes a time when a well-written contract is a necessity.

Getting Your Agreement in Writing

Many artists wonder if they must insist on a written document, especially if an oral contract is agreed upon and the individual gives you his or her word to follow through. Unfortunately, I believe movie mogul Sam Goldwyn had it right when he said, "Oral contracts are not worth the paper they're written on."

I have spoken to gallery dealers who refuse to use written contracts, and when pressed, defend their decision with the argument that they are trustworthy and don't need them. I've never understood why, if they are truly so trustworthy, that they *resist* putting their agreements in writing — even in the form of a letter or e-mail.

Verbal agreements on their own actually complicate transactions because they have the appearance, but seldom the reality, of an agreement. Human beings have an infinite capacity to rationalize their positions in an argument, particularly after the fact. If people are not held accountable in an irrefutable manner (like with a contract), they tend to hear what they *want* to hear and remember only what they *wish* to be true. Legal agreements, documented in the form of a contract, protect the integrity of those agreements against the vagaries and partialities of memory.

Because you are an artist, and you sell objects people *want* rather than *need*, contracts are a necessary part of your business. Remember that the words in a contract are the end result, not the beginning, of building relationships with people who buy, represent or license your art.

If you've started to exhibit your work beyond your studio, or you're considering marketing your art in "alternative" spaces like coffee houses or cafés, you may find yourself working with people who are unfamiliar with the normal conventions of art sales and display (not to mention art care, maintenance and safety). Despite the popularity of a certain famous phrase, ignorance usually *isn't* bliss, as illustrated in the following scenario:

> *You're thrilled when "Chi-Chi Café" wants to display your work on their walls. It's such a beautiful space — friendly and warm, but classy at the same time. You've always admired the artists they display, and now you're going to be one of them! Is there any way, the manager asks, that you could bring some pieces by tomorrow morning? One of their artists has to "pull" his work right away and they'd hate to leave the walls bare. Plus, they're going into the weekend, their busiest time...*

You rush off to your studio and start madly going through your inventory, looking for your best pieces — after all, they're very upscale for a café and with their prices it's clear they have wealthy diners. This is just the break you've been hoping for! You carefully wrap the chosen pieces for transport (those frames were expensive!) and pack them into your van. They only have room for six pieces, but you're taking ten so the manager can choose which ones will work best. Who knows, maybe she'll like them so much that she'll find another spot for the extras. Since you don't know which pieces they'll actually hang, you don't prepare an inventory list; that's easy enough to do it after she makes her selections.

When you arrive with your work the next morning, however, the manager isn't there (she had to handle some emergency at the bank). She's told the assistant manager to expect you, and to have you leave the art in the employee break-room — she'll go through it when she gets back. Disappointed that you won't see her reaction to your art, you" hang out" for almost an hour. but finally decide you'd better get back to your studio and get some work done. You head for home after asking the assistant to have the manager phone you when she can, figuring it will be after the noon rush.

Unfortunately, it isn't until Monday morning that you hear anything — the manager is "so sorry" about not getting back to you, and explains they booked a last-minute bridal shower Saturday afternoon so everyone was scrambling and Sunday was her first day off in ten days. Wanting to sound friendly and supportive, you tell her you "know how that is," and that you "used to wait tables in art school to help make ends meet." She then gushes about the work you delivered (she was able to look at it Saturday morning before all the "craziness started") and then mentions that the owner will have to make the final decision about which pieces get hung in the café.

This is a surprise to you — you thought the work was already hanging (for the weekend crowd, and all) but you don't say anything. The manager assures you that the owner will be "in" the next day to go through your work and make selections. When Tuesday comes and goes with no word from the manager, the owner or anyone else at the café, you decide to go there in person. Walking in on Wednesday morning, you're surprised to see they only have one of your paintings on the wall — the rest of the space is still hung with work by the artist who was "leaving," and by another artist whose work you've not seen before.

"Well," you think, "maybe the timeframe has changed." You look around for the manager... or the owner... or even the assistant. Finally a guy in the kitchen says he "thinks they decided to go with someone else" but that "your work is really cool — he saw it in the break room a few days ago." When you make your way back to the break room to retrieve your art, you find the pieces haphazardly arrayed around the room, stacked against the walls in such a way that the canvases now have "pressure marks" and several of the frames have been 'dinged.' When you inquire about the damage to the owner, he claims he has no knowledge of any "arrangement" you might have made to display your work (which indeed he might not) and that he's not responsible.

Does this scenario scare you? I hope so! While there are certainly many reputable, responsible, trustworthy people (and businesses) in the world, it's all too easy — particularly as a "young" artist — to get used or even *unintentionally* harmed by entering into arrangements without a contract.

Even if you plan on using a contract to define your agreement, if you deliver your artwork *in advance* of its signing, you can leave yourself "up a creek" without the proverbial paddle. More often than not, artists are damaged because *they don't ask* for a contract, or because they hand over their work before the contract is finalized. Don't let it happen to you!

Just as good fences make good neighbors, good contracts make good business partners. As long as you hold yourself and the other party to the security of a signed contract, you'll avoid a fair share of heartache.

This is not to say that legal documents will completely protect you from hardship, because legal agreements are only as "good" as the relationships they describe. However, I believe the process of working out these agreements builds trust rather than negates it, and doing so will serve as a cornerstone for a healthy business relationship.

Whether you decide on a simple letter of agreement or a multi-page document, supporting your business relationships with paperwork notifies people that you understand your rights as an artist and are prepared to uphold them — while also respecting their rights as a buyer or business partner.

In addition, did you know that creating a business contract helps acknowledge and legally document the value of your work? Contracts inherently make it easier to protect your rights and ownership of your work, and retain your rights for compensation (particularly with licensed work).

Of course, a contract will also help you avoid or resolve potential disputes with business partners. Here are four ways they do that:

1. Contracts create mutual understanding

Drawing up a contract forces both sides to think through and discuss their mutual expectations. If you can agree in advance about what each party will do, the chance of a misunderstanding is reduced and the odds of building a trust-based relationship are increased.

2. Contracts serve as a record of your agreement

When an issue arises, the parties involved can consult the document to "refresh" their memories. We all know that our memory can play tricks on us. Like witnesses to a car crash, each individual may see and remember details differently, so put your trust in a contract rather than your memory.

3. Contracts provide the foundation for new agreements

If a dispute arises that seems irresolvable, your contract may provide a means of re-establishing the business relationship. Ask the other party to review the contract with you as you explain, in good faith, what you understood it to mean. By using the document as a source of "talking points," you may be able to defuse the dispute and find a mutually satisfactory resolution.

4. Contracts are a final legal recourse

Although legal action should only be used as a last resort, in court your contract will serve as an "impartial witness" and provide definitive proof of the responsibilities of both parties in fulfilling your business agreement.

If you must hire a lawyer to resolve a conflict, do so before the situation escalates or becomes desperate. Naturally, one of the primary benefits of having an attorney review all of your contracts before signing is to help in the event of conflicts. Not only will you feel more peace of mind knowing your contract was carefully crafted and that your attorney is already familiar with the agreement, but you may be on better legal footing as well.

Typically, contracts tend to favor the "drafting party." By involving your attorney when the contract was written, it may already be worded in favor of your position.

Don't assume just because you're an artist with limited funds that you won't be able to afford a lawyer's fees. Like you, there are many attorneys who are just starting in their careers. A good number of them would be happy to gain a client whose billings, though initially small, will likely build over the years.

If you don't have a lawyer yet, search for one. Check with fellow artists, contact the local bar association or consult Volunteer Lawyers for the Arts (http://www.vlany.org/) online.

Negotiating Your Contracts

While having your attorney review your contracts before signing is always recommended, it's likely he or she won't be present for every stage of the negotiations going into the agreement.

I often review contracts for clients in order to prepare them for further discussions with agents, galleries or even non-traditional representatives. Many times, what's left out of a contract causes the most problems later.

When a contract is on the table, know the deal you are making. If someone asks you to sign his or her contract, read every single word. If you don't understand the entire agreement, don't sign it until you do... and if you can imagine a scenario in which bad things could happen to you as a result of a particular term in a contract, you *must* raise it with the other side.

Negotiations are an integral part of contracts — without discussing the points important to you, you won't get the terms you need, and you could end up worse off than not having any contract at all.

Remember, when you sign a contract you're agreeing to *everything* it says, and courts will hold you to that agreement. When reading a potential contract, a good safeguard is to continually ask the question, "What is the worst thing that could happen to me, if I agree to this particular deal point?" If the answer makes you uncomfortable or in any way uncertain, make a request to have that line of the contract amended.

In order to help you speak from a position of strength during the negotiation process, it's wise to familiarize yourself with some of the usual requests, objections and rebuttals you may hear. Here are three common replies you'll face when you ask to change part of a contract:

1. "Don't worry, we would never do that."
This type of verbal guarantee doesn't mean anything if the contract says otherwise. Your response can be friendly, but assertive at the same time. Say something like, *"Okay, if you'd never do what this term seems to allow, then let's take it out — because clearly, it's not needed."*

2. "But this is the standard form that we use with all our exhibitors."

Assure your partner of your faith in good intentions, while reiterating your request. Appeal to their professionalism by saying, *"Since you use this contract form routinely, I'm sure you want it to be as good as it can be. I believe that the agreement would be a lot better if we remove this particular ambiguity. Let's change it to this…"*

3. "I don't have time to make a bunch of changes. Take the contract or leave it."

If you're feeling pressured by an ultimatum like this, one of your best tactics is to again praise the other party's integrity in your reply. Try, *"I know you're a reasonable person, and I believe this is a reasonable request. I'm sure we can work it out."*

If your request is still rejected after you respond courteously to their first objection, at least you've gained some valuable insight: this person is unreasonable. Are you sure you want to do business with someone like that?

When a potential business "marriage" doesn't appear to be made in heaven, don't fret — but don't give up and just accept the original contract, either. So far you've lost nothing but time, but by signing a bad contract you could lose far more. If you still wish to try to salvage the deal, ask to reschedule at a later time when you can bring some help or advice to the negotiating table.

If you can't make any headway at all, just walk away. If negotiating the contract is that troubled, the odds are that everything else about the business partnership would have been too. Better to "lose" a deal and save your art, your reputation and perhaps some of your sanity.

Avoiding "Contract Legalese"

Contracts are notorious for having complicated language and extensive legal terminology, making them difficult to read and even harder to understand. This well-deserved, "bad" reputation is so universally acknowledged that contract verbiage served as the inspiration for one of the Marx Brothers' most famous skits in *A Night at the Opera*.

Here's an excerpt:
(Note: http://www.offbalance.com/art4.html)

> **Groucho Marx:** *(Reading from a contract) All right. It says, "The first part of the party of the first part shall be known in this contract as the first part of the party of the first part, shall be known in this contract…"—look, why should we quarrel about a thing like this, we'll take it right out, eh?*
>
> **Chico Marx:** *Yes, it's too long anyhow. (They both tear off the tops of their contracts). Now what have we got left?*
>
> **Groucho Marx:** *Well, I've got about a foot and a half. Now, it says, "The party of the second part shall be known in this contract as the party of the second part." Now what's the matter?*
>
> **Chico Marx:** *I don't like the second party either.*
>
> **Groucho Marx:** *Well, you should have come to the first party. We didn't get home till around four in the morning. I was blind for three days.*

While it's easy to laugh at the Marx Brothers' antics, there's nothing funny about the needless "legalese" obscuring the meanings and intentions of contracts. There's simply no need for such complicated language when plain everyday English will do just as well. In truth, legal jargon isn't evidence of a good contract — just evidence of bad writing.

Writing Your Own Contract

When working with artists on contracts, I strive for simple, declarative sentences using ordinary words in the active voice:

Example: *"Doe will pay," (active voice)* instead of, *"There will be a payment," (passive voice).*

Unfortunately, much of government and contractual writing is in the passive voice, giving those documents their recognizably wordy, bureaucratic tone. When you write in the active voice you eliminate unnecessary verbiage and clarify your meaning by naming both the person AND the action they are taking, in the same sentence. Whether you're using a contract template you've downloaded from the Internet or you're drafting your document from scratch, make the effort to write in the active voice so your finished contract is simpler and easier to read.

Of course, each deal is unique. While you probably have a good *general* understanding about any business arrangement you're making, you may not have looked very closely at the specific details needed to make it work. Spend some time at this point, before you begin writing and revising your contract, to determine just what your needs are for every step of the process. If you begin drafting a contract before taking this step, it's very easy to overlook crucial details.

Once you're clear about your wants and needs, insist on using contract terms that are specific and clear. If every detail, intention and responsibility isn't plainly spelled out, then the contract needs more work.

Test your finished contract by seeing if the document passes the "journalist's" test (as you read it, ask who, what, where, when, why and how). Then find someone without legal training (preferably a neutral "outsider" who isn't familiar with your negotiations) to read the contract and explain it back to you in their own words, going over each party's commitments and responsibilities. When they can do that, your contract may be ready.

Understanding Contract Structure & Terms

If contracts and legal terms are new to you, make sure to study the following guide and familiarize yourself with the standard formats and terminology:

Parties
The "parties" mentioned in a contract are the people involved. For example, *"This Contract is made by Jane Doe (DOE) and Richard Rom (ROM)."*

Date
Every contract should include the date the contract was written. A simple sentence will work, such as, *"This Contract is dated for reference on September 18th, 2013.*

Outline
In the outline, or "recitals," of a contract, you will present the big picture of the deal to set the context for what is included or excluded. It might look something like this:

> *a.* DOE is a graphic artist specializing in finger painting.

> *b.* ROM is a consignment art broker who operates under the fictitious name of Rom Gallery in Big Smoke, New York.

c. *DOE has agreed to place ten paintings ("the Paintings") in the Rom Gallery for retail sale. The Paintings are identified and their corresponding prices are given in Exhibit A to this Contract.*

d. *ROM has agreed to display DOE's Paintings in his gallery for sale.*

e. *The purpose of this contract is to carry out the foregoing agreement.*

Definitions

The "Definitions" section is used to define the people or items that will be discussed multiple times within the contract. To explain this concept, let's say you're dealing with a gallery that has multiple locations. Rather than having to specify which location is being referred to every time the word "gallery" is mentioned, you could write something like, *"it is agreed that "gallery" will always mean the locations specified here."*

Avoid using ambiguous terms in your definitions, such as "prominent," "advertisement," "consignment" or "installment sale agreement," which defeat the purpose of the definitions. Instead, strive for clear, specific language. Here are a few good examples:

a. *"Broker" means Richard Rom, Rom Gallery or any business entity used to market the Paintings that is owned or controlled by Richard Rom.*

b. *"Gallery" means Rom Gallery located at 999 Tommy Kinkade Avenue, Big Smoke, New York.*

c. *"the Paintings" means ten oil paintings by Jane Doe identified in Exhibit A to this Contract.*

Substance or Agreement

In the main body of the contract, usually titled "Agreement," you will need to describe the specific terms of the deal for each person involved. It will look something like this:

DOE agrees to do the following:

a. *Ship the Paintings not later than ten (10) days preceding Saint Swithen's Day in even numbered years or February 29 in Leap Years. Paintings will be individually shrink-wrapped, crated and shipped to Smallville, via XYZ courier service.*

b. Insure the Paintings with an insurance carrier with a Standard and Poor's rating of AA or better at the values listed in the inventory attached to this Contract as Exhibit A.

c. Supply any documents, photographs or other records reasonably requested by ROM.

d. Assign to ROM fifty percent of the retail sales receipts from sale of the Paintings. (You can add far more detailed payment terms if you'd like.)

ROM agrees to do the following:

a. Use his best efforts to sell the Paintings. This includes, without limitation, hanging the paintings in the central gallery facing Sweet Smell of Success Ave., maintaining advertisements in Rich & Famous magazine and Condo Painting News, insuring the paintings at the value indicated in Exhibit A as further provided in section __ from delivery date until sold or returned to DOE.

b. Pay DOE 50% of the sales proceeds within thirty days of sale of each painting sold. Payment is to be made by direct electronic transfer to DOE's account with the Left Bank of Smallville, Account No. 99999999.

The Parties mutually agree to the following:

a. DOE will retain the common law copyright and may establish a statutory copyright without ROM's consent.

b. After a Painting is sold, DOE may make and market limited editions of the paintings without permission from or obligation to ROM or the buyer

c. ROM may return the Paintings in the manner described in section __ at any time at ROM's expense without obligation to DOE.

Term
"Term" refers to the beginning and ending dates of the contract, and may have several qualifiers. The example below includes conditions in the case of bankruptcy or death:

"This contract begins on the earlier of: a) when ROM places an original signed copy in the U.S. mail, postage paid, b) the date indicated at the beginning of the contract, or d) when DOE receives the fully executed contract. It will end on the earlier of: a) twelve months from execution, b) when DOE receives payment from ROM for all of the paintings, c) upon return of the unsold paintings to DOE in the same condition as when shipped to ROM, d) thirty days after either party delivers a notice of termination to the other party, e) death or disability of either party, or f) when ROM Gallery files a proceeding in the Bankruptcy Court. . ." etc.

Insurance

This is where you'll specify the type of insurance you require for your artwork, including policy limits, deductible amounts and which party (or parties) will be paying for it. If costs are being shared, specify percentages for each. Also, make sure to include insurance provisions if the artwork needs to be returned to the artist at the end of the contract term (return shipment typically falls to the gallery or licensing entity) and ask for proof of insurance in a document called a "certificate of indemnification." Here is an example:

"From and after receipt of the paintings, ROM agrees to maintain comprehensive insurance coverage for the Paintings insuring against all casualties including, without limitation, theft, fire, negligent loss or damage, water damage and hostile critical review, especially in Condo Painting News. Policy limits for such coverage shall be not less than the agreed retail price listed in Exhibit A. Deductible amounts may not exceed ten percent (10%) of the retail sales prices in Exhibit A. DOE must be named as an additional insured on the insurance policy(s)."

Assignment

"Assignment" refers to the transfer of a contract to someone else (you may be most familiar with the concept in the mortgage and loan industry, where assignment occurs frequently).

Because the relationships between artists, galleries and agents are so personal, and the artist's reputation is so closely linked to the people who represent them to the public, most artists would prefer that their contracts be non-assignable. However, most contracts are generally considered to be assignable to another person unless specifically noted otherwise.

Check every contract for a non-assignment clause, and ask that it be added if missing. This will prevent your customer, agent or gallery from assigning your contract to another party without your permission.

> *"Neither party may assign their rights or obligations under this contract without the prior written consent of the other party. Consent to assignment may be withheld for any commercially reasonable reason. Standards for denying consent to assignment include, without limitation, whether the assignee has the necessary financing, experience, sound business reputation, training and credit rating."*

Dispute Resolution and Attorneys' Fees

Litigation is an impractical, expensive way to handle disputes, and will almost always cost more than the value of the art in question. For that reason, most contracts include terms for negotiation should a seemingly irresolvable dispute arise — typically by mediation. While it's always preferable for the two parties to resolve their issues on their own, a thorough contract will include a passage to protect you from having to go to court, should the worst occur.

Along with terms for negotiation, contracts often include provisions for attorneys' fees. Keep in mind, a lawsuit can be initiated by either party — if an unreasonable lawsuit is brought against you, just defending yourself could be very costly.

If you're using one of the many basic artist contracts available on the Internet, check the wording in this area very carefully. Many of these downloadable forms state that the right to recover attorneys' fees goes to the "aggrieved party."

This isn't clear enough to protect you — by the time two parties in a lawsuit exchange nasty looks in a courtroom, they are both well and truly "aggrieved." Instead, be sure that your contract assigns the right to recover attorneys' fees to the "prevailing party." In other words, this is the party that the court determines to be "in the right."

Agreement to Agree

In a contract, the phrase "agreement to agree" means that there are conditions of the deal that still need to be worked out and defined later. In other words, an agreement to agree is NOT an agreement, just the promise of one.

To be enforceable, a contract must specify the terms of the deal. Agreeing to settle issues such as price, payment terms, advertising and promotion and so forth at a later date offers insufficient protection. Until those critical terms are spelled out, there is no contract.

Don't allow your desire to appear trusting and helpful (or your eagerness to gain representation) lure you into signing a contract with one or more "agreements to agree." A good lawyer will tell you that "flexible" contracts with dangling, unresolved issues spell trouble: each side is usually anticipating an eventual resolution that favors them, not the other party. Resolve all issues *before* you sign.

Indemnification

The term "indemnify" means to "insure against." Do NOT sign a contract in which you agree personally to indemnify, defend or hold the other party harmless from contract-related claims.

Delete any clause that looks something like this:

> *"Artist agrees to indemnify and hold harmless "Owner" of and from any and all claims, demands, losses, causes of action, damage, lawsuits, judgments, including attorneys' fees and costs, arising out of or relating to the work of the artist."*

If you must indemnify the opposite party from lawsuits or damages, stipulate that the indemnity applies ONLY if caused by your own negligence and insist that the indemnification is reciprocal.

In other words, make sure that *you* have the same protection in the event of their negligence (and be sure to discuss the indemnity clause with your insurer, so you have proper coverage).

An amended clause that would be more acceptable might read:

> *"Artist agrees to indemnify and hold harmless "Owner" of and from any and all claims, demands, losses, causes of action, damage, lawsuits, judgments, including attorneys' fees and costs, **but only to the extent** caused by, arising out of, or relating to the work of the Artist. Furthermore, "Owner" extends…."*

Here's the bottom line when it comes to contracts:

If someone asks you to sign his or her contract, read every single word. If you don't understand the entire agreement, ask for clarification until you do. If you don't like a term, negotiate for what you *would* like. Negotiating is perfectly acceptable; it doesn't mean you're untrusting, it means you're a good business partner. By discussing the terms up-front and working towards an agreement that satisfies everyone involved, you'll improve the business relationship immensely — and that's well-worth the price of a little discomfort at the beginning.

Keep in mind that the terms you include in a contract are only as good as the other party's integrity and the size of their bank account. A large part of the value of having a contract rests in your ability to collect damages if the contract is broken. Even the most carefully worded and considered contract becomes useless if one of the parties falls on "hard times" and decides to break the terms. If the negligent party has no funds — even if they are entirely at fault — they are said to be "judgment proof," meaning that no monetary compensation can be assigned because they have no ability to pay it.

Never assume that you know how an individual will act under extreme financial duress, or that a signed contract will always protect you from loss. Should a situation arise in which contract terms are being broken (for example, if a gallery owner is a few months behind on payments) then your contract could be useless. If faced with the choice of paying artists or defaulting on the mortgage, concerns about "breaking a contract" would likely pale in the face of losing a family home.

A Quick Note on Copyright Law

Like contracts, copyright protection is another area that seems to create a fair amount of confusion for artists. So to gain a better understanding, let's start by defining what copyright protection actually is.

Essentially, copyright law secures (for the maker of a creative work) the exclusive right to choose who can make copies of that work or make other works *derived* from it. While there are nuances and variations within the law itself, that is its primary purpose — to grant you control over who can reproduce your original creation.

The "creation" being copyrighted must be in a tangible form — for example, a painting or sculpture, and not just the *idea* for a painting or sculpture. Copyright protects the *expression* of an idea, but not the idea itself. Similarly, you cannot copyright a *style*. Whatever you copyright must be a physical *expression* of that style, in tangible form.

Your creative work is considered to be under copyright protection from "the moment it is created and fixed in a tangible form." Technically, you don't even need to add the familiar symbol of the "c" within the circle — ©. Since 1989 in the U.S., nearly all privately-created original works have been considered protected by copyright, whether that copyright notice is displayed or not. This means if someone copies your work without your express written permission, you have the right to take them to court.

Sounds simple, right? Well… not necessarily.

You've probably heard that you can formally register your copyrighted artwork with the U.S. government, and wondered if you need to do that too. The answer is a resounding "No. And yes."

You see, as the creator of your art, you automatically own the copyright — but unless you've registered that ownership with the government, the range of legal actions you can take against someone who infringes on your rights and misuses your art is fairly limited.

Let's say that you didn't register one of your pieces, and must go to court to prove that another party has infringed upon your copyright.

Not only must you bear the burden of proof that your work was in existence *before* that of the infringer, but you are limited in the amount of monetary damages you can recover from the infringer (who may have profited greatly from using your artwork). In addition, you cannot receive statutory damages or recover your legal fees.

With prior registration, on the other hand, you automatically have court-acknowledged proof of your rights-of-origination, you're eligible for statutory damages of up to $150,000 per incident of infringement, and you can be awarded attorney's fees and other costs related to the litigation.

So why not register every piece of art you produce? You certainly can (and some artists do). Using online registration options, the entire filing process now takes about 2-3 months from start to finish, which is far superior to filing by mail — that can take two years or longer. The cost of registering is low, and if you have multiple pieces to copyright you can take advantage of "batch processing." The cost to register one artwork is the same as registering a hundred, or even more, as long as they're all in the same filing.

However, just because you *can* register the copyright for all of your artwork doesn't necessarily mean that you need to, or that you should. While submitting a filing does offer extra protection, the fact is that very few artists are truly at risk. The chance that someone will copy your art and reproduce it in a very large manner (and make a substantial sum of money on it) is just not very likely. While there's always the chance someone might use your art without permission on a smaller scale, if there's no money being made that you can recover, going to court for the infringement just isn't worthwhile.

Clearly, though, choosing to register your copyright is a very personal decision. Artists with proven commercial appeal whose works can easily and inexpensively be reproduced might choose to err on the side of caution. Similarly, if your art contains creatures, characters or settings that could potentially be translated into films, comics or video games, or if your work is very expensive, you have additional reason to consider registering your work.

Whatever your decision, be sure you at least give clear notice of copyright on all of your materials. Your original artwork, giclées, prints, website, print media and all photographs of your work should include the copyright symbol, date and your name. For example, I use "© 20XX Aletta de Wal, Artist Career Training."

Here are some insights from a fellow artist who has a very practical view of copyright registration — both the realistic potential for damage and his personal approach to prevention:

> *"My best defense is to keep creating pieces that are so richly textured and layered that they cannot be easily copied. The truth is, there are people out there who may try to copy your work, but think about it... wouldn't someone intent on plagiarizing an artist for profit target someone who's making hundreds of thousands, or millions, of dollars worth of work worldwide? Unless you're in that category, I think an undue amount of fear and energy put into that area can dilute your focus, and keep you from producing at your potential. With that said, being a business professional, if I did find an individual or company illegally using my work for profit, I would take proper legal action and go after them. Beyond that, do your best to ensure you're doing business with honest and reputable people, whether they're licensing companies, galleries, or collectors. Use smart business practices, and be kind, honest, and fair in all your dealings."*
>
> *~Bruce Marion, painter*

If you do an Internet search you'll find links to detailed information on U.S. copyright registration and proposed amendments to copyright law, as well as some copyright alternatives, such as Creative Commons licenses.

Creating Business Systems

Once you get your art business going (but before it's running at high speed, if at all possible) it's a good idea to put some systems in place to track important information related to your business. This information should include:

- Details about your clients, galleries and other art business relationships
- Resources for future growth, like potential suppliers, galleries, licensing opportunities or even new creative directions
- Records of past sales, finances and your art inventory

When you're just starting out, it's easy to think that this level of documentation is unnecessary or even excessive. You've spent your whole life dreaming about being a professional artist. Now that you are one, every person you meet, every piece you create and ship to a gallery and every sale you make is indelibly etched in your mind — it's that important to you.

But… here's the catch. As your art business flourishes and your success continues to grow, believe it or not, some of those details *will start to slip from your memory*. It's not a sign that you're jaded, forgetful, or that you don't care — it's a sign that you're a small business owner! You carry the workload of many people, in many different business roles, all while trying to refine your singular artistic vision.

No need for systems? Think again.

Good systems put in place early on will help you make the most of your art business without creating undue stress. They will free you to focus on what you do best: create great art and build relationships.

Choosing a Database

Databases are flexible information systems designed to store data, keep track of information and make it easy to reference later. Among other things, you can use information databases to save mailing lists, manage your inventory and tracking prices and sales.

Another important reason to set up an effective, efficient database is to help you keep track of contacts: this includes people who have bought your work, who are interested in your work or who can help your career.

I truly believe that the "bedrock" of sales is relationships, and in order to build the kinds of relationships that lead to sales, you'll need to keep careful track of who you know, how you know them, what you know about them and what they know about you.

Whether the people you meet are potential gallery reps or future art collectors, the ability to recall details about them and the topics you discussed can mean the difference between a thriving art career and a painful disappointment. It doesn't matter *how* you do it — the important part, for others, is that they feel specially and singularly remembered by you.

Nearly any information you can gather will help you grow and build relationships to support a viable living making art. Even seemingly unimportant details that you can "remember" at a crucial moment will help you gain momentum and sales. No one needs to know that a computer program "helped" you recall the important specifics of your relationship. You took the time to record them, and made a point to make them important to you.

If you think long-term when you first set up your information systems, you'll save time, money and grief later on. The way you store information should be able to grow and expand right along with your business. As your career grows, you'll need to add new contacts and add new information to existing contacts. Perhaps you'll even group those contacts under various headings, as your relationships change.

Envision the career of your "future self" and think about those future database needs now. You don't want to invest time and energy setting up a system and collecting a lot of data only to find you need to start over in a few years because it wasn't set up correctly to handle your expanding needs. Most computers come equipped with basic software and will have some form of digital address book. This may be adequate for temporary record-keeping, but your art business will quickly outgrow what a simple address book can do. If you go this route, make sure that you can at least search your address book by category or keyword: you may need to look up dates, purchase categories, or future wants. Most importantly — make sure that you can "export" the information for use elsewhere.

With database software programs like Excel, Access or FileMaker you can do much more, like sort and filter your data, make formulas for calculations, view your information in tables and charts, work with it interactively (for example, to mass-produce address labels) and even import files from other databases. If you have experience with any of these spreadsheet programs, you can easily set up a simple information database for your own use.

Of course, there are also software systems developed specifically for artists and galleries. In addition to allowing you to search your database by specialized filters, many of these programs include features for artwork inventory and website management. Although they were relatively expensive a decade ago, these programs are much more reasonably priced today, with an ever-expanding array of tools.

One major drawback to these specialized programs is the steeper learning curve (compared to basic spreadsheet software). Also be sure to consider are the level of support you'll receive and the potential longevity of the company. If it's the type of service where your information is kept on their servers, and the company goes out of business, it could leave you without your information.

Before making a purchase, here are my suggestions to help you make a wise choice:

- Research all possible software and think about who will use it most often. If you're lucky enough to have a spouse or assistant helping you manage your files, you'll want to get their input too.

- While it's always advisable to check reviews online, keep in mind that unless you're considering a program specifically designed for artists or gallery owners, most reviews will be from other industries that may not have the same requirements as your art business.

- If possible, talk with other artists as part of your product research. Find out what programs they use and what advantages or difficulties they've encountered.

- Finally, download a trial version (if available) to see for yourself if it's right for you. You may find one system easier to view, easier to navigate or easier to control — all of which can save you time and effort down the road.

Even if you don't plan on purchasing specialized software today, just reading about the features they offer can help you plan for the future or give you ideas for your own system.

Tracking Your Art Inventory

Your art is your number one tangible asset, so having a system for tracking it is especially important.

At any given time, you should be able to see how much artwork you have available, where it's located and how it's priced. You should also have a ready list of available art and a record of your income from past sales. For business, financial, legal and tax considerations, you need to have as detailed, accurate and up-to-date records as possible — you never know when you'll need documentation to track down a missing piece, file a damage claim or sue for restitution in court.

Again, I encourage you to get your inventory database "in place" as soon as possible. It doesn't matter how few pieces you've created or whether or not you've lined up any galleries for representation. I guarantee that when you *do* land your first exhibition, you'll have more than enough to handle without having to start from scratch documenting your inventory.

Plus, when your inventory is still small, it's much easier to set up a system and build a habit of good maintenance by entering each new piece as you go. As soon as you create a new work of art, and especially before it heads out on its way to a gallery, juried exhibition or (best of all) hanging in a collector's home, photograph it and get the record in your database.

However, it's not enough just to document each piece as you create it. You need to continue to log its whereabouts and any changes in its status until it's been sold, shipped and delivered to its new owners. Think about it… as your career becomes more active, you'll be sending artwork out regularly to even more destinations: invitational events, museum exhibitions, licensing agents and more. Imagine if you were to let a week or two go by without documenting all of that movement in your database. You'd have no idea where half of your precious art is!

Your job isn't done even when a piece has been shipped to a reputable gallery. You must manage your most important assets no matter *where* in the world they are, or under whose care. Your records must be accurate, extensive *and* timely or you'll soon have chaos on your hands. Consider this: while you are trying to monitor your work as it ships out to multiple destinations, galleries are trying to monitor work coming in from an even larger number of places. The fact that 99% of the time all this valuable art ends up in the right place, properly accounted for, is a testament to the systems that are in place and the people who manage them.

Taking snapshots of each piece just before delivery or shipping to the gallery, along with shipping records and snapshots of the piece hanging in the gallery (if possible) will help you document the location and condition of each piece. And, by keeping accurate records about your work, you'll have a documented history of the appearance, value and provenance of your art. There are several distinct financial benefits to keeping an accurate inventory system:

- You'll be able to submit your work for copyright registration.
- You'll know the value of your work for insurance purposes. If you ever have a fire or flood, you can determine the value of the lost goods and what exactly was lost.
- You'll be prepared to handle disagreements about damaged or missing inventory.
- You'll have a way to assess the value of your inventory at year-end.

Unfortunately, the occasional piece can still "go missing," and trying to discover its whereabouts is often difficult. Could it still be buried in a gallery's back stock? Was it lost in transit from the shipper? Is it at the framer's being repaired? Or sold, but never recorded?

Don't count on being able to reference the records of your galleries, shipping agents or framers. If you ever have to deal with damaged or missing inventory, it will be up to you to produce accurate records and be able to trace the work to its last known locale. If you need to file an insurance claim, you'll need to have proof of the artwork's movement history as well as documentation showing its total value, including casting, mounting, framing and so on.

Check with your insurance company to make sure you're documenting your inventory thoroughly enough according to their specifications (they may require written estimates, photographs, sales records or other additional documentation). Don't wait until you want to file a claim to document your work — in all likelihood it will be too late.

The other reason to know the value of your inventory is for your taxes. The IRS requires you to value your inventory at the beginning and end of each year so that you can determine your Cost of Goods Sold (COGS). This number is significant because when you deduct it from your gross art receipts you get the gross profit of your art business for the year. This gross profit, in turn, determines the income tax you owe for your business. Naturally, figuring your Cost of Goods Sold is much easier if you have accurate inventory records.

The Basics of an Art Business

As mentioned earlier, you can set-up your inventory records in a spreadsheet program (like Excel) or use software designed specifically for inventory management. If you're not using specialized software, you can start creating your inventory spreadsheet by establishing column headings for the following:

- Title
- Inventory number
- Creation date (if not included in inventory number)
- Medium (wood, bronze, multi-media, acrylic, oil, etc.)
- Dimensions: height x width (x depth, if applicable)
- Price (with options, if applicable, such as framed or unframed)
- Matte/frame material, size and cost (if applicable)
- Status (S=Sold D=Donation C=Consigned R=Rental L=Loan E=Exhibition)
- Current location
- Date out/date back
- Exhibit history
- Copyright registration information
- Insurance
- Shipping

ABC ART COMPANY
ART INVENTORY

Title	Inventory Number	Creation date (if not included in inventory number)	Medium (wood, bronze, multi-media, acrylic, oil, etc.)	Dimensions height x width (x depth, if applicable)	Price (with options, if applicable, such as framed or unframed)	Matte/frame material, size, and cost (if applicable)	Status S=Sold, D=Donated, C=Consigned, R=Rental, L=Loan, E=Exhibition	Current location	Date out/date back	Exhibit history	Copyright registration information	Insurance	Shipping
"If Only"	012-2015-P		Acrylic	27x32x9	$1000 unframed, $1350 framed	Wood frame, $500	E	Smith Gallery	out: 12/15/15				Pick-up
"Wait"	013-2015-5		Bronze		$5,000		S	Jack O. Trades					FedEx
"Tomorrow"	014-2015-P		Oil	12x12	$350		R	Jill Smith	out: 12/20/15, back: 1/20/16				USPS

Try to consider every conceivable bit of information you might want to include in your inventory database. While you may not need to reference certain information now, it could be an invaluable tool in the future.

If you use inventory software that came as part of a packaged office suite, be sure it can handle all of your future needs. Some of these programs appear excellent "on the surface" but don't have the growth potential you might think, particularly if they weren't created specifically for art management.

One especially important feature (which is almost always included in art-industry software but frequently missing from others) is the ability to store a photo or "thumbnail image" along with the written inventory description.

It's sometimes hard to believe in your early days as an artist that there'll come a time when your mind will "draw a blank" as you read the titles of your work — but it *will* happen. Look for this feature as you make your software selection.

In addition, make sure the manufacturer has a solid track record in the software industry… you want them to still be in business and prepared to issue upgrades when technology takes another leap forward. Otherwise, you could face starting over with hundreds of works needing to be re-entered by hand into a new software program.

Once you've chosen your database software and started your inventory system, you'll also need to connect each file record to the art piece it references. One of the best ways to do this is to assign each piece an inventory number as well as a title, and record that information on the back or bottom of the physical work of art.

Your inventory numbers can help in more ways than you might think. I suggest that you create your inventory numbers by assigning each piece a "unit" number that also serves as a running production-tally for each year, to let you know if an artwork was the fourth, twelfth or thirty-second piece you created. This is very helpful in tracking your production rate from year to year, and makes it much easier to see if you're capable of supplying additional shows or galleries.

Before or after the unit number, put the current year and (if you work in more than one medium) add a letter to indicate whether it's a sculpture, painting, etc. You can arrange these numbers and letters in whatever order you find convenient — my personal preference is to put the unit number first, followed by the year and medium, like so:

> **"012-2012-S"** represents "Piece #12 - created in 2012 - Sculpture"
> **"010-2013-P"** represents "Piece #10 - created in 2013 - Painting"

You'll notice in these examples that the unit numbers (012 and 010) re-set to zero with each new calendar year. The other option is to keep a running career total with your unit numbers, which would look something like this:

> **"012-2011-S"** represents "Career piece #12 - created in 2011 – Sculpture"
> **"147-2013-S"** represents "Career piece #147 - created in 2013 – Sculpture"

Some artists find tracking their career production in this manner very gratifying and don't mind having to "do the math" to see their year-to-year comparisons. The choice is yours, though keep in mind this system is not as effective if you work in more than one medium.

Some artists also prefer to keep the date of origin obscured from potential collectors so that no works are considered "newer" or "older" (and thus less or more desirable). One easy way to do this is to assign a letter of the alphabet for each calendar year. To explain how this would work, let's imagine the letter "A" corresponds with the year 2000. This would mean inventory numbers that begin with the letter "G" were created in 2006, those beginning with the letter "L" were created in 2011 and so forth:

> **"M-272-P"** represents "2012 - Career piece #272 - Painting"
> **"N-324-P"** represents "2013 - Career piece #324 - Painting"

Other artists like to go one step further in tracking production by adding two more numbers to represent the month of creation in addition to the year. You can do this by using 01 for January, 02 for February, and so on, just as if you were writing a date. This method looks as follows:

> **"M-03-47P"** represents "2012 - March - Piece #47 - Painting."

Adding the month of origin can help you track even more specific information about your rates of production. For example, you can check periodically to see if you're "on pace" to create the same number of works as in the previous year. Since many pieces take considerably more time than others and artist's work schedules aren't always consistent, this information can be extremely helpful in keeping you from getting behind. It may also help you see shifts in color or style that occur over the course of a few months' time.

Collecting Contact Information

When collecting contact information, your collectors, supporters and art "fans" are just the first of many important people to build relationships with. You also need to keep track of gallery owners and their staff (of current and potential future locations), art fair events and organizers, art magazine editors, writers and bloggers, licensing reps, museum curators, supply resources, fellow artists... and the list goes on and on.

As you build your contact database, keep the following three types of information readily accessible, so you can initiate contact at any time and in a timely fashion:

1. Information about people

Nothing creates feelings of goodwill or builds relationships faster than showing people that they genuinely matter to you. Being able to recall the "little" details of a person's life makes a great impression and puts you well on your way to a trusting relationship.

By referring to the notes in your database each time you make contact with someone, you'll instantly have those important personal details (including any specific interests they have in your art) to talk about. You'll come off looking very professional, and they'll be impressed with your great memory.

At minimum, collect and record the following information:

- Where and when you met, and under what circumstances
- Contact details such as name, address(es), email(s) and telephone number(s)
- General information about their life, including occupation, family or significant others, birthdays and anniversaries (or other gift-giving occasions) and so forth — basically anything they feel comfortable sharing that will help you personalize future communication
- Notes on all transactions or communications, including dates
- Any purchases they've made, artwork they've admired, favorite styles or colors and any future opportunities (for example, when a move or remodel will be completed)

2. Information about places

As you build relationships with people who want to see your art, you will always need more places to exhibit your work. Gather information about potential venues — not just locally, but while traveling as well. Even if you don't yet have a body of signature work to show, make note of locations where you think your work might fit in the future and where you would be proud to exhibit. Once you do begin to show your work, your list will come in handy.

Make sure to record at least the address, the name of a contact person, their contact information, future show themes, submission details and any important financial considerations.

3. Information about you for the media

In order to help your reputation grow beyond your immediate circle, it's important to build relationships with the media. As your career blossoms, your awards, exhibits and shows will all present opportunities for coverage in newspaper articles, magazine features, blog posts, social media shares and radio or TV appearances.

Make sure to record any information on regular art features, special coverage opportunities and submission deadlines.

As you build, update and use your information systems and contact database, here are some helpful hints to keep in mind:

- When you spend time with people talking about your art, make detailed notes about the meeting or phone call including the day and time and a recap of what you discussed. If you're at an event and find yourself meeting several new contacts in a row, jot down a few notes after each encounter lest they all "run together" by the end of the night. (A small notebook or digital tablet is perfect for this). Afterwards, enter your notes into your primary database as soon as possible. If you use a digital device, you may be able to "sync" directly to your database, making the entire process easier still.

- Don't just note the date you initially added a person or venue to your database — document every subsequent contact as well. Include the shows they attended, dates of purchases, phone calls made and so on. Dating each time and method of contact allows you to track the duration of your marketing strategies and prevent embarrassing duplications.

- Having out-of-date information can make you look unprofessional, so make a habit of updating frequently, particularly if someone has asked to be removed from your database. The more often you update, the less of a chore it will be and the more likely your updates will be detailed and accurate because the information is fresh in your memory.

Of course, just having all of this information without using it is pointless. Taking the time each week to follow up with some of your contacts is an important part of selling your art. You can follow up with people for many reasons — to offer birthday or anniversary wishes, to inquire after an important event they mentioned or to ask if they've decided on a color scheme for their new home, just to name a few.

If you're genuine and sincere in your follow-up, you won't be seen as a pest — in fact, your contact will probably think just the opposite. By acknowledging an important occasion or offering a solution to something you remember from past conversations, they'll likely feel that you're both kind and caring.

Art representative Margaret Danielak is the "queen of follow-up," and her efforts directly result in many sales. She sometimes makes eight or more personal contacts with prospective clients over a period of several months to a year before they reach a buying decision. Of course, it's her attention to people combined with meticulous record of previous calls and contact information that lets her "pick up where she left off" and build those productive relationships.

Another artist I know devotes two hours every Friday to follow up with her contacts. She searches her database's follow-up field and then either calls or emails depending on the results of her last contact. For example, when one of her collectors mentioned the possibility of purchasing a piece of art for his wife's Christmas gift in the coming year, she wrote it down in her database. Then, right after Thanksgiving, she contacted him with some pieces in his wife's favorite colors, also gleaned from information stored in her database. Not only did this artist make a sale, but she made a life-long fan of the collector, whose usual gift dilemma was successfully solved quickly and easily. None of this would have happened had she not taken thorough notes and then followed up on them.

The most important message to take away from this section?

Have a detailed system in place, check it regularly and "follow-through" on following up. This single habit can make the difference between enjoying a thriving business with consistent earnings and struggling to stay in business because of spotty sales.

The End of This Book is the Beginning of Your Journey

So now you have information … maybe you've even done a few of the things I suggested. That's a great start! Perhaps you've already seen the benefits of the steps you've taken. Even better. Now comes the hard part — you have to keep on going.

Because just knowing, without doing, won't get you where you want to go.

Grow your career intentionally, step-by-step, and continue to use this book as a reference source while you advance to each new stage. Whether you're starting as a hobbyist with dreams of your first sale or as an emerging artist who has just quit his "day job," you have the tools you need right here at your fingertips. Take the time to discover your true signature style, build a solid body of art, develop consistent work habits and forge a strong business foundation so you can achieve the art career and lifestyle of your dreams! Then, proudly look people in the eye and tell them, "My real job is being an artist!"

I hope my words will touch and inspire all who read them, and help guide you to rewards of which you've only dreamed.

Aletta

My Personal Journey

My clients often ask me how I came to help artists make a better living making art and still have a life. The short answer is that I followed my instincts as I responded to what life offered. The longer answer follows.

When I work with artists, I consider them professional colleagues. Because I work with each one in a way that suits them as individuals, I ask them many questions about who they are, what they want from life and how they got as far as they are. Every artist has a unique life story behind the art they create. I am always interested in that story because it helps me connect to the artist so I can better help them. In the course of our work, I often share stories from my life in general and own experience as an artist, educator and entrepreneur in particular.

I'm the second oldest daughter in a family of five children. I was born in Indonesia to Dutch parents. I've lived in Holland, English–speaking and French-speaking Canada, the South of France, New Zealand and California. As a result, I don't really identify with any particular culture. My culture is more of a hybrid, which serves me well in my work as an artist advisor. I consider myself a "global nomad" — a term used to describe anyone who has grown up in several cultures.

As a child, each time my family moved I didn't fit in. I was always on the outside looking in, along with all the other "misfits" from other countries. Because of those circumstances I became a lot more interested in school than I might otherwise have been. I had a very rich inner life. All of this was great training for becoming an artist. I developed my own unique perspective on what I saw and how I interpreted it. All human beings do this, but in my case, it became fodder for my art.

As I lived in different countries, I became a "cultural detective" so I could understand how things worked. It honed my curiosity. I had no choice but to adapt to whatever new situation our travels brought us. That allowed me to build resilience — a skill that has stood me in very good stead. Resilience is an essential attribute for every artist. We are like moths that struggle out through a pinhole to fly into the world. The struggle makes us stronger.

My childhood experiences with art were no different than most children's. Unlike many artists, I was not one of those who knew from childhood that I was destined to be an artist.

When I was little more than a toddler, I had my first art experience. From my playpen on the floor, I was just the right height to see — and touch, when my mother wasn't around — a fine wood carving of a goddess head from Indonesia. She sat on the wide window ledge surrounded by my mother's African violets. The warm wood tones lit her beautiful face. The patterns of intricate detail in her headdress added elegance and serenity that captivated me. The three-dimensional beauty mesmerized me. Motionless, I could spend an hour just looking at her and meeting her steady gaze.

This art experience filled me with awe, fascination and curiosity. Who is she? How old is she? Where does she live? What does the rest of her body look like? My hands explored every part of the finely carved surface. I can still feel the smoothness of her "skin" and the edges of the folds in her headdress.

The thought that someone had made her never crossed my mind until I became an artist. Knowing the imagination, craft and persistence it takes to make such a fine carving magnified my love of this treasured piece of art. To this day, I always have to restrain myself when I am near sculpture. I want to touch it, so I can share the tactile experience of the sculptor.

My first memory of making art was finger painting in second grade. Coming from a pristine home where everything was so neat you could eat off the floors, I found this a wonderful new experience. I had never liked having sticky hands but this was different. I loved the feel of my fingers moving the paint around on the special paper. There were no rules.

Third grade brought art "assignments" to replicate objects. We began by recreating an image projected on the wall. Next, we used grid lines to reproduce an image we brought from home. I brought a Three Little Pigs comic. I worked hard to get each curve exactly right or as close as possible without tracing it. It was satisfying but no longer fun.

Fourth grade art class killed my joy in making art for the next thirty years. I was happily drawing my favorite Linden tree from my back yard. The art teacher came alongside our desks to check each student's progress. It was the 1950s so imagine a buxom woman wearing a cotton print dress with matching cloth belt. The rollers had been carefully removed from her hair to preserve the "do" for a week. She asked me "What is that?" It was obvious to me that my drawing was the tree I loved. She grabbed the pencil from my hand and firmly told me that my drawing was wrong. "This is the way you draw a tree," she demonstrated.

For many years after that, the only art I did was "paint by numbers" so I could be sure to get it right. I still loved the painting process, but I was following someone else's idea of "right."

So I did the "sensible" thing — I focused on school and got on with my life. I was only nineteen years old when I graduated with a Bachelor of Arts in English and French Literature in the early 1970s. I applied to sixty-five different companies and finally got a job as a management trainee with a bank in Montreal after they learned that I spoke French. After many other positions, I eventually held a challenging job where I was in charge of management, operations training and development for 30,000 employees worldwide with a $600,000 budget. It brought all my education and experience together and I was finally able to do work that improved people's daily work lives.

I thought I had arrived. All of that changed in a heartbeat. In 1989, I discovered that some persistent health problems I had been having were from NSLE (Neuro Systemic Lupus Eurythematosis). One minute, I was at the top of my game in business and personal life. The next minute all of that was gone. I had two strokes that left me without the ability or mobility I had always taken for granted — to use my head to make my way in the world and to get up and go anywhere I pleased anytime. I was thirty-eight years old and instead of climbing the corporate ladder, my daily job was to learn to walk and talk all over again. While I would never have chosen that experience, I am grateful for all the good that has come out of that difficult time. I would not be working with artists now and you would not be reading this book.

A couple of years later, I was waiting for a friend to drive me home after a doctor's visit, I noticed an ad on the bulletin board outside her office for a class called "Drawing for the Absolute Beginner." I thought "That would be me!" I needed to do something beyond working at getting better. I signed up and learned from Ose and Zeisha, two very generous teachers, along with other women who had chronic or terminal illnesses. Art became part of healing my body, mind and spirit. As my creative talents returned, I soon resolved to make art the core of my life, instead of a sideline.

Fast forward to 1993. During the day, I coached executives to be more creative. Nights and weekends, I made art, taught art workshops and sold my own art and the work of other artists in alternative spaces and my own space in a renovated textile factory, which I called The Loft Gallery.

Since then, I have worked to help fine artists make a better living making art. I have no doubt that I am now doing what I was meant to do — helping artists turn their talents into businesses that are sustainable and earns them a long-term, healthy income.

Thanks for being fellow travelers as you embark on the next leg of your own journey.

Aletta

Acknowledgements

Nothing in the world gets done by just one person. We're all in this together. The list of everyone who has enriched my life and helped me throughout my life and with this book would take hundreds of pages. I am forever appreciative of their caring, influence and support in my life.

Here are a few of the people who directly helped make this book possible. Each one deserves a whole story so I promise to write more about them in my book blog. They are listed here in alphabetical order. If I've left anyone out, it is only from the list and not from my heart.

Featured artists I've interviewed over the years and whose wise words I included to inspire you: *Cristina Acosta, Eric Armusik, Wm. Kelly Bailey, Susan Birkenshaw, Peter Bragino, Connie Bransilver, Frank de Las Mercedes, Bruce K. Haley, Jr., B.J. Katz, Lori McNee, Bruce Marion, Huguette Despault May, Patrice Federspiel, Pat Fiorello, Jennifer Mason, Carol Mackay Mertz, Nicholas Petrucci, Barbara Riche, Karen Schmidt, James Thatcher, John T. Unger, Amy Ventura, Bilhenry Walker.*

Artist peer reviewers, master readers, and author reviewers who read earlier versions of this book and added their hearts, eyes and hands to improving my text as I went through countless rewrites and revisions. *Eric Armusik, Beth Barany, Susan Birkenshaw, Peter Bragino, Connie Bransilver, Frank de Las Mercedes, Huguette Despault May, Patrice Federspiel, Pat Fiorello, Jennifer Mason, Magella Sergerie*

Judy Baker, my creative marketing coach, who encouraged me to write this book and helped me find members of my book team.
www.creative1.com/creative_coach

Margaret Danielak, author of the sold-out book "Gallery Without Walls," artist representative and follow-up queen, who invited me to talk about my work when I first arrived in California. www.danielakart.com

Suzi Elton, my writing coach who asked great questions throughout the many drafts, pulled the rest of the content out of my mind jumps and who contributed to the business section of this book. www.wowfactorwriting.com/about-suzi

Martin Finesilver and Mark Smith of Finesilver Design Inc. for being able to take bits of ideas and create a beautiful cover design that communicates what I meant to say but could not express in words. www.finesilverdesign.com

Lin Lacombe, Strategic Partner in Communications, Public Relations and Marketing, & Literary Publicity, who helped me understand book publicity one step at a time and gave hands-on advice and conversations that were the equivalent of a martini when I needed encouragement. www.frompassiontopublicity.net

Rachel Ann Lindsay, whose gesture drawing perfectly captures the spirit of this first book about embarking on the journey of a professional art career. www.rachelannlindsay.com

Christina Merkley, my Biz-Life accelerator coach, who granted me certification as a Shift-It Visual Coach, and link to my soul family mastermind group who all have huge hearts, great minds and client success-oriented business. www.shift-it-coach.com

Robin Sagara, the "wizard behind the scenes" who is my "other half" at Artist Career Training who along with her husband Harry Sagara quietly and competently makes me, my work and my clients look good in print and on the Internet. www.sagaradevelopment.com

Lee Silber, an author whose prolific writings and infectious enthusiasm inspired me to write in the first place. www.leesilber.com/

Nina Yablok, business attorney unlike many others who gives great advice with a sense of humor.

And for keeping me on the road to the best book I could write, last but certainly not least my editors.

Lee Wright, major domo editor who took care of my vision and my words as she thoroughly and methodically edited my 100· version into the heartfelt and informative book you have just read. She also contributed examples from her experience managing her husband Bruce Marion's career.

Dan Duhrkoop, final editor who smoothed out the wrinkles in the 101· version so you could read without tripping over errors and omissions (Any that remain are down to me, so please let me know if you find any.)

I owe so much gratitude and respect to all the artists and arts professionals I have worked with through Artist Career Training, who have used the information in this book and contributed to its realism.

And of course, invisible but essential to making this book go from my computer through the many hoops of publishing to your hands, Jiliane Patriarca, Professional Organizer & Founder, *The Organization Organization*. www.theorganizationorg.com

Author Biography

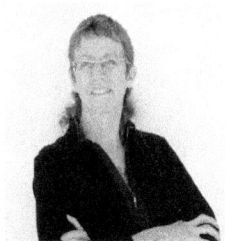 Aletta de Wal, Artist Advisor at Artist Career Training guides fine artists to make a better living making art in any economy. Aletta works with part-time, emerging and full-time artists who are serious about a career in fine arts. She makes art marketing easier and the business of art simpler. Equal parts artist, educator and entrepreneur, Aletta has worked with over 4,000 artists in groups and 450 artists in one-to-one consultations. Her clients say that she inspires them to do the work to be successful, offers detailed advice on specific action and supports them through the ups and downs of life and art.

Aletta de Wal, M, Ed.
Artist Advisor & Certified Visual Coach for Fine Artists
I'll help you build a better living from your art - and still have a life.

Aletta de Wal, M.Ed.
Artist Advisor & Certified Visual Coach
Artist Career Training
http://www.artistcareertraining.com
http://www.artistcareertraining.com/realjobartist
250-549-2615 Pacific Time
Aletta@ArtistCareerTraining.com
http://www.facebook.com/pages/Artist-Career-Training
https://plus.google.com/+ArtistcareertrainingAlettadeWal
http://www.linkedin.com/in/alettadewal
http://www.pinterest.com/artistcareer
http://www.twitter.com/artmktgmentor

Artists like to be different. I understand and respect that — it's part of our creative nature, after all — but I also know that every art business need structure. I show each artist how to run a business that is as individual as their art, while still being focused, organized and confident in all art business matters.

I share insider information and step-by-step instructions in lively group telephone classes, on-site workshops, seminars and personal consultations to allow in-depth work on specific projects. You also have independent study options through recordings and e-book.

I realize that you probably have "other duties as assigned," so I take that into account too.

Bottom line: Friendly, focused guidance to get you where you want to go as a real artist.

Appendices

Thank you again for purchasing "My Real Job is Being an Artist."
I hope that you are finding out what you are already doing right and what
you need to do next.

There is an (over) abundance of information online about the "nuts and bolts"
of small business. I've created a starter list for you
at *http://www.artistcareertraining.com/realjobartist*

I highly recommend that you create an active living document by adding
your own discoveries of useful information. You can also bookmark these
websites on your computer. I personally find it useful to have a document
that collects all the web addresses and my comments in one place.

If you have any questions about what you've learned from this book, please
contact me at *Aletta@ArtistCareerTraining.com*

Index

Note: Page numbers in italics followed by "t" denote tables.

inland marine insurance, 229
inspiration. *see also* creativity
    need to channel, 63–64
    sources of, 146, 148–149
insurance, 227–236
    business property insurance, 229–230
    consideration in contracts, 248
    general liability insurance, 230
    misconceptions about, 227–228
insurance, artists on
    Bailey, Wm. Kelly, 233–235
insurance, in contracts, 248
internships and apprenticeships, 155–156
inventory
    at various career stages, *39t*
    emerging artists and, 54
    mid-career artists and, 74–75
    established artists and, 91–92
    cost of goods sold, 205, *206t*
    effect of, on sales, 82 (*see also* signature style, dangers of changing)
    production schedules and, 173
    tracking, 258–262, *260t*
IRS resources, regarding taxes, 225
IRS Video Portal (online resource), 225

J
John Seed
    on art professionals, 132
Jorgensen, Robin
    on criticism (the "inner critic"), 150
    on discipline, 150
journals (for ideas), 170
juried exhibits and shows, 154–155, 159–163

K
Katz, B.J.
    on professionalism, 20

L
land use permits, 196
lawyers
    need for, 241–242
legal assistance, 241–242
legal assistance, finding, 241–242

ORDER FORM FOR USE BY MAIL

You can also order the soft cover book online at
http://www.artistcareertraining.com/realjobartist

✂ ---

I want _____ copies of *"My Real Job Is Being An Artist": How to produce a body of signature art and build the foundation of an art business* by Aletta de Wal, MEd.

Payment: _____ quantity x $29.95 USD (or $24.95 CAD) = _____ Total

Payment method: ☐ Check ☐ Money order ☐ Visa/MasterCard/American Express

Check No.: _____ Cardholder name: _____

Card Number: ☐☐☐☐ ☐☐☐☐ ☐☐☐☐ ☐☐☐☐

Exp. Date: _____ CV Code: _____

Signature: _____ Date: _____

Billing Address	Mailing Address
Name:	☐ *Check if same as Billing address.*
Address:	Name:
City, State/Province:	Address:
ZIP/Postal code:	City, State/Province:
	ZIP/Postal code:

Scan and submit by e-mail to: Aletta@ArtistCareerTraining.com.

Due to the excessive shipping costs, this book is only available in North America. However, please visit our website http://www.artistcareertraining.com/realjobartist to order eBooks online.

www.ingramcontent.com/pod-product-compliance
Lightning Source LLC
Chambersburg PA
CBHW072130170526
45158CB00004BA/1321